AT

THE ROBERTS ENGLISH SERIES

SECOND EDITION

THE ROBERTS ENGLISH SERIES

SIXTH BOOK

A LINGUISTICS PROGRAM

PAUL ROBERTS

CHARLES S. ROSS

JULIAN BOYD

HARCOURT BRACE JOVANOVICH, INC.

New York   Chicago   San Francisco   Atlanta   Dallas

ACKNOWLEDGMENTS: *For permission to reprint copyrighted material, grateful acknowledgment is made to the following publishers, authors, and agents:*

Atheneum Publishers and *Collins Publishers:* From *The Territorial Imperative* by Robert Ardrey, copyright © 1966 by Robert Ardrey.

Brandt & Brandt: "Wilbur Wright and Orville Wright" by Stephen Vincent Benét from *A Book of Americans* by Rosemary and Stephen Vincent Benét, copyright 1933 by Stephen Vincent Benét; renewed © 1961 by Rosemary Carr Benét. Published by Holt, Rinehart and Winston, Inc.

Dodd, Mead & Company, Inc.: From *Scott's Last Expedition* by Robert F. Scott, copyright 1913, 1941 by Dodd, Mead & Company, Inc.

Doubleday & Company, Inc. and *Faber and Faber Ltd.:* "The Coming of the Cold (Part 3)," copyright 1941 by Theodore Roethke, from *The Collected Poems of Theodore Roethke.*

Harcourt Brace Jovanovich, Inc. and *MacGibbon & Kee:* "In Just-," copyright, 1923, 1951, by E. E. Cummings, from his volume *Poems 1923–1954.* Published in England under the title *Complete Poems.*

Harper & Row, Publishers, Incorporated: "The Purple Cow" by Gelett Burgess from *A Little Book of Necessary Nonsense,* compiled by Burges Johnson, copyright 1929 by Harper & Brothers; renewed © 1957 by Burges Johnson. From page 6 in *The Blue Nile* by Alan Moorehead, copyright © 1962 by Alan Moorehead.

Holt, Rinehart and Winston, Inc. and *Laurence Pollinger Limited:* "The Runaway" by Robert Frost from *Complete Poems by Robert Frost,* copyright 1923 by Holt, Rinehart and Winston, Inc.; copyright 1951 by Robert Frost. Published in England by Jonathan Cape Limited.

Alfred A. Knopf, Inc.: "Dream Variations" and "The Negro Speaks of Rivers" by Langston Hughes, copyright 1926 by Alfred A. Knopf, Inc. and renewed 1954 by Langston Hughes, from *Selected Poems* by Langston Hughes.

The Macmillan Company, New York, Macmillan & Co. Ltd., London and *The Trustees of the Hardy Estate:* "When I set out for Lyonnesse" from *The Collected Poems of Thomas Hardy.*

The New Yorker: From "Wallace" by Richard H. Rovere from *The New Yorker,* February 4, 1950.

W. W. Norton & Company, Inc. and *The Bodley Head Ltd.:* From *A History of Polar Exploration* by L. P. Kirwan, copyright © 1959 by L. P. Kirwan. Published in England under the title *The White Road.*

Oxford University Press, London: "The Harbor of Fowey" by Sir Arthur Quiller-Couch.

Penguin Books Ltd.: "Problem Child" by J. E. Faulks from *More Comic and Curious Verse.*

Random House, Inc.: "Ascent to the Sierras" by Robinson Jeffers, copyright 1928 and renewed 1956 by Robinson Jeffers, from *Cawdor and Other Poems* by Robinson Jeffers.

Charles Scribner's Sons and *The Hamlyn Publishing Group Limited:* From *My Early Life: A Roving Commission,* pages 15–17, by Winston Churchill, copyright 1930 Charles Scribner's Sons; renewal copyright © 1958 Winston Churchill. Published in England by Odhams Books Limited, Publishers and Proprietors of the copyright.

The Society of Authors, representing The Literary Trustees of Walter de la Mare: "Silver" by Walter de la Mare.

The Viking Press, Inc.: From *Americans Before Columbus* by Elizabeth Chesley Baity, copyright 1951, © 1961 by Elizabeth Chesley Baity.

Mary Yost Associates, John Murray, and *The Trustees of the Estate of Sir Arthur Conan Doyle:* From "The Croxley Master" from *Croxley Master and Other Stories of the Ring and Camp* by Sir Arthur Conan Doyle. Also published in his book *The Conan Doyle Stories.*

Illustrations in this book are by the following artists:

Huntley Brown, pp. 148, 180; Paul Calle, pp. 39, 41, 44, 282; Joseph Cellini, pp. 30, 68, 70, 71, 273; Joseph Giordano, p. 292; Manny Haller, p. 50; Gordon Laite, pp. xvi, 4, 88, 106–07, 124, 126; Robert J. Lee, pp. 18, 168, 218; Allen Mardon, pp. 60, 228, 230, 242; G. Charles McBarron, pp. 156, 159; George Parrish, p. 76; Ray Porter, pp. 96, 98; Rich Schreiter, p. 116; Shannon Stirnweis, pp. 9, 11, 188, 198; Hans Zander, pp. 210, 251, 253.

Photo Credits:

Louis Goldman from Rapho Guillemette, p. 80, Aramco World Magazine, p. 81.

Copyright © 1970, 1966 by Harcourt Brace Jovanovich, Inc.

ISBN   0-15-312710-4

Contents

PART 2 Section 1

Section 2

Section 3

PART 3 Section 1

Section 2

Section 3

PART 4   Section 1

Section 2

Section 3

PART 5   Section 1

Section 2

Section 3

PART 6   Section 1

Section 2

Section 3

PART 7 Section 1

Section 2

Section 3

PART 8 Section 1

Section 2

Section 3

PART 9 Section 1

Section 2

Section 3

PART 10 Section 1

Section 2

Section 3

THE ROBERTS ENGLISH SERIES

PART

1

A Poem

The poems and stories you will study in this book have several purposes. One is to give you practice in careful reading. You will not usually be asked to tell why you like them or dislike them. Instead you will be asked to tell what they say.

If the selection is read aloud, listen to it very carefully. Even if it is read aloud, read it to yourself afterward, trying to understand the meaning of one part before you go on to the next. The questions that follow will help you to understand the selection better. Often you will be able to guess meanings from context — that is, from other things that are said in the selection.

This first poem is about a horse.

The Runaway

Once, when the snow of the year was beginning to fall,
We stopped by a mountain pasture to say "Whose colt?"
A little Morgan had one forefoot on the wall,
The other curled at his breast. He dipped his head
And snorted to us. And then he had to bolt.
We heard the miniature thunder where he fled
And we saw him or thought we saw him dim and gray,
Like a shadow against the curtain of falling flakes.
"I think the little fellow's afraid of the snow.
He isn't winter-broken. It isn't play
With the little fellow at all. He's running away.
I doubt if even his mother could tell him, 'Sakes,
It's only weather.' He'd think she didn't know.
Where is his mother? He can't be out alone."
And now he comes again with a clatter of stone
And mounts the wall again with whited eyes
And all his tail that isn't hair up straight.
He shudders his coat as if to throw off flies.
"Whoever it is that leaves him out so late,
When other creatures have gone to stall and bin,
Ought to be told to come and take him in."

ROBERT FROST

1

► At what time of year does this take place? Where does it take place, as far as the poem tells you?

► What kind of animals might one see in a mountain pasture? Which of these kinds is a **colt?** If you don't know that, think which of these kinds might snort, dip its head, and stand with one forefoot on the wall. Then look up **colt.** Is it a young animal or an old one? From what you have read, tell what a **Morgan** is.

► The colt had to **bolt.** Miniature means a small-scale like-ness of something. So what is **miniature thunder?** The poem says the colt fled. Then what does **bolt** mean here? Check your guess by using a dictionary.

► How does the poet say that it was hard to see the colt run-ning in the snow?

► We may say that a horse isn't broken to the saddle. What isn't the colt broken to? **Sakes** is short for the expression "For goodness' sakes!" How does the poet express surprise that the colt's mother isn't with him?

► What is there in the colt's appearance that shows how frightened he is? What verb tells what he does to his coat?

► Who do the people think is to blame for the colt's fright? What other creatures might have gone to stall and bin? What do the people think ought to be done?

Single Quotation Marks

As you know, these are quotation marks: " ". We put the actual words that someone says between quotation marks. Find the quotations in the poem that show what actual words were said by the people who were watching the colt.

Sometimes what a person says may include his report of what another person says. When that happens, the words of the second person are enclosed in single quotation marks: ' '.

Mary said, "I heard the swimmer shout 'Help me!'"

► Find in the poem the single quotation marks that show what the poet thinks the mother horse might have said.

▶ 1. Stress is the degree of loudness with which we pronounce syllables. For instance, when we say **barber,** we say the **bar** part louder than we do the **ber** part. Tell which is the louder syllable, the first or the second, in the following words.

golden   alive   beyond   dictate   loudness

In these words we can hear two degrees of stress. Some syllables are louder and some weaker. However, we have more than two degrees of stress in English. Pronounce this expression: **telephone bill.**

▶ 2. How many syllables are there in the expression **telephone bill?** Of these, which one do you think is pronounced most loudly? Which is pronounced most softly? Do you think the other two have the same degree of loudness or different degrees?

The expression **basketball game** has the same stress pattern as **telephone bill.** In both expressions, the first syllable is the loudest, and the second is the weakest. In both, the fourth syllable is louder than the third. Both have four degrees of stress.

3. Although expressions like **basketball game** may have as many as four degrees of stress, simple words don't. You have seen that in two-syllable words like **barber** there can be two degrees of stress. In words of three or more syllables there can be as many as three degrees of stress.

▶ Say **masquerade.** How many syllables has this word? The first syllable is louder than the second, and the third syllable is loudest of all. We say that **masquerade** has three degrees of stress.

▶ 4. Say **volleyball.** Which syllable has the loudest stress? Which has the weakest? Which has a stress between the other two in loudness?

▶ 5. How many degrees of stress does **satisfaction** have?

We will be studying stress in single words, not expressions, so only three degrees of stress concern us here. We will use the following terms for these three degrees of stress: **first stress** for the loudest; **middle stress** for the next loudest; and **weak stress** for the softest.

3

The poem "The Runaway" tells about a frightened colt. Here is a prose account of a frightened animal.

The Fawn

My berry pail was nearly full of the wild strawberries that grew in profusion in the mountain meadow we called "The Red Shell," meaning, I guess, "red shale." My sister Mary contentedly picked in one spot, but I moved from one rich bed of berries to another, picked a handful, and moved on. Our dog Shep roamed the meadow's edge, searching the stone walls for wood-chucks.

In one of my moves, I nearly stepped on a soft, spotted wild creature lying curled chin on forefeet like a sleeping dog, hidden within a nest-like depression in the tall meadow grass. It was a new-born fawn.

The timid creature, eyes closed, lay motionless, holding its breath until it could do so no longer. Then it panted, terror-stricken, but obedient to its mother's orders to lie still no matter what. Mary came over to look. The fawn did not move. Then Shep came over to investigate, sniffing its spotted coat. The fawn quivered in fright, but made no move to escape, nor did Shep make a sound or movement to threaten it. Confident that the doe would return when we left, we tiptoed silently away, leaving the helpless fawn where we had found it. But for many days afterward, we marveled at this infant of the wild, which had the courage to be motionless in a time of desperate fear.

■ Many of the sentences in the story about the fawn explore several ideas. Find and copy single sentences that express about the same thing as the groups of sentences below.

1. I nearly stepped on a creature in one of my moves. The creature was wild. It was soft. It was spotted. It was lying. It was curled. Its chin was on its forefeet. A dog sleeps. A dog lies like this. Something hid within a depression. The depression was like a nest. The depression was in the meadow grass. The grass was tall.

2. The creature was timid. It lay motionless. Its eyes were closed. It held its breath until a time. Then it could do so no longer.

3. We were confident (of something). We would leave. Then the doe would return. We tiptoed away silently. The fawn was helpless. We had found the fawn (in some place). We left the fawn there.

■ Choose one or more of the other sentences in "The Fawn" and try writing a group of simpler sentences that express all the ideas of the longer sentence.

■ Think of a frightened animal that you have seen, and write a paper telling about it. Tell what it was that frightened the animal. Describe what the animal looked like, how it showed its fear. Tell how you think it must have felt.

Put a title at the beginning. In a title, we capitalize the first word and all the other words except words like **and, the, a, into.** Indent the first line of each paragraph. Leave wide margins on both sides of the paper and at the top and bottom.

English sentences are made up of certain kinds of words or groups of words that are used in certain ways. We call the kinds of words or word groups **structures.** We call the ways in which they are used **functions.**

You are probably already familiar with a number of structures and with some of their functions. (If you need more explanation or review than is given here, turn to pages 302–21 at the back of the book.) The two main structures of a sentence are a **noun phrase** and a **verb phrase.** The noun phrase functions as the subject of the sentence and the verb phrase functions as the predicate. Thus, in the sentence "The man rode a horse," the noun phrase **the man** functions as the subject, and the verb phrase **rode a horse** functions as the predicate. In "He was a policeman," the noun phrase **he** functions as the subject, and the verb phrase **was a policeman** functions as the predicate.

► Point out the structures that function as subject and predicate in the following sentences:

1. The lady carried a fan.
2. He smiled.
3. Joan passed the examination.
4. Everybody felt fine.
5. A catbird sings many songs.
6. Someone moved.
7. Mrs. Taylor signed this note.
8. She knows your teacher.
9. Miss Smith lives near the school.
10. Someone dropped some books.
11. An elephant led the parade.
12. Some squirrels built that nest.

► Tell whether each noun phrase that functions as subject in the sentences above is (1) a determiner plus a common noun — **the lady,** (2) a proper noun — **Joan,** (3) a personal pronoun — **he,** or (4) an indefinite pronoun — **everybody.**

► Some of the predicates of the sentences above contain noun phrases. Name them. Tell what kind they are.

► Find all the noun phrases in the sentences above that have determiners. Name the determiners. Name the nouns.

6

There are several kinds of determiners. Here are some of them:

Articles: the, a (an), some, null
Demonstratives: this, that, these, those
Numbers: one, two, three,etc.
Quantifiers: several, many, much, a few,etc.
Possessives: my, your, his, her, its, our, their

► Point out the determiners in the noun phrase subjects of the following sentences and tell what kind each one is:

1. The colt was frightened.
2. Two people were working it.
3. Your friend was here.
4. This box looks big enough.
5. Several boys turned out.

The articles are of two kinds, **definite** and **nondefinite.** The only definite article is **the.** Two of the nondefinite articles are **a** and **some.** **An** is the form of **a** that we use before vowels.

The nondefinite article **some** goes with nouns that refer to a group or quantity of something:

Group: Some puppies chewed the rug.
Quantity: Some mud spattered the windshield.

When common nouns like these are used without **some** or **the,** they do not refer to a group or quantity of something, but to that thing in general:

General: Puppies chew rugs.
General: Mud is dirty.

We say that plural common nouns and nouns like **mud** have a null (Ø) determiner before them when they are general in meaning, although they don't have an actual word before them.

► Each sentence below contains two noun phrases, each with an article. Tell what the articles are.

6. The car hit a telephone pole.
7. Some youngsters found the money.
8. Horses eat barley.
9. The newcomer made trouble.
10. Darkness overtook the travelers.

▶ Common nouns may be either of two kinds — **countable** or **noncountable.** A countable noun is one like **puppy, boy, sheep** that refers to something that can be counted. We can say **one puppy, three puppies, ten boys, sixteen sheep.** Give five other examples of countable nouns.

▶ Noncountable nouns refer to things that cannot be counted, or at least aren't usually. Mud is a noncountable noun. We don't usually say "two muds." **Furniture, blood, courage** are noncountable nouns in their usual meanings. Name five others.

■ Write the noun from each noun phrase below. Tell whether it is countable or noncountable. Write the article that is the determiner for each noun. Your answers will look like this:

1. Rain ruined the picnic.
1. rain noncountable Ø; picnic countable the
2. A man delivers milk.
3. Cream comes in cartons.
4. The fog covers the city.
5. Some frost whitened my window.
6. Three boys played tennis.

■ Find the countable nouns in the following list and write the plural form of each. Do not write noncountable nouns.

girl	oil	child	spy	soap
woman	sheep	ice	side	goose
health	weather	baby	tooth	inch

Often a word can be either a countable noun or a noncountable noun, depending on the use that is made of it. **Meal** is a word like this:

The **meal** was delicious.

Here we don't know whether **meal** means grain ground into flour or breakfast, lunch, or dinner.

Write two sentences, using **meal** as a countable noun in one and as a noncountable noun in another. Then write two similar sentences for **lamb** and for **goose.**

Mary had a little **lamb.** The **goose** was not very good.

8

An Exploration

Over sixty years ago Admiral Robert E. Peary of the United States Navy, accompanied by his faithful friend Matthew Henson, set out to discover the North Pole. Read L. P. Kirwan's account of the last and most hazardous part of their exploration.

The Conquest of the North Pole

Peary and five men — four Eskimos and Matthew Henson, who was almost as skillful as they in the technique of swift Arctic travel — faced two great hazards as they set out on April 2 on the last stage of the Polar journey. A twenty-four hour gale might spring up and open wide and impassable leads in the ice, dangerously delaying them. But more dangerous still was the imminent approach of the full moon and of the spring tides. These, Peary feared, might "stir the great ice fields around us into restlessness" and create a network of water leads across the path, some open, some perhaps thinly and deceptively coated with new ice whose strength would have to be gauged to a nicety if dogs and sledges were not to plunge into the deep and icy water below. Nevertheless, as

he climbed a great pressure ridge behind his snow-house and looked toward the north, he was swept by a sudden surge of excitement. "I felt," he wrote, "the keenest exhilaration, and even exultation, as I climbed over the pressure ridge and breasted the keen air sweeping over the mighty ice, pure and straight from the Pole itself. . . . It was a fine marching morning, clear and sunlit, with a temperature of minus 25°, and the wind of the past few days had subsided to a gentle breeze. The going was the best we had had since leaving land. The floes were large and old, hard, and level, with patches of sapphire-blue ice (the pools of the preceding summer). While the pressure ridges surrounding them were stupendous, some of them fifty feet high, they were not especially hard to negotiate, either through some gap or up the gradual slope of a huge drift of snow. The brilliant sunlight, the good going save for the pressure ridges, the consciousness that we were now well started on the last lap of our journey, and the joy of again being in the lead, affected me like wine. The years seemed to drop from me, and I felt as I had felt in those fifteen years before, when I headed my little party across the great ice cap of Greenland. . . ."

In continuous daylight they traveled for ten hours at a stretch, racing against the approach of the full moon. The ice appeared motionless. But they could hear the floes grinding and groaning on all sides as they neared the 89th parallel. It was not the bitter wind they feared, though it lashed their faces like a whip of steel, nor the pressure ridges which rose dark and massive in the distance. The water leads were the greatest menace. "I was in constant dread," Peary confessed, "lest we encounter an impassable one toward the very end. With every successive march, my fear of such impassable leads had increased," and indeed at every ridge he hurried forward fearing to see from its summit a broad, black stretch of water barring their way to the Pole. Early

in April clouds obscured the sun and left them to march on in a gray and colorless and melancholy light. But they were not depressed, for they were near now, near enough to be certain of success.

On April 6, 1909, Peary with Matthew Henson and four Eskimos reached the North Geographical Pole. "The Pole at last. The prize of three centuries. My dream and goal for twenty years." Five flags were planted: the American flag, the Navy League flag, the Red Cross flag, the "World's Ensign of Liberty and Peace," and the colors of the Delta Kappa Epsilon Fraternity at Bowdoin College, of which Peary was an alumnus. In a crack in a nearby ridge Peary then placed a bottle containing a strip of his national flag and a brief record of the journey, due credit being given to Herbert L. Bridgman and the Peary Arctic Club of New York City whose strenuous efforts had made possible the acquisition "of this geographical prize for the honor and prestige of the United States of America." In another document he, Robert E. Peary of the United States Navy, claimed the entire region in the name of the President of the United States.

► How many people were in the party? Who was nearly as skillful as whom in Arctic travel?

► What does **hazard** mean? (Use a dictionary for any words you don't know.) Describe the first hazard they faced. A **lead,** which rhymes with **bead,** is a channel of water through the ice. Why would leads cause trouble?

► Describe the second hazard. What does **imminent** mean? What is meant by "gauged to a nicety"? What had to be so carefully gauged?

► A **pressure ridge** is a hill of ice built up by pressures in the ice pack. What did Peary do when he climbed the pressure ridge behind his snowhouse? How did he feel? What sort of morning was it? What was the temperature?

► A **floe** is a large, level piece of floating ice. How does Peary describe the floes? What does he say of the pressure ridges surrounding them? What does **negotiate** mean here? At the end of the paragraph, Peary says that he felt much younger. How does he say it?

► Why was the daylight continuous? How long did they travel at a time? What were they racing? What were the floes doing? The 89th parallel is the **latitude** north of the equator that they had reached. You may know what latitude is from the study of geography. If not, use a dictionary. At what latitude is the North Pole? About how many miles were they from the Pole at latitude 89° N.?

► We are told of two things that the explorers did not particularly fear. What were they? What was the greatest danger? What word is used in place of **danger?** What does Peary say he was in constant dread of? What did he do at the top of every pressure ridge?

► On what day did the party reach the North Pole? What do you think might be meant by "the prize of three centuries"? What flags did they plant at the Pole? What is an **ensign** in the sense the word is used here? What is a **fraternity?** What is an **alumnus?**

► Peary left two documents at the North Pole. What is a **document?** What were the documents that he left?

▶ 1. Every syllable, whether it is a whole word or part of a word, has one vowel sound in it. Tell how many syllables each of these words has: **work, workman, workmanship.**

▶ 2. Say the word **porter.** Which syllable has first stress, **por** or **ter?** We say that the syllable that has first stress, **por,** is **accented.** Tell which syllables are accented in these words:

seldom   revive   because   diplomat   silence

▶ 3. In a dictionary, words of two or more syllables are printed in syllables to show how the syllables are spelled. After each word there is a **respelling** of the word, printed in parentheses. The respelling is divided into syllables too, and first stress is shown by an **accent mark: ′.** The respelling shows how the syllables are pronounced. Study the following:

a·live (ə·līv′)   gold·en (gol′dən)

Which syllable is accented in **alive?** In **golden?** Is **golden** divided into syllables for spelling exactly the same way that it is divided for pronunciation? What is the difference?

▶ 4. The words above have two syllables and two degrees of stress. One syllable is accented, and one is not. Now study a word with three degrees of stress: first, middle, and weak.

Say **copycat.** How many syllables are there in **copycat?** Which syllable has first stress? Which has weak stress? Which has middle stress?

Notice that the respelling of **copycat** has two accent marks — a **heavy accent mark** and a **light accent mark:**

cop·y·cat (kop′ē·kat′)

Which accent mark does the syllable with first stress have? Which accent mark does the syllable with middle stress have? Does the syllable with weak stress have an accent mark?

▶ 5. Tell how many degrees of stress each word below has, and tell which syllable has first stress, which weak, and which middle stress (if there is a syllable with middle stress).

ob·tain (əb·tān′)   sil·ver·smith (sil′vər·smith′)
mo·tor·boat (mō′tər·bōt′)   mag·ic (maj′ik)

13

A large part of the trouble people have in spelling comes in spelling syllables with weak stress, because the vowel sound in these syllables gives no clue to the letter to be used in spelling the vowel sound. So weak stress is the degree of stress that we will now be most interested in.

▶ Say these words in which the second syllable has weak stress, and listen to the vowel sound in that syllable:

grammar   baker   actor   murmur

▶ Are the vowel sounds in the last syllable all the same? How does the spelling of the vowel sound differ?

The syllables with weak stress have the vowel sound schwa — the vowel sound we have in words like **fir, heard, word.** This sound tells us nothing about the spelling.

▶ One thing that may help us remember the spelling is the fact that in some words syllables pronounced with weak stress and schwa may be pronounced instead with middle stress and another vowel. For example, the second syllable of **ruin** is usually pronounced with weak stress and schwa. But it may be pronounced with middle stress and the vowel /i/. Try pronouncing **ruin** that way. Then write the word without looking at it.

▶ Pronounce these words twice each. The first time pronounce the second syllable with middle stress and the vowel /i/. The second time pronounce it the usual way, with weak stress and schwa.

goblin   bobbin   coffin   cousin   Latin

■ Close your books and write the words from dictation.

We normally pronounce **doctor** with weak stress and schwa in the last syllable. But we can pronounce it with middle stress and /ō/ in the **or** part. Try pronouncing it this way. Write the word without looking at it.

▶ Pronounce these words twice, first with the vowel /ō/ in the second syllable, then with schwa:

actor   pastor   sector   tailor   terror

■ Close your books and write these words from dictation.

Some noun phrases contain words called **determiners.** These may be any of several particular structures: articles, demonstratives, numbers, quantifiers, possessives. Give an example of each of these.

Even some of these can be broken down into more particular classes. Thus articles are of two kinds:

definite: **the**   nondefinite: **a(n), some, Ø**

We use the nondefinite articles in the following way. Give another example of each:

a(n)	with singular count nouns —	{ **a flower** **an insect**
some	a. with plural count nouns —	{ **some flowers** **some insects**
	b. with noncountable nouns —	{ **some furniture** **some sugar**
Ø (null)	a. with plural count nouns —	{ **Ø flowers** **Ø insects**
	b. with noncountable nouns —	{ **Ø furniture** **Ø courage**

▶ The noun phrase that functions as subject in each sentence below contains an article as the determiner. Name the article. Tell whether it is definite or nondefinite. Tell whether the noun in the noun phrase is a singular count noun, a plural count noun, or a noncountable noun. If the noun phrase contains no other article, the article is null (Ø).

1. The depth was twenty feet.
2. An albatross is a bird.
3. Ships anchor in the harbor.
4. Some jam spotted his necktie.
5. A telegram brought the news.
6. Music fills the air.
7. Some people joined us.
8. The gasoline evaporated.
9. Molasses comes from sugar cane.
10. Automobiles filled the road.

▶ Point out the noun phrases in the predicates of these sentences. They all function as **complements.** After verbs the complement function has a special name — **object of a verb.**

1. Sam likes everybody.
2. The cat caught the mouse.
3. We helped Ben.
4. The colt showed fear.
5. Bill saw him.

▶ In sentence 5, the noun phrase **him** is the object form of the personal pronoun **he.** Say the sentence "Bill saw _____" six times, but each time substitute a different personal pronoun until all have been used. Which personal pronouns have special forms for the object function?

▶ Complete each of the following sentences in four different ways. Use first a proper noun as object, then a personal pronoun, then an indefinite pronoun, then a determiner plus common noun.

6. He likes _____.
7. We found _____.
8. They need _____.

Another function of a noun phrase is in what is called a **prepositional phrase.** This is a group of words made up of a preposition and a noun phrase. A preposition is a word like **in, at, by, near, under. In the house, at the desk, by the table** are prepositional phrases. The noun phrases that follow the prepositions are said to function as objects of the prepositions. If they are personal pronouns, the object forms are used.

▶ Point out the prepositional phrases in the following. Point out the noun phrase within each prepositional phrase.

9. John was in the yard.
10. Jane sits near me.
11. It was under a stone.
12. We found the button behind the box.
13. It may be inside his desk.
14. Bill was waiting around the corner.
15. There is a beetle on your collar.

The fourth function of a noun phrase is its use after one of the forms of the word **be — am, is, are, was, were, may be,** etc. A noun phrase used in this position is said to function as a **verb phrase complement.**

▶ Point out the noun phrases that are used as complements in the following sentences. Tell what kind of noun phrase each one is.

16. Angelo was the winner.
17. It was she.
18. The principal is Mr. Rudolph.
19. The accident was nothing.
20. These animals are marmosets.

▶ We have, therefore, four different kinds of noun phrases and four possible functions. The functions are (1) subject, (2) object of a verb, (3) object of a preposition, (4) complement. Find the noun phrases in the following sentences. Tell of each what kind it is and what its function is.

21. I sat near the chalkboard.
22. That girl is his sister.
23. Marmosets are animals.
24. David bought a record.
25. They drank the milk.
26. Everybody enjoyed the talk.
27. Peary reached his goal.
28. He saw it from a ridge.
29. The food was on the sled.
30. Henson helped him.
31. Eskimos travel on the ice.
32. They use dogs.
33. The dogs pull sleds.

■ The blanks in the following sentences are positions for noun phrases in one of the four functions. Tell what function is marked by each blank. Then write each sentence four times, each time filling the blank with a different kind of noun phrase.

34. _____ laughed.
35. _____ is near _____.
36. _____ watched _____.
37. It was _____.

A Poem

Read this poem about moonlight. Notice the verbs in it. Find the answers to the questions that follow.

Silver

Slowly, silently, now the moon
Walks the night in her silver shoon;
This way, and that, she peers, and sees
Silver fruit upon silver trees;
One by one the casements catch
Her beams beneath the silvery thatch;
Couched in his kennel, like a log,
With paws of silver sleeps a dog;
From their shadowy cote the white breasts peep
Of doves in a silver-feathered sleep;
A harvest mouse goes scampering by,
With silver claws, and silver eye;
And moveless fish in the water gleam,
By silver reeds in a silver stream.

WALTER DE LA MARE

Silver

► The first two lines of the poem are a sentence, even though the poet uses a mark called a **semicolon** at the end instead of a period. What noun phrase functions as subject? Two words that end in **ly** tell the way in which the moon walks. What are the words? Do you remember what kind of adverbs they are?
► The word **shoon** is an old plural noun. What is the modern plural form of this noun?
► What is the subject of Sentence **a** below? Of Sentence **b**?
    a. She peers this way and that.
    b. She sees silver fruit upon silver trees.
► Read the two lines of the poem that say the same things as Sentences **a** and **b** above. Can you see that the two lines you

read are a single sentence? What is the subject? How many verb phrases are there in the predicate? What word connects the verb phrases?

► What is meant by **casement?** Look the word up if you don't know it. What do the casements catch? What is a **thatch?**

► Find the two lines in the poem that express all of these ideas:

A dog sleeps. The dog is couched in his kennel. The dog is like a log. The dog has paws of silver.

What is the subject of lines 7 and 8?

► What is the sentence which has the following as subject?

the white breasts of doves in a silver-feathered sleep

The predicate is the rest of the sentence. What is the predicate of this sentence? What is the shadowy **cote** that the doves have?

► A **harvest mouse** is one that appears in harvest time. What time of the year would that probably be? How does the moon affect the harvest mouse?

► We would be likely to describe the fish as "motionless." What word does the poet use instead? What are **reeds?**

► What word does the poet use again and again to show the effect of moonlight on the objects he names? Which of our five senses is the poet appealing to all through this poem?

■ Poetry and Prose

Write a **prose version** of the poem on page 19. A prose version is something expressed in the usual way, not in a poetic way. For example, in poetry we may use rhyme, but in prose we do not. Poets often turn sentence structure around in complicated ways. For instance, the poet Walter de la Mare said, "Couched in his kennel, like a log, with paws of silver sleeps a dog." In prose we would do it more straightforwardly. We might say something like this: "The dog is sleeping in his kennel with his paws colored silver by the light of the moon."

Describe the things described in the poem "Silver," but describe them in the ordinary prose way. Write your version as a single paragraph.

20

A **morpheme** is a word or a part of a word that has a meaning. Fox is a morpheme because it means a bushy-tailed wild animal. **Foxes,** however, contains two morphemes — two units of meaning. The **es** part means "more than one," so **foxes** contains the morpheme fox and the morpheme plural.

When we are talking about a morpheme, and not just a word or syllable, we underline the morpheme: fox, plural.

Foxes is a two-syllable word and it is made up of two morphemes. The word **cats** is a one-syllable word, but it is made up of two morphemes: cat + plural.

▶ Tell of the following words how many morphemes and how many syllables they have:

    bears   witches   monkey   monkeys   tiger

One kind of morpheme is just the simple base meaning of a word. We show that we are thinking of this base meaning when we underline the base form of the word: fox, witch, monkey. Another kind of morpheme is a meaning like "more than one." We show that we are thinking of this kind of morpheme when we underline the name of the morpheme: plural.

▶ Morphemes like plural are not always spelled the same. For instance, the ending **es** in **foxes** stands for the morpheme plural. But **men** has two morphemes also: man + plural. How is the morpheme plural spelled in the word **men?** In **boys?**

▶ How many morphemes and how many syllables are there in each of the following?

    mice   children   tooth   geese   teeth

Now look at the word **boy's** as in "The boy's coat is on the hook." This word contains the meaning of "having," as in "The boy has a coat." We call this the possessive morpheme.

▶ How many syllables and how many morphemes are there in **boy's?** How many in **man's?** How many in **fox's?** What is the difference in meaning between **foxes** and **fox's?** What is the difference in meaning between **boys** and **boy's?**

▶ Name the morphemes that each of the following contains:

    dog's   dogs   girl's   girls   mothers   mother's

21

► Consider now the word **men's.** This has three morphemes: the base meaning of <u>man</u> + <u>plural</u> + <u>possessive</u>. How is the <u>plural</u> morpheme shown? How is <u>possessive</u> shown?

► **Boy** contains one morpheme; it has the meaning "a male child." **Boy's** contains two: <u>boy</u> + <u>possessive</u>. **Boys** also contains two: <u>boy</u> + <u>plural</u>. But **boys'** contains three. What are they?

► Tell how many morphemes each of the following nouns has and what they are:

goats   table   girls'   John's   children's   ladies'

We will call words made up of just one morpheme **base words.** Words like **fox, boy, monkey, lady, mother** are base words. Other morphemes — like <u>plural</u> and <u>possessive</u> — may be added to base words to widen their meanings.

► There are a large number of morphemes that can be added to base words. Consider the word **teacher.** This is made up of the base word **teach,** a verb, plus the meaning "one who does" what the verb says. In the word **teacher,** the "one who does" morpheme is spelled **er. Teacher** means "one who teaches."

► What does **writer** mean? How many morphemes does the word have? What are the morphemes?

► What does **carrier** mean? How many morphemes does the word have? What are the morphemes?

► The "one who does" morpheme is not always spelled **er.** In many words it is spelled **or: actor, creator, editor.** In a very few it is spelled **ar: liar, beggar.**

► The word **actor's** contains three morphemes — the base word <u>act</u>; the "one who does" morpheme, which we will call <u>er</u>; and the <u>possessive</u>. How many morphemes does **teacher's** contain? What are they?

► The word **sweeper** means "someone or something that sweeps." It contains <u>sweep</u> + <u>er</u>. How many morphemes are there in **sweeper's?** What are they? How many are there in **sweepers'?** Name them.

► Tell what morphemes each of the following contains:

child	children's	worker's	riders'	conductor
tutors'	helpers'	teeth	maker's	losers'
swimmer's	men's	whistler	copiers'	berries

▶ We can show that groups of morphemes are to be rewritten as words by using plus signs and an arrow.

$$\underline{build} + \underline{er} + \underline{plural} + \underline{possessive} \rightarrow$$

The word we would write after this arrow is **builders'.** Explain why.

■ Write the word for each group of morphemes below:

goose + plural →   man + plural + possessive →
girl + possessive →   girl + plural + possessive →
own + er + plural →   own + er + possessive →
own + er + plural + possessive →
paint + er + plural + possessive →
drive + er + plural + possessive →
carry + er + plural + possessive →

Structures in the Verb Phrase

You have seen that **noun phrase** is the term for the general structure that may function as subject, object, or complement. A noun phrase is always composed of one of several more particular structures. In a simple sentence these more particular structures are the following: determiner + common noun, proper noun, personal pronoun, and indefinite pronoun.

Similarly, a **verb phrase** is a general structure. In a simple sentence, a verb phrase functions as the predicate. A verb phrase may be composed of one particular structure — a verb — or of several particular structures — verb + object, verb + adverbial of place, etc. A verb phrase doesn't always contain a verb. But if it doesn't contain a verb, it must contain one of the forms of **be.**

▶ Point out the form of **be** or the verb in each sentence:

1. Bob helped me.
2. Everyone is ready.
3. They ruined the car.
4. Barbara smiled.
5. Mr. Brightfield was a sailor.
6. They are in the garage.
7. My brother mows the lawn.
8. The farmer found the colt near the fence.

► In each of the following sentences, point out the verb phrase and tell whether it contains a verb or a form of **be:**

   9. The dog was in its kennel.
  10. Nancy swallowed the medicine.
  11. Everyone rushed to the rail.
  12. I am an outdoorsman.
  13. The swallows were on their nests.
  14. He is ticklish.
  15. Trucks roared over the highway.
  16. Beetles are insects.

If the verb phrase contains a verb, you know that it may consist of the verb alone, as in "Barbara smiled." If the verb phrase contains a form of **be,** however, the **be** has one of the following structures as complement after it: (1) a noun phrase, (2) an adjective, (3) an adverbial of place.

► What is the function of a noun phrase occurring after a form of **be** in a verb phrase?

► Point out the verb phrases in the following sentences, and tell which noun phrases function as complements:

  17. He is the loser.
  18. The brothers are carpenters.
  19. I am her brother.
  20. Somebody was the hero.
  21. The pets were kittens.

► Adjectives are words like **wise, tall, efficient, courageous.** Which verb phrase contains an adjective?

  a. The judge was wise.   b. The judge was Mr. Ford.

► Point out the adjectives in the predicates of the following sentences:

  22. John was angry.
  23. The gym was empty.
  24. It is elastic.
  25. Her feet are tiny.
  26. People were hungry.

Adverbials of place are of two kinds. They may be single-word adverbs like **outside, upstairs, away, here, there.** Or they may be prepositional phrases, like **in the house, on his desk, near me.**

▶ Which verb phrase contains a prepositional phrase?

    a. He was inside.   b. He was in the kitchen.

▶ Point out the adverbials of place in the following sentences and tell of each whether it is an adverb or a prepositional phrase. If it is a prepositional phrase, point out the noun phrase that functions as object of the preposition.

    27. John was in the gym.

    28. Sheila is outside.

    29. The eggs are inside the refrigerator.

    30. Everyone is here.

    31. They were under the stairs.

▶ Complete each of the following sentences three ways: first with a noun phrase, next with an adjective, third with an adverbial of place.

    32. David was _____.

    33. I am _____.

    34. They are _____.

    35. The people were _____.

▶ Tell what kind of structure follows a form of **be** in each of the following sentences: a noun phrase, an adjective, or an adverbial of place. It may help to know that you can use the word **very** before an adjective: **very angry, very tiny.** But **very** cannot be used before noun phrases or most adverbials of place. We do not normally say "very inside," "very an idea," "very children." Try using **very** if you are in doubt whether the structure is an adjective.

    36. John is angry.

    37. John is outside.

    38. John is the winner.

    39. The turtles are in the pond.

    40. Turtles are animals.

    41. His turtles are friendly.

    42. Cynthia was hungry.

    43. Mr. Evans is a poet.

    44. The other bedroom is upstairs.

    45. I'm tired.

    46. The horses were wild.

    47. Herbert was away.

    48. That lady is my mother.

► 1. There are many ways to make comparisons. One is simply to say that something is like something else. Robert Frost said that the runaway colt looked "like a shadow." Make comparisons using **like** to answer the following questions:

    a. What does a jet plane sound like?

    b. What does a heavy shower of rain look like?

► 2. Another way to make comparisons is to say that something **is** something else. Robert Frost talks about "the curtain of falling flakes" as though the falling snow was really a curtain. Make comparisons in this way with the following.

    a. falling apple blossoms   b. wind in trees

► 3. Suppose someone asked you, "How strong is Harry?" You could use a word like **very, quite,** or **somewhat** to answer the question: "He's very strong." Another way is to think of something or someone with the same amount of strength as Harry and make a comparison. When we do this we put one simple sentence into another. Study the following sentences:

    a. Harry is strong.   b. A weight lifter is strong.

If we want to say that Harry has the same amount of strength as a weightlifter, we must use the morpheme of <u>comparison,</u> and put Sentence **b** into Sentence **a**. This is called the **comparison transformation.**

    a. Harry is strong + <u>comp.</u> + S⎫
    b. A weightlifter is <u>strong.</u>   ⎬ →
                         ⎭
    c. Harry is as strong as a weightlifter is strong.

► The arrow after Sentences **a** and **b** shows that these sentences are to be rewritten as a single sentence — Sentence **c.** In this example, **as . . . as** takes the place of <u>comp.</u> What adjective follows the first **as** in Sentence **c?** Where does the second **as** come? The symbol **S** in Sentence **a** stands for "Sentence." What takes the place of **S** when Sentences **a** and **b** are rewritten?

To complete the comparison transformation, we must drop the repeated adjective **strong** and we may drop the entire predicate of Sentence **b:**

    d. Harry is as strong as a weightlifter is, or

    e. Harry is as strong as a weightlifter.

Make comparisons by using **as ... as** for comp. and making up **b** sentences to replace **S.** Drop the repeated adjective.

    4. Ruth is pretty + comp. + S

    5. George is honest + comp. + S

    6. The lake is quiet + comp. + S

▶ 7. To tell how strong Harry is, we could also compare Harry to someone who isn't as strong as Harry:

    a. Harry is strong + comp. + S ⎫
    b. Bob is strong. ⎬ →
                  ⎭
    c. Harry is stronger than Bob is strong.

To replace the morpheme comp., we add **er** to the adjective **strong** and put in **than.** What replaces the symbol **S?** What must we drop from Sentence **c?**

▶ Make comparisons by using **er than** to replace comp. and making up **b** sentences to replace **S.** Drop the repeated adjective.

    8. The girls are happy + comp. + S

    9. That mountain is high + comp. + S

   10. The dog is lazy + comp + S

▶ 11. Now suppose someone asked you "How beautiful is Sally?" Again, you could use words like **very, quite,** or **extremely:** "She's quite beautiful." You could also say "She's as beautiful as Helen." But would you say "She's beautifuller than Jane?" Why not?

    A number of longer adjectives like **beautiful** and **courageous** don't take **er than.** With such adjectives, we use **more ... than** to replace comp., rather than **er than:**

    a. Sally is beautiful + comp. + S ⎫
    b. Jane is beautiful. ⎬ →
                  ⎭
    c. Sally is more beautiful than Jane is beautiful.

▶ Notice where **more** comes. What replaces **S?** What must be dropped from Sentence **c?** What may be dropped?

▶ Make comparisons by using **more ... than** to replace comp. Drop the entire predicate of your **b** Sentence.

   12. His story was unusual + comp. + S

   13. The boy was serious + comp. + S

   14. Her idea was original + comp. + S

   15. Work is important + comp. + S

T E S T S

1. Copy the following words and put an accent mark ' over the vowel of the syllable that has first stress. If you make mistakes, study pages 3, 13.

above	compare	Saturday	October
wooden	Sally	beside	introduction

2. Study each word below and tell how many syllables it has by writing a numeral. Write the vowel letter in the syllable that has weak stress. If you make mistakes, study pages 3, 13, 14.

obtain	motorboat	golden	grammar
telephone	murmur	paragraph	cousin

3. Copy the following words and after each write a numeral to show how many morphemes it has. If you make mistakes, study pages 21–23.

desks	monkey	girl's	foxes	man
men	men's	teacher	children	actors'
women's	diver's	beggar	kittens'	teeth

4. Write words containing the following morphemes. If you make mistakes, study pages 21–23.

woman + plural →   boy + plural + possessive →
child + possessive →   drive + er + plural →
carry + er + plural + possessive →

5. Copy each noun phrase and write a numeral after each to show whether it functions as (1) a subject, (2) a complement after **be,** (3) the object of a verb, or (4) the object of a preposition. If you make mistakes, study pages 6, 16–17.

a. Ralph smiled.
b. We found them.
c. She was behind everyone.
d. His car is in the alley.
e. These animals are woodchucks.
f. She was very angry.
g. His father is a policeman.
h. They buried the treasure.
i. Turtles lay eggs.

6. Copy each noun phrase below and write the determiners. Write Ø for null. If you make mistakes, study page 7.
   a. An ostrich laid the egg.
   b. Colts eat grass.
   c. Some girls gave a party.

7. Write **Countable** and **Noncountable** as headings. Write each noun below under the heading which tells what kind of noun it is. If you make mistakes, study page 8.
   tiger   mud   mistake   health   blood   lady

8. For each of the sentences below write a numeral to show whether the structure that follows the form of **be** is (1) a noun phrase, (2) an adjective, or (3) an adverbial of place. If you make mistakes, study pages 23–25.
   a. His uncle is a burglar.
   b. The treasure was under the floor.
   c. The colt was nervous.

Write **c** sentences for each of the following, replacing comp. with **as . . . as.** Omit the entire predicate of the **b** sentence. If you make mistakes, study pages 26–27.
   9. a. The boy was nervous + comp. + S ⎫ →
      b. A cat is nervous.   ⎭
  10. a. The girl is pretty + comp. + S ⎫ →
      b. Her mother is pretty.   ⎭

Write **c** sentences for each of the following, replacing comp. with **er than.** Omit the repeated adjective. If you make mistakes, study pages 26–27.
  11. a. The cat was quick + comp. + S ⎫ →
      b. The mouse was quick.   ⎭
  12. a. The play was funny + comp. + S ⎫ →
      b. The movie was funny.   ⎭

Write **c** sentences for each of the following, replacing comp. with **more . . . than.** Omit the entire predicate of the **b** sentence. If you make mistakes, study pages 26–27.
  13. a. The crown was splendid + comp. + S ⎫ →
      b. The throne was splendid.   ⎭
  14. a. The math test was difficult + comp. + S ⎫ →
      b. The science test was difficult.   ⎭

29

PART

2

A Poem

The poet never says what the narrow fellow is, but you should be able to guess easily enough.

A Narrow Fellow in the Grass

A narrow fellow in the grass
Occasionally rides;
You may have met him — did you not?
His notice sudden is.

The grass divides as with a comb,
A spotted shaft is seen;
And then it closes at your feet
And opens further on.

He likes a boggy acre,
A floor too cool for corn.
Yet when a child, and barefoot,
I more than once, at morn,

Have passed, I thought, a whiplash
Unbraiding in the sun —
When, stooping to secure it,
It wrinkled, and was gone.

Several of nature's people
I know, and they know me;
I feel for them a transport
Of cordiality;

But never met this fellow,
Attended or alone,
Without a tighter breathing,
And zero at the bone.

EMILY DICKINSON

► Have you guessed who the narrow fellow in the grass is? In the first stanza the poet says that the narrow fellow **rides** in the grass. Can you think of a reason to say **rides** instead of **crawls** or **wriggles?**

► The poet says "His notice sudden is." Where would we put the form of **be** if this were ordinary prose? What does the poet mean by **sudden notice?**

► How does the poet describe the passage of the narrow fellow through the grass and the glimpse of him as he passes? Read this stanza and decide what **it** refers to in "then it closes at your feet."

► In the third stanza, what does the poet mean by a **boggy acre?** What is the floor of the boggy acre? Why is the **floor** too cool for corn?

► In the days of horse-drawn vehicles, drivers carried whips made of braided leather. Why might the child think the narrow fellow was a whiplash in the sun? What did the child try to do with the whiplash? How did the whiplash move when it disappeared?

► A **transport of cordiality** means a very warm and friendly feeling — affection. What are some of "nature's people" that the poet might feel this way about? Does she feel this way about the narrow fellow?

► In the last stanza what do you think **attended** means? What do you think the poet means by **tighter breathing?** By **zero at the bone?**

► Emily Dickinson sometimes uses rhyme, but very often she simply uses words that are somewhat similar in their final sound or sounds. One example of this similarity in sound rather than rhyme is the use of **rides** and **is** in the first stanza. What consonant sound is the same in these two words? Find two other examples of this similarity of sound in the poem. Find the three pairs of rhyming lines in the poem.

► The poet did not actually describe the narrow fellow, but she made him seem very real. Tell the ways in which you think she accomplished this.

■ Try writing an actual description of one of these narrow fellows in ordinary prose.

You have seen that the "one who does" morpheme, which is most frequently spelled **er,** is also spelled **or** in many words and **ar** in two very common ones. Say the following words and listen to the vowel sound in the syllable that represents the morpheme <u>er</u>:

teacher editor beggar

► Can you tell by the sound how to spell the vowel sound in the last syllable of these words?

The weakly stressed syllable in **teacher, editor,** and **beggar** all have the same vowel sound — schwa (/ə/). Although the sound /ə/ does not help us with the spelling, there are some clues that do. One thing we can do is to decide whether the syllable with /ə/ represents a morpheme. If so, there may be some rules for spelling that morpheme.

As you know, most words with the "one who does" morpheme have the spelling **er** at the end. The only two common words that end in **ar** are **beggar** and **liar.** So this leaves the "one who does" words that end in **or** as spelling problems. There are about five hundred of these.

► When we add the "one who does" morpheme to verbs that end in **ate,** like **create,** we usually spell the final /ə/ sound with the letter **o: creator.** Add the "one who does" morpheme to the following verbs:

educate dictate elevate liberate
separate operate orate demonstrate

► Verbs that end in **ct,** like **collect,** usually use the spelling **or** for this morpheme: **collector.** Add the "one who does" morpheme to the following verbs:

inspect direct protect conduct
contract act prospect instruct

Another way to remember these **or** words is to pronounce this syllable with the middle stress and the vowel /ō/ when you are learning them, rather than with weak stress and /ə/.

► If the final syllable is part of the **er than** that represents the morpheme of comparison, <u>comp.</u>, we regularly add the ending **er.** Add the **er** of comparison to these adjectives:

quiet cold large happy red
pretty sad hot gray big

Tense

> You know that a predicate can begin with a verb or a form of **be.** Tell whether the predicates of these sentences begin with a verb or a form of **be.**

1. Henry was unhappy yesterday.
2. His ears were cold.
3. He played in the park.
4. I am here.
5. Joe is upstairs.
6. The girls are in the garden.
7. The boys play very well.
8. Henry plays baseball.

A verb or a form of **be** that begins a predicate always expresses tense. Usually it has a form which is different for **past tense** than for **present tense.** Past tense usually indicates past time, but present tense usually does not indicate past time.

> The past tense forms of **be** are **was** and **were.** Find them in sentences 1 and 2. Now find the three present tense forms of **be** in sentences 4, 5, and 6. What are they?

> Verbs have one past tense form and two present tense forms. Find the past tense form of **play** in sentence 3. Find the two present tense forms in sentences 7 and 8.

The present tense form **play** is the **simple form.** We use the simple form when the subject is a plural noun phrase, like **the boys,** or when the subject is one of the four personal pronouns **I, we, you,** or **they.** For other subjects we use the **s form: plays, walks, rides, studies.**

> Tell whether the tense of the verb or form of **be** in each sentence is past or present.

9. Donald roped a calf.
10. It is in the closet.
11. We were helpless.
12. Max hunted buffalo.
13. Mrs. Danby drinks tea.
14. The radio was on the shelf.
15. He came late yesterday.
16. I'm sorry.

Study these strings, or sets, of morphemes and the sentences made from them.

Donald + past + rope + a + calf   (*Donald roped a calf.*)
he + pres. + wait   (*He waits.*)

The morpheme <u>past</u> means past tense. It is applied to the verb (or **be**) that follows it. In this case the verb **rope** is changed to the past tense form — **roped.**

► The morpheme <u>pres.</u> means present tense. <u>Pres.</u> is an abbreviation of <u>present</u>. Tense is always applied to what follows it. Why is **wait** changed to the **s** form **waits?** In the third morpheme string, what is the tense morpheme <u>pres.</u> applied to? Why is the form **work** used?

■ In each of the following sentences, apply the tense morpheme to what follows it, and write the sentence.

1. <u>they</u> + p<u>ast</u> + <u>be</u> + <u>late</u>
2. <u>Harry</u> + <u>pres.</u> + <u>ride</u> + <u>a</u> + <u>pony</u>
3. <u>the</u> + <u>girl</u> + <u>plural</u> + <u>past</u> + <u>serve</u> + <u>lunch</u>
4. <u>a</u> + <u>kitten</u> + <u>pres.</u> + <u>be</u> + <u>cute</u>
5. <u>some</u> + <u>people</u> + <u>past</u> + <u>be</u> + <u>sad</u>
6. <u>we</u> + <u>pres.</u> + <u>like</u> + <u>pie</u>
7. <u>I</u> + <u>pres.</u> + <u>be</u> + <u>behind</u> + <u>you</u>
8. <u>Mr. Hance</u> + <u>past</u> + <u>be</u> + <u>there</u>
9. <u>she</u> + <u>past</u> + <u>drop</u> + <u>the</u> + <u>cup</u>

► Study the following sentence:

Mr. Smith sings in the tub.

What is the tense? Does the sentence mean that singing in the tub is a regular habit of Mr. Smith's — something he does right along?

If you want to say that Mr. Smith is singing now, at this moment, we can add <u>be</u> + <u>ing</u>:

a. <u>Mr. Smith</u> + <u>pres.</u> + <u>sing</u> + <u>in</u> + <u>the</u> + <u>tub</u>
b. <u>Mr. Smith</u> + <u>pres.</u> + <u>be</u> + <u>ing</u> + <u>sing</u> + <u>in</u> + <u>the</u> + <u>tub</u>

If we make a sentence out of **b,** we apply the morpheme <u>present</u> to **be** to get **is,** and <u>ing</u> to **sing** to get **singing:**

b. <u>Mr. Smith is singing in the tub.</u>

▶ What is the tense in this sentence: "Mr. Smith sang in the tub"? Here we are saying that at some time in the past Mr. Smith sang in the tub.

▶ But suppose you were telling about walking by Mr. Smith's house at 6 A.M. and that at that exact time you heard the singing in the tub going on. Then you would probably add be + ing to your sentence:

c. Mr. Smith + past + sing + in + the + tub

d. Mr. Smith + past + be + ing + sing + in + the + tub

Notice that past goes with **be.** What does ing go with? What is the actual sentence for **d?**

▶ In the **e** string below, for the sentence "He is brave," the tense morpheme applies to **be.** See what happens when be + ing is added just after tense and before the original **be:**

e. he + pres. + be + brave

f. he + pres. + be + ing + be + brave

In **f,** pres. goes with the **be** of be + ing to give **is,** and ing goes with the original **be** to make **being.** What is the sentence for **f?**

■ Write finished sentences for the following:

10. a. you + past + be + kind

    b. you + past + be + ing + be + kind

11. a. she + pres. + bake + bread

    b. she + pres. + be + ing + bake + bread

12. a. I + pres. + be + careful

    b. I + pres. + be + ing + be + careful

■ Rewrite each sentence string below, adding be + ing after tense. Then write the finished sentence. Remember that tense and ing apply to what follows them.

13. Willis + past + wash + the + car

14. everyone + past + talk

15. the + girl + plural + pres. + be + quiet

16. John + pres. + walk + to + school

17. he + past + sit + down

18. we + past + be + funny

19. a + goat + pres. + eat + grass

36

Expansion of Predicates with have + participle

The participle form is the form of a verb or of **be** that we use after any form of **have** in a simple sentence, as in **had eaten, has talked, have sung, has been.**

Most verbs have participle forms that are the same as the past tense forms — "I talked" and "I had talked," "I thought so" and "I have thought so." We can show this another way by adding the morpheme past and the morpheme participle (part.) to the same verb:

    past + talk → talked   and   part. + talk → talked
    past + think → thought and part. + think → thought
    past + drink → drank   but   part. + drink → drunk

Some verbs have special forms for the participle:

    past + eat → ate   but   part. + eat → eaten
    past + run → ran   but   part. + run → run

► Give the participle forms of the following verbs. Just think what form you would use after **have.**

    play   fall   wait   grow   spend
    drink   seem   forget   drive   write

Study this account of something Bob did yesterday.

    a. He ate lunch.

Then he went to see Tom. Tom's mother invited him to lunch. But he had already had his lunch.

    b. He had eaten lunch.

► What is the tense in Sentence **a?** Sentence **b** tells about something that happened before something else happened. To make Sentence **b,** we add have + part. to **a:**

    a. he + past + eat + lunch
    b. he + past + have + part. + eat + lunch   →

In **b,** have + part. is inserted between tense and the verb. Tense applies to **have:** past + have → had. The morpheme part. applies to the verb **eat:** part. + eat → eaten.

■ Here is an example in which the tense is **present:**

    a. Sue + pres. + help + us *(Sue helps us.)*   →
    b. Sue + pres. + have + part. + help + us
    (Sue has helped us.)

In **b,** pres. goes with have to make **has;** part. goes with help. What is the participle form of **help?**

Here is another example in which have + part. are put into the morpheme string between tense and be:

a. Dan + past + be + there   (*Dan was there.*)

b. Dan + past + have + part. + be + there
(*Dan had been there.*)

▶ What does past go with in **b?**   What word does this make? What does part. go with?   What word does this make?

■ Add have + part. to each of the following, after the tense. Then write the finished sentence.   Remember that tense and part. apply to what follows them, so tense will apply to have, and part. will apply to the verb or to be.

1. John + pres. + see + it
2. we + past + object
3. everyone + pres. + take + the + bus
4. his + mother + past + finish + the + book
5. they + pres. + be + sick
6. the + dog + past + die
7. Millie + pres. + do + the + dish + plural
8. I + pres. + forget
9. someone + past + move + it
10. Murchison + past + go + home

As you have seen, a predicate always contains tense — present or past.   It also always has a form of a verb or **be.** It *may* also have the morphemes be + ing or have + part. Tense is always expressed by the first word in the predicate, which may be a verb, **be,** or **have.**

■ Write a finished sentence for each of the following strings of morphemes.   The arrows show what goes with what.

11. the + bus + past + be + ing + wait
12. I + past + know + about + it
13. they + past + have + part. + memorize + it
14. she + pres. + be + ing + be + kind
15. Ed + pres. + have + part. + drink + the + milk
16. everyone + past + be + ing + watch
17. he + pres. + be + ing + work + here

Read this account by Elizabeth Chesley Baity of people who saw America five hundred years before Columbus.

The Vikings Find America

It was a cold day in the late summer of A.D. 986, and a blustering wind from the north lashed the Atlantic Ocean into great waves. The storm had been raging for days. The men in the battered little boat with the dragon carved on the prow were dead tired and half starved; they wished with all their hearts that they had never left their comfortable homes in Iceland to set sail for Greenland. Even Bjarni Herjolfsson, to whom the dragon ship belonged, had to admit that the lashing winds had blown them off their course. They should long before have reached Greenland, where he was going to join his father, who had followed Eric the Red when this quick-tempered adventurer had had to leave Iceland.

At last they saw land ahead, but their hearts sank when they reached it. The shore stretched empty before them: no masts of ships, no feast-hall roofs. They were hungry for their own kind, for feasts and meetings with friends and relatives, for food and wine

and songs, and for the sagas, or stories of Viking heroes, which the music-making *skalds* sang to the sound of the harp. None of these things was here. When the winds died down, they turned back north again and after many days reached Greenland.

During the long winter evenings in Greenland, Bjarni Herjolfsson often told of the unknown land that he had discovered. Among the people who asked him eager questions about it was young Leif, one of Eric's sons. As he listened, Leif's mind began to burn with the desire to explore this unknown country. Years later he bought a boat from Bjarni, fitted it with provisions, and persuaded thirty-five of his friends to set off on the adventure with him. He even induced old Eric the Red to lead the expedition, in order to bring it luck. Eric protested that he was too old to go, but Leif out-talked him. At last, the day came when they rode down to the shore to set sail. But Eric's horse stumbled, and the old explorer fell and hurt his foot. Eric took this as a bad sign. "I am not destined to discover more countries than this in which we are now living," he told his son. "We shall no longer keep one another company."

Leif sadly said good-bye to his father and turned the dragon prow of his ship toward the land which Bjarni had sighted. They found the new land and went ashore, but it was a poor, cold place of glaciers and flat rock. Leif said, "Unlike Bjarni, we have not failed to come ashore in this country, and I shall now give it a name and call it 'Helluland' (land of flat stones)." Then the party pushed on to discover a new coast with long white beaches backed by woods. Here Leif said, "This land shall be given a name after its nature and shall be called 'Markland' (woodland)."

Again Leif turned his ship to the open sea and sailed with a northeast wind for two days. Again land was sighted.

And such land! Rich grassy meadows for the cattle, tall trees that would make wonderful ships' masts,

waters that swarmed with fish. Scholars now think that this land, which Leif called "Vinland," was the coast of North America somewhere south of the Saint Lawrence River.

Leif divided his party into two groups; each day one group went exploring while the other group rested and took care of the camp. Leif ordered his men to stick together, since it would be a serious thing to be lost in this vast country. But one night the exploring party came home without Thyrker, whom Leif had loved almost as his own father since childhood. Furious and frightened, Leif started out with a searching party of twelve men. After a while they came across Thyrker, who told them in great excitement that he had discovered wild grapes. Now they could make wine! Calling his men together the next day, Leif told them, "We will now do two things. Each day we will gather grapes or we will fell trees for a cargo for my ship."

When the ship was loaded with grapes and timber, they set sail back to Greenland. His adventures earned him a new name — Leif the Lucky.

The year was A.D. 1003.

▶ On a globe or map locate Iceland, Greenland, and the St. Lawrence River. The **j** in Bjarni is pronounced with the sound /y/. Where were Bjarni and his men going? How did it happen that they got to North America instead?

▶ What is the **prow** of a ship? What was carved on the prow of the **Viking** ship? What is a Viking? Look up the word.

▶ Why did their hearts sink when they saw the land? Name some of the things that they had been looking forward to. The word **saga** is defined for you in the story. What is a saga? A **skald** was a minstrel.

▶ Whose son was Leif? Bjarni was called Herjolfsson because he was the son of Herjolf. What do you think Leif's full name was?

▶ Why did Leif persuade his father to lead the expedition? What made Eric change his mind?

▶ What kind of land did Leif and his companions first find? What did they do there that Bjarni had not done? What did Leif name the land? Why? What sort of place was the second coast that they discovered? What did they name that?

▶ Describe the third land that they found. Where do scholars think it was? Leif named it Vinland. Can you figure out from the rest of the story why they called it that?

▶ What two things did the Vikings take back with them?

▶ In what year did Leif discover America? It is interesting that, having discovered this fine new land, the Vikings never returned to it. They never did, though, and it waited for Columbus five hundred years later.

A Point of Spelling

We add **s** to most nouns with the ending **o** to spell the plural. But note the spelling of **heroes.** We always add **es** to some of these nouns. Here are the main ones:

> hero   tomato   potato   echo   Negro

We may add either **es** or **s** to a few others:

> motto   cargo   hobo
> tornado   volcano

You have found that when a syllable containing schwa stands for a morpheme, there may be rules that help with the spelling.

A large number of words end in sounds usually pronounced /ən/. Such endings may represent one of these morphemes, or they may be just part of a word, not separate morphemes at all.

One morpheme that is sometimes represented by /ən/ is what we have called <u>participle</u> (<u>part.</u>). This morpheme has the meaning "what we do to a word to make it a participle." When we apply <u>part.</u> to certain irregular verbs, what we do is add a syllable pronounced /ən/. This is always spelled **en.** Thus <u>part.</u> + <u>eat</u> is **eaten.**

▶ Apply the morpheme <u>part.</u> to the following verbs:

fall	drive	write	forget	choose	ride
take	give	shake	freeze	speak	rise

Another morpheme that is represented by the sounds /ən/ and the spelling **en** makes verbs from adjectives and a few nouns. We will call this morpheme <u>v–en</u>:

<u>red</u> + <u>v–en</u> → **redden**   <u>strength</u> + <u>v–en</u> → **strengthen**

▶ Apply <u>v–en</u> to the following adjectives and nouns:

Adjectives

bright	rough	wide	thick	deaf	black
dark	light	sweet	broad	damp	ripe

Nouns

length   height   heart

The third morpheme that is represented by the sounds /ən/ and the spelling **en** makes adjectives out of nouns. We will call this morpheme <u>adj–en</u>:

<u>oak</u> + <u>adj–en</u> → **oaken**   <u>wool</u> + <u>adj–en</u> → **woolen**

▶ Apply <u>adj–en</u> to the following nouns:

wood	lead	ash	earth
silk	hemp	flax	wax

In words in which /ən/ is not a morpheme, /ə/ may be spelled **e, a, o, i,** or **ai.** But if /ən/ represents a morpheme, schwa is usually spelled **e.**

Studying and Writing Paragraphs

"The Vikings Discover America" contains nine paragraphs varying in length from a single line to a half page. It is difficult to say just how long a paragraph should be or what it should contain. But you will learn something about paragraphing by answering the following questions.

▶ We try to limit the paragraph to the development of a single idea. Which paragraph in the selection on pages 39–41 develops the idea that the Vikings had been blown off course by a storm? Make a list of the ideas in this paragraph that develop this main idea.

▶ When we move into a new, though related, idea, we start a new paragraph. What paragraph of the selection is built around the idea that Bjarni and his crew were disappointed in the land they accidentally found?

▶ The American poet Henry Wadsworth Longfellow read about an ancient tower that was discovered in Newport, Rhode Island, and a skeleton in armor that was found near Fall River, Massachusetts, a town not far from Newport. Seizing on a report that these were relics of the Vikings, he wrote a story in verse called "The Skeleton in Armor." In the poem, the skeleton tells Longfellow of the adventure that brought him to America. You may be interested in finding the poem in a library and reading it.

■ Here are the main ideas behind the story of "A Skeleton in Armor," told briefly in prose and not paragraphed. Read these statements. Then retell the story in your own words, dividing it into paragraphs as you think best. Try to use longer, more interesting sentences. You may wish to add to the story by giving details, either real or imaginary. For example, you can add the real information that a corsair is a sea raider who captures other ships or coastal towns. Or you can describe Hildebrand and his daughter.

The Story the Skeleton Told

1 I was a Viking. I joined a corsair's crew. We led a wild life. We killed many men. 2 I fell in love with a beautiful maiden. She was the daughter of Hildebrand. He was a powerful prince. I asked for permission to marry his daughter. He laughed at me in scorn. He refused to give his consent. 3 Her room was unguarded that night. I carried her away to my ship. We sailed out to sea in a storm. 4 Hildebrand and his men pursued us in another ship. We turned about. We rammed Hildebrand's ship. It sank in the storm. Hildebrand and his men drowned. 5 We sailed westward through the storm. We sailed for three weeks. We came to land at last. I built a tower by the sea. My lady and I lived there for many years. We had children. We were happy. At last my wife died. I buried her beneath the tower. I did not want to live without her. I fell upon my spear and ended my life.

You know that a predicate may begin with one of these:

(1) a form of **be:** James was waiting.

(2) a form of **have:** James had waited.

(3) a verb: James waited.

A fourth structure that may begin the predicate is what is called a **modal.** There are five modals in English. Their present tense forms are **can, may, will, shall,** and **must.**

▶ Point out the modals in the following sentences:

1. John may like it.
2. We must hurry.
3. His father can tame lions.
4. I shall think about it.
5. They will be here soon.

▶ A modal is followed by the **be** form of **be.** What form of a verb follows a modal?

The meanings of the modals are tricky. For instance, when we say "He **may** know," we mean it as possible that he knows. But when we ask "**May** I go to the movies?" we are asking permission to go to the movies. In which sentence below does **must** mean that somebody has to do something? In which does it mean that something is certainly true?

a. Bob must pass the test.

b. Bob's grades must be pretty bad.

▶ The modal **must** is always present tense; it has no past tense form. But the other four modals do have past tense forms:

may, might; can, could; will, would; shall, should.

The past tense forms of the modals are not real past tense in the way that past tense forms of verbs are. "He might go" just means that there is some possibility that he will go. If we want to put the idea of past tense into the sentence, we add have + part.: "He might have gone yesterday."

▶ Point out the past tense forms of the modals in the following:

6. We shall hurry.
7. The lions could be dangerous.
8. The children might enjoy the ride.
9. Nobody would help us.

Tense — past or present — is always expressed by whatever comes first in the predicate — a verb, a form of **be,** a form of **have,** or a modal.   The modals differ from verbs, **have,** and **be** in that they have just one form of the present tense. Pres. + <u>can</u> is always **can,** no matter what the subject is.

■ Write sentences for these strings of morphemes:

10. <u>I</u> + <u>pres.</u> + <u>can</u> + <u>do</u> + <u>it</u>
11. <u>I</u> + <u>past</u> + <u>can</u> + <u>do</u> + <u>it</u>
12. <u>I</u> + <u>past</u> + <u>shall</u> + <u>watch</u> + <u>it</u>
13. <u>I</u> + <u>pres.</u> + <u>must</u> + <u>see</u> + <u>it</u>
14. <u>I</u> + <u>past</u> + <u>may</u> + <u>like</u> + <u>it</u>
15. <u>I</u> + <u>pres.</u> + <u>will</u> + <u>name</u> + <u>it</u>
16. <u>I</u> + <u>past</u> + <u>will</u> + <u>reject</u> + <u>it</u>
17. <u>I</u> + <u>pres.</u> + <u>may</u> + <u>double</u> + <u>it</u>
18. <u>John</u> + <u>pres.</u> + <u>work</u> + <u>hard</u>
19. <u>John</u> + <u>past</u> + <u>work</u> + <u>hard</u>
20. <u>John</u> + <u>pres.</u> + <u>can</u> + <u>work</u> + <u>hard</u>
21. <u>John</u> + <u>past</u> + <u>can</u> + <u>work</u> + <u>hard</u>
22. <u>John</u> + <u>pres.</u> + <u>be</u> + <u>ing</u> + <u>work</u> + <u>hard</u>
23. <u>John</u> + <u>past</u> + <u>be</u> + <u>ing</u> + <u>work</u> + <u>hard</u>
24. <u>John</u> + <u>pres.</u> + <u>have</u> + <u>part.</u> + <u>work</u> + <u>hard</u>
25. <u>John</u> + <u>past</u> + <u>have</u> + <u>part.</u> + <u>work</u> + <u>hard</u>

► Name the verbs in Sentences 10–25.

In strings of morphemes such as these, tense may apply to a modal, a **have,** a **be,** or a verb.   <u>Part.</u> and <u>ing</u> may apply to a **be** or a verb.   Modals do not have <u>ing</u> forms or participle forms.

■ Write sentences from the following:

26. <u>the</u> + <u>girl</u> + <u>plural</u> + <u>past</u> + <u>may</u> + <u>be</u> + <u>angry</u>
27. <u>the</u> + <u>girl</u> + <u>plural</u> + <u>pres.</u> + <u>have</u> + <u>part.</u> + <u>be</u> + <u>busy</u>
28. <u>the</u> + <u>girl</u> + <u>plural</u> + <u>past</u> + <u>have</u> + <u>part.</u> + <u>leave</u>
29. <u>the</u> + <u>girl</u> + <u>plural</u> + <u>pres.</u> + <u>be</u> + <u>ing</u> + <u>wait</u>
30. <u>the</u> + <u>girl</u> + <u>plural</u> + <u>pres.</u> + <u>must</u> + <u>be</u> + <u>ing</u> + <u>wait</u>
31. <u>the</u> + <u>girl</u> + <u>plural</u> + <u>past</u> + <u>shall</u> + <u>have</u> + <u>part.</u> + <u>wait</u>

▶ The morpheme comp. may be represented by **as . . .as, er than,** or **more . . . than,** depending on the comparison we wish to make and the adjective that is used. What kind of word belongs where the dots are in **as . . . as** and **more . . . than?**

Not all comparisons are made by using one of the forms of the morpheme comp. The morpheme comp., in the forms **er than** and **more . . . than,** is used to compare one person or thing with one other person or thing:

> Bob is wiser than Joe.
>
> The story was more serious than the poem.

■ Apply the comparative transformation to the following:

1. a. Sue is busy.
   b. Jane is busy. } →

2. a. Tom is courageous.
   b. Ed is courageous. } →

If we want to compare more than two persons or things, we usually apply a different morpheme of comparison, called the superlative morpheme and abbreviated sup.

With adjectives that take the **er than** form of comp. we can use the **the . . . est of** form of sup.:

a. Jill is pretty + sup. + S
b. The three girls are pretty. } →
c. Jill is the prettiest of the three girls.

▶ We call this form of comparison the **superlative transformation.** What word comes before the adjective in the **c** sentence? What is added to the adjective? What structure in the **b** sentence must be dropped?

With adjectives that require the **more . . . than** form of comp., we use a corresponding form of sup.: **the most . . . of.**

a. Bill is serious + sup + S
b. All the boys are serious. } →
c. Bill is the most serious of all the boys.

▶ What two words come before the adjective in the **c** sentence? Is the form of the adjective changed? What word follows the adjective in the **c** sentence? What structure is dropped from the **b** sentence?

■ Apply the superlative transformation to the following, using the form **the ... est of** if you can do so with the adjective given. If not, use the form **the most ... of.**

3. a. A monkey is foolish + <u>sup.</u> + S
   b. The animals in the zoo are foolish.
4. a. Mr. Brown is old + <u>sup.</u> + S
   b. The men in the club are old.
5. a. Miss Kimball is patient + <u>sup.</u> + S
   b. The teachers are patient.
6. a. The bee is busy + <u>sup.</u> + S
   b. Insects are busy.
7. a. A dog is faithful + <u>sup.</u> + S
   b. Pets are faithful.
8. a. Mrs. Ellis is gentle + <u>sup.</u> + S
   b. The nurses are gentle.

The **c** sentence for Exercise 8 is "Mrs. Ellis is the gentlest of the nurses." In **c** sentences, we can normally leave out the **of** or the **of the:** Mrs. Ellis is the gentlest nurse. How was the noun **nurses** changed when this was done? Rewrite the **c** sentences for 1–6 above, omitting **of** or **of the.**

■ Apply either the comparative or the superlative transformation to the following, depending on whether the comparison is between two or more than two. A question mark is included in the **a** sentence where <u>comp.</u> or <u>sup.</u> would normally be. You must also decide for yourself which forms of <u>comp.</u> or <u>sup.</u> to use. Do not use **as ... as** in these exercises.

9. a. Mr. Brown's work is dangerous + <u>?</u> + S
   b. Mr. Smith's work is dangerous.
10. a. Corn is cheap + <u>?</u> + S
    b. Wheat is cheap.
11. a. That boy is friendly + <u>?</u> + S
    b. The boys in our class are friendly.
12. a. Your plan is practical + <u>?</u> + S
    b. The three plans are practical.
13. a. Bill is popular + <u>?</u> + S
    b. The sixth-grade boys are popular.
14. a. The apple jelly is sweet + <u>?</u> + S
    b. The mint jelly is sweet.

Some Nonsense Rhymes

It is fun to play with words and achieve comical little surprises in poetry. Here are some poems of this sort.

There was a young lady of Niger
Who smiled as she rode on a tiger;
They returned from the ride
With the lady inside,
And the smile on the face of the tiger.

COSMO MONKHOUSE

I never saw a Purple Cow,
I never hope to see one;
But I can tell you, anyhow,
I'd rather see than be one.

GELETT BURGESS

The Rhymes

► The first of these is a **limerick.** A limerick is a five-line poem in which the first, second, and fifth lines rhyme and the third and fourth lines rhyme. The first, second, and fifth lines have three first stresses each. What syllables have the first stress in the second line of the limerick? The third and fourth lines have two first stresses each. What syllables have the first stress in the third line?

Morphemes, Spellings, and Word History

▶ English spelling represents sounds and morphemes, as you have seen. Also, it often shows the histories of words.

The ending al in many words represents a morpheme that makes adjectives out of nouns. We will name this morpheme by using as its symbol the letters that represent it: al.

person + al → **personal**   region + al → **regional**

■ 1. Make adjectives from the following nouns by adding the morpheme al. Copy the sentences **a–c** and put the adjectives into them to replace the blanks.

nation   season   tribe

a. The Indians built a _____ headquarters.
b. Harvesting strawberries is a _____ occupation.
c. Washington is our _____ capital.

2. If we do not know the nouns to which al is added, we may not think that the al represents a morpheme. For example, **animal** was originally an adjective made from the noun **anima,** a Latin word that meant soul or life. **Animal** means having life.

■ Here are some Latin nouns and their meanings. When the morpheme al is added, an adjective is formed. Copy sentences **a–f** and replace the blanks with the adjectives. Notice that the morpheme al is always spelled al, even though the original noun may be changed in the English spelling.

Latin Origin	Meaning	Adjective
vita	life	vita + al → **vital**
totus	all	totus + al → **total**
oris	mouth	oris + al → **oral**
duo	two	duo + al → **dual**
vocis	voice	vocis + al → **vocal**
mentis	mind (brain)	mentis + al → **mental**

a. An opera singer must receive long _____ training.
b. Care of the mouth is called _____ hygiene.
c. Facts about births and deaths are called _____ statistics.
d. If you spend all your savings you have spent the _____ amount.
e. An insane person suffers from _____ illness.
f. A car with two tail pipes has _____ exhausts.

■ The predicate of a simple sentence may begin with **be** or a verb. In this case, tense applies to the **be** or verb. Write sentences for these strings:

1. John + p$\overset{\frown}{\text{ast}}$ + b$\overset{\frown}{\text{e}}$ + foolish
2. John + pr$\overset{\frown}{\text{es}}$. + e$\overset{\frown}{\text{at}}$ + pie

■ We can, as you know, expand a predicate by adding a modal, a <u>have</u> + part., or a <u>be</u> + <u>ing</u>. When we do this, tense applies to the modal, <u>have</u>, or <u>be</u>. Write sentences for these:

3. John + p$\overset{\frown}{\text{ast}}$ + m$\overset{\frown}{\text{ay}}$ + be + foolish
4. John + pr$\overset{\frown}{\text{es}}$. + h$\overset{\frown}{\text{ave}}$ + p$\overset{\frown}{\text{art}}$. + e$\overset{\frown}{\text{at}}$ + the + pie
5. John + p$\overset{\frown}{\text{ast}}$ + b$\overset{\frown}{\text{e}}$ + i$\overset{\frown}{\text{ng}}$ + be + foolish

Here are the five tense-carrying structures as illustrated by the predicates of the sentences you wrote from the morpheme strings:

a. *A form of be:* **was foolish**
b. *A verb:* **eats pie**
c. *A modal:* **might be foolish**
d. *The <u>have</u> of a <u>have</u> + part.:* **has eaten the pie**
e. *The <u>be</u> of a <u>be</u> + <u>ing</u>:* **was being foolish**

If we add a modal and a <u>have</u> + part., the modal comes first, and therefore carries the tense:

6. John + p$\overset{\frown}{\text{ast}}$ + c$\overset{\frown}{\text{an}}$ + have + p$\overset{\frown}{\text{art}}$. + w$\overset{\frown}{\text{ait}}$

▶ What finished sentence does 6 stand for? What does <u>past</u> apply to? What does <u>part.</u> apply to? Does any other morpheme apply to <u>have</u>? What form of <u>have</u> appears in the finished sentence?

If we add a modal and a <u>be</u> + <u>ing</u>, the modal comes first, and once again the modal carries the tense:

7. John + past + can + have + part. + be + ing + wait

▶ What sentence does 7 stand for? What does <u>past</u> apply to? What does <u>part.</u> apply to? Does any other morpheme apply to **be?** What form of **be** appears in the sentence?

Now look at the following string that contains a modal, a have + part., and a <u>be</u> + <u>ing</u>:

8. John + past + may + have + part. + be + ing + wait

What is the finished sentence for 8?

► Tell of each of the following whether the predicate contains (1) a modal, (2) be + ing, (3) have + part. If the predicate contains more than one of these structures, say so, and identify them. Then give the finished sentence for the string.

9. Jane + past + may + be + outside
10. Bill + pres. + must + have + part. + leave
11. she + past + can + be + ing + work
12. we + pres. + have + part. + be + lonely
13. they + pres. + be + ing + raise + tomato + plural
14. he + past + shall + have + part. + be + ing + wear + a + hat
15. Mr. Smith + past + have + part. + be + ing + think

■ Add have + part. to the following and write the finished sentences. If the string contains a modal, where does have + part. come? The arrows have been omitted.

16. Sally + pres. + see + it
17. Jerry + past + be + here
18. Andy + past + may + do + it
19. Tommy + pres. + will + finish + the + cake
20. Judy + past + shall + stop + it

■ Add be + ing to the following strings and write the finished sentences. When do you *not* add be + ing after the tense?

21. Sam + past + feel + happy
22. Sam + pres. + study + history
23. Ron + pres. + must + wait
24. she + past + may + argue
25. Tim + past + will + play + ball

■ You know that when you add a modal and have + part. or a modal and be + ing, the modal comes first. Figure out which comes first, have + part. or be + ing, when you add both. Then add both have + part. and be + ing to the following strings and write the finished sentences.

26. he + past + dance
27. she + pres. + knit
28. they + past + may + act + silly
29. George + pres. + whittle
30. Nan + past + can + sleep + upstairs

The Possessive Transformation

■ 1. A sentence with a form of the verb **have,** such as the following, shows possession: **The girl has a brother.** We can express the same idea by rewriting the "have" sentence as a possessive noun phrase: **the girl's brother.** What was added to the noun phrase **the girl** to show possession? Does a possessive noun phrase like **the girl's brother** have tense?

Write a possessive noun phrase to replace each of these "have" sentences:

   a. The dog has a dish.
   b. Somebody had a wallet.
   c. The lady has a hat.
   d. Jack had a cousin.

■ 2. The subject of the following "have" sentence is plural:

   The boys have a playground.

We can express the same idea by using a possessive noun phrase: **the boys' playground.** What was added to the noun phrase **the boys** to show possession? How could you rewrite the following "have" sentence as a possessive noun phrase?

   The women have an organization.

Write a possessive noun phrase to replace each of these "have" sentences:

   a. The men had lockers.
   b. The farmers have trucks.
   c. The babies have cribs.

■ 3. What kind of noun phrase functions as subject of the following "have" sentence?

   They have some horses.

To rewrite such a "have" sentence as a possessive noun phrase, we use the possessive form of the personal pronoun: **their horses.**

Write a possessive noun phrase to replace each of these "have" sentences:

   a. He had an ice cream cone.
   b. We have some ribbon.
   c. You had a bicycle.
   d. She has a typewriter.
   e. It had a toy.
   f. I have some money.

4. We can make these two sentences into a single sentence by changing the "have" sentence to a possessive noun phrase:

    a. The teacher read the notebooks.

    b. The students have some notebooks.

We will replace a noun phrase in the **a** sentence with a possessive noun phrase made from the "have" sentence. Which will we replace, **the teacher** or **the notebooks?**

We can rewrite the pair of sentences as follows. The symbol **NP** shows which noun phrase will be replaced. Then we will express the ideas of **a** and **b** in a single sentence, **c:**

    a. The teacher read the notebooks → The teacher read + NP

    b. The students have some notebooks → the students' notebooks

    c. The teacher read the students' notebooks.

▶ Where does the first part of Sentence **c** come from? Where does the last part come from?

■ 5. Sentence **c** is called a **transform.** The way we make a transform like **c** from two sentences like **a** and **b** is called the **possessive transformation.** Here is another example:

    a. The teacher read the notes.

    b. The girl has a teacher.

Now, which noun phrase in Sentence **a** will be replaced by the possessive noun phrase made from the "have" sentence? We will use the symbol **NP** to show this:

    a. The teacher read the notes. → NP + read the notes.

    b. The girl has a teacher. → the girl's teacher

Write the transform, Sentence **c.**

■ Apply the possessive transformation to the following pairs of sentences. Write just the transforms — the **c** sentences:

    6. a. The boys shared the candy bars.

       b. The girls have some candy bars.

    7. a. The change belt was out of order.

       b. The conductor has a change belt.

    8. a. The race will be held at the club.

       b. The men have a club.

    9. a. They borrowed the sled.

       b. I have a sled.

   10. a. The boat tipped over.

       b. They have a boat.

The Morpheme <u>have</u> and the Verb "have"

There are two kinds of **have.** One is the <u>have</u> of <u>have</u> + <u>part.</u> that you have been using with the participle form of a verb or of **be.** This <u>have</u> is a morpheme, but it is not a real verb. It is simply the morpheme that we use before participles. If this morpheme <u>have</u> follows the tense morpheme, tense applies to it: <u>pres.</u> + <u>have</u> → **have** or **has;** <u>past</u> + <u>have</u> → **had.**

The other **have** is a real verb — the **have** of "have" sentences. It is followed in simple sentences by a noun phrase:

They have a car.   He had a tractor.

Both the morpheme <u>have</u> and the verb **have** carry tense and do so with the same tense forms: <u>pres.</u> → **have, has;** <u>past</u> → **had.**

► Tell which is which in the following sentences. Say "verb" if the **have** is the regular verb kind. Say "morpheme" if it is the kind used in <u>have</u> + <u>part.</u>

1. We have a pony.
2. Mabel has left.
3. The team has a water boy.
4. They have run.
5. I had been carrying the ball.
6. No one has left.
7. They had a color TV.
8. Mr. Royce has an office in that building.

► Some sentences have both kinds of **have.** Tell which is which in the following:

9. They have had an argument.
10. He could have been having a haircut.
11. We should have had a fishing pole.

Add <u>have</u> + <u>part.</u> to each of the following strings and write the finished sentences:

12. <u>John</u> + <u>past</u> + <u>may</u> + <u>have</u> + <u>chicken pox</u>
13. <u>Alison</u> + <u>pres.</u> + <u>have</u> + <u>three</u> + <u>gumdrop</u> + <u>plural</u>
14. <u>they</u> + <u>pres.</u> + <u>have</u> + <u>the</u> + <u>information</u>
15. <u>I</u> + <u>past</u> + <u>can</u> + <u>have</u> + <u>a</u> + <u>vacation</u>
16. <u>she</u> + <u>past</u> + <u>shall</u> + <u>be</u> + <u>ing</u> + <u>have</u> + <u>a</u> + <u>party</u>
17. <u>he</u> + <u>pres.</u> + <u>may</u> + <u>be</u> + <u>ing</u> + <u>have</u> + <u>a</u> + <u>chill</u>

56

The Meanings of the Verb "have"

You have seen that the <u>have</u> of <u>have</u> + <u>part</u>. is a morpheme that always comes before a participle and never stands alone as a verb.

The other **have,** the one that never has a participle after it, is a verb. But the verb **have** has different meanings. One meaning is possession:

a. She has a motorbike.

Another meaning is not to possess, but to have something happen to one:

b. She had an accident.

Another way to state **b** is this: She suffered an accident.

► Tell whether the verb **have** in each sentence is the "possess" **have** as in **a,** or the "suffer" **have** as in **b:**

1. He had a headache.
2. He had a pony.
3. They have a houseboat.
4. They have the measles.
5. I have a cold.

We also use the verb **have** to mean "take" or "accept":

c. She had a soft drink.

► Tell whether the verb **have** in each sentence below is the "possess" **have** as in **a,** the "suffer" **have** as in **b,** or the "take" **have** as in **c.**

6. She has a kitten.
7. She has cereal for breakfast every morning.
8. He had an orange with his dessert.
9. He had a bad scare.
10. They have tea with their cake.

Another meaning of **have** is to cause something to be done:

d. My father has his hair cut once a week.

► Tell what the meaning of **have** is in each of the following:

11. She will have the dress cleaned.
12. They have a swimming pool.
13. We had some candy at Bob's house.
14. Tom had his friend help him.
15. Alice might have a disappointment.
16. We must have the lock on this door changed.

T E S T S

1. Add the "one who does" morpheme er to the verbs in each of the following sets and write the nouns that result. If you make mistakes, study page 33.

> **Set a:** lie beg **Set b:** direct dictate edit
> **Set c:** work teach follow paint

2. Apply morphemes to the words below as indicated. If you make mistakes, study page 43.

Set a: part. + fall →   part. + take →   part. + freeze →
Set b: wide + v–en →   fat + v–en →   rough + v–en →
Set c: wool + adj–en →   silk + adj–en →   wood + adj–en →

3. Apply the adjective-making morpheme al to the following. If you make mistakes, study page 51.

> nation + al →   vita + al →   oris + al →

4. Apply the morpheme poss. to each of the following. If you make mistakes, study page 54.

> dogs   puppy   he   men   they

5. Copy the first word in the predicate of each sentence and after it write a numeral to tell whether the predicate begins with (1) a verb, (2) a form of **be,** (3) a form of the have morpheme, or (4) a modal. Tell the tense also, by writing present or past. If you make mistakes, study pages 52–53.
   a. John painted the chair.
   b. We were in a hurry.
   c. Joan has finished the book.
   d. They may come later.
   e. Ed had forgotten all about it.
   f. Mark leaves next month.

6. Expand the strings by adding be + ing. Write the finished sentences. If you make mistakes, study pages 35–36, 46–47, 52–53.
   a. everyone + past + help
   b. you + past + joke
   c. somebody + past + be + silly
   d. they + pres. + sell + furniture

7. Expand these strings by adding <u>have</u> + <u>part</u>. Write the finished sentences. If you make mistakes, study pages 37–38, 46–47, 52–53.

    a. <u>Mr. Wheeler</u> + <u>past</u> + <u>miss</u> + <u>the</u> + <u>bus</u>
    b. <u>he</u> + <u>pres.</u> + <u>do</u> + <u>the</u> + <u>work</u>
    c. <u>Jenny</u> + <u>past</u> + <u>have</u> + <u>an</u> + <u>accident</u>
    d. <u>they</u> + <u>past</u> + <u>shall</u> + <u>help</u>

Apply the superlative transformation to the following, using the form **the . . . est of** if you can do so with the adjective given. If not, use the form **the most . . . of.** If you make mistakes, study pages 48–49.

  8. a. Alice is beautiful + <u>sup.</u> + S
     b. The three sisters are beautiful.
  9. a. That street is dark + <u>sup.</u> + S
     b. The streets in that neighborhood are dark.
10. a. The tiger is fierce + <u>sup.</u> + S
     b. The big cats are fierce.
11. a. Elwood seemed anxious + <u>sup.</u> + S
     b. The boys in the principal's office seemed anxious.
12. a. That ring is unusual + <u>sup.</u> + S
     b. All the rings are unusual.
13. a. Mr. Mack is kind + <u>sup.</u> + S
     b. Men are kind.

Apply the possessive transformation to the following. Write just the transforms. If you make mistakes, study pages 54–55.

14. a. The sailboat tipped over in the storm.
     b. We had a sailboat.
15. a. The fathers built the clubhouse.
     b. The boys have a clubhouse.
16. a. Someone stole the car.
     b. The policemen have a car.
17. a. The raincoat leaked.
     b. She had a raincoat.
18. a. We know the husband.
     b. The lady has a husband.
19. a. The pocketbook fell on the sidewalk.
     b. Somebody had a pocketbook.
20. a. The tree fell on the house.
     b. Our neighbors have a house.

PART

3

A Poem

This is a famous poem by a great English poet, Percy Bysshe Shelley. Read it carefully.

Ozymandias

I met a traveler from an antique land
Who said: Two vast and trunkless legs of stone
Stand in the desert. . . . Near them, on the sand,
Half sunk, a shattered visage lies, whose frown,
And wrinkled lip, and sneer of cold command,
Tell that its sculptor well those passions read
Which yet survive, stamped on these lifeless things,
The hand that mocked them, and the heart that fed.
And on the pedestal these words appear:
"My name is Ozymandias, king of kings:
Look on my works, ye Mighty, and despair!"
Nothing beside remains. Round the decay
Of that colossal wreck, boundless and bare
The lone and level sands stretch far away.

Ozymandias

▶ What does **antique** mean in line 1? See a dictionary.

▶ A **trunk** means a body without the head, arms, or legs. What parts of the original statue still stand?

▶ **Visage** means face. Lines four and five tell three things about the face which reveal the character of the king. What are they? The **sculptor** who made the statue "read well" the king's passions. What does **read well** mean?

▶ The king's passions survive the **hand that mocked them.** This was the sculptor, who mocked them by carving them in stone. They also survived **the heart that fed** (them). What does this mean?

▶ There is a great contrast between the words on the king's statue and what the traveler saw in the desert. Look up **irony** in the dictionary. Is this poem ironical?

Poems have different forms.   One form you know is the limerick, used in humorous verse.

"Ozymandias" is a form called a **sonnet.**   Sonnets always have the same number of lines.   How many?

▶ In a sonnet, there is usually a break between the eighth and ninth lines.   In the first eight lines the poet may describe something, and in the rest he may make a point about it or a comment on it.   In the first eight lines of "Ozymandias," he describes the remains of the statue in the desert.   How does he comment on this in the rest of the sonnet?

In a sonnet, every second syllable usually has first or middle stress, and there are usually five such stressed syllables in a line.   Thus, if we use the mark ' over the vowel of the syllable with first or middle stress, the first line goes like this:

I mét a tráveler fróm an ántique lánd

■ Copy the second line and see if you can mark the five prominent stresses in the same way:

Who said: Two vast and trunkless legs of stone

Sometimes, to keep the rhythm from being too monotonous, the poet may change it a little.   The third line goes like this:

Stánd in the désert. . . .   Néar them, ón the sánd,

■ The line below is regular.   Copy it and mark the prominent stresses:

The hand that mocked them, and the heart that fed.

■ Writing Paragraphs

The two parts of a sonnet are something like paragraphs because each part deals with a group of related ideas.   The two groups together make a complete composition.   Retell the content of "Ozymandias" in two prose paragraphs.   Use these beginning sentences:

1. A traveler once told me about the remains of a statue in the desert.   (Then describe the remains.)

2. There was a strange contrast between the proud words on the pedestal and the place where the statue lay.   (Tell about the words and the place.)

1. You have learned that the ending **al** in many words represents a morpheme that makes adjectives out of nouns. Some of these nouns to which the **al** is added are familiar English words. Make adjectives from the following nouns by adding **al:**

> section   margin   navy   front   tide

Use each adjective you made in a sentence.

2. You have also seen that the part of the word to which **al** has been added may not be a familiar English word at all. In a great many English adjectives ending in **al,** the first part of the word is Latin. Some words of this kind were given on page 51. Others are given below.

■ Study the following Latin nouns and their meanings. See how they are made into adjectives. Then copy sentences **a–i** and replace the blanks with the adjectives. Once more you will notice that words with the morpheme <u>al</u> regularly end with the spelling **al.**

Latin Origin	Meaning	Adjective	
ordinis	order	<u>ordinis + al</u>	ordinal
manus	hand	<u>manus + al</u>	manual
dentis	tooth	<u>dentis + al</u>	dental
visus	sight	<u>visus + al</u>	visual
annus	year	<u>annus + al</u>	annual
mortis	death	<u>mortis + al</u>	mortal
norma	rule	<u>norma + al</u>	normal
ruris	country	<u>ruris + al</u>	rural
socius	friend	<u>socius + al</u>	social

a. Every year adds an _____ growth ring to a tree trunk.
b. First, second, third, and so on are _____ numbers.
c. A _____ school is located in the country.
d. Hard labor is _____ labor.
e. A _____ injury is one that results in death.
f. An examination of the teeth is a _____ examination.
g. A _____ event is one that is expected — that happens according to rule.
h. A friendly get-together is a _____ gathering.
i. When we see something, we get a _____ impression of it.

63

The sentences that we have studied so far in this book are **affirmative** statements. This means that they affirm the truth of something — they say that something is so. The opposite of **affirmative** is **negative**. A negative statement says that something is not so. We make an affirmative statement into a negative statement by changing, or transforming it, using the word **not.**

You recall that a verb phrase may begin with one of four structures: a modal, a form of **have,** a form of **be,** or a verb. If the verb phrase begins with one of the first three, we make it negative by simply adding the word **not** after the modal or the form of **have,** or the form of **be.**

> *Modal:* a. he + pres. + must + refuse
> b. he + pres. + must + not + refuse
> *Have:* a. he + pres. + have + part. + refuse
> b. he + pres. + have + not + part. + refuse
> *Be:* a. he + pres. + be + ing + refuse
> b. he + pres. + be + not + ing + refuse

▶ What word does **not** follow in each of the **b** strings above? Give the finished form of each of the six sentences above. Remember that the morphemes pres., past, ing, and part. apply to whatever follows them in a string of morphemes.

■ Make negative strings of morphemes from the following affirmative strings by rewriting the string and putting **not** into it in the proper place. Then write the actual negative sentence.
   1. John + past + be + here
   2. we + past + can + do + it
   3. the + child + plural + pres. + have + part. + eat

■ Now rewrite the following affirmative sentences, making them negative. Do not write the morpheme strings.
   4. I should stay.
   5. Edith is paying attention.
   6. Mr. Wheeler had forgotten.
   7. Mrs. Burbank must like potatoes.
   8. I am going.

If the verb phrase begins with a verb instead of a modal, a form of **have,** or a form of **be,** we make it negative in quite a special way.

The verb phrase of the sentence below begins with a verb:

a. John + past + go + home

We might try putting **not** after the verb, just as we did with modals, **have,** and **be:**

b. John + past + go + not + home

This will give us the sentence "John went not home." People once made negative statements that way, but they don't anymore.

We might try putting **not** after the tense morpheme:

b. John + past + not + go + home

But this leaves the tense with nothing after it that it can apply itself to.   **Not** cannot express past.

► What one can actually do in English is to put in **do** after the tense morpheme and then put in **not.**   The **do** expresses the tense.   Add **do** + **not** after the tense:

b. John + past + do + not + go + home

This will give us the sentence "John did not go home."

► What morphemes would you add to the following affirmative string to make it negative?   Where would you put them?

she + past + sell + the + pony

What would the negative statement be?

■ Write negative strings from the following.   Then write the finished negative statements.

9. he + past + find + it

10. Sylvia + pres. + may + like + it

11. Amy + past + be + in + her + room

12. Pablo + pres. + leave + early

13. Ellen + past + have + part. + try + hard

14. the + sculptor + past + finish + the + statue

Rewrite the following affirmative statements, making them negative:

15. Mike likes watermelon.

16. Barbara is going with us.

17. Ann should do that.

18. Ellen had tried hard.

For every affirmative statement there is a matching question that can be answered with **yes** or **no.** "Yes/no" questions, like negative statements, are made one way with modals, forms of **have,** or forms of **be.** They are made another way with verbs. Study the following. In each pair, **a** is the statement, **b** the question.

Modal: a. he + pres. + can + win
            b. pres. + can + he + win
Have: a. he + pres. + have + part. + win
            b. pres. + have + he + part. + win
Be: a. he + pres. + be + ing + win
            b. pres. + be + he + ing + win

▶ When the verb phrase of string **a** begins with a modal, **have** or **be,** what two morphemes are at the beginning of the **b** string? What does the tense morpheme apply to in the question strings? What are the finished questions?

◼ Write "yes/no" questions to match the following strings:
1. Ed + past + be + here
2. they + pres. + have + part. + finish
3. he + past + will + sing + for + us

Now study the following strings:
Verb: a. he + past + win   (He won.)
          b. past + do + he + win   (Did he win?)

▶ When the first word in the predicate of the statement is a verb, what morpheme appears at the beginning of the question string? What morpheme do we insert after the tense morpheme?

▶ This transformation is the **"yes/no" question transformation.** How does it compare to the negative transformation?

◼ Write the matching "yes/no" question strings for the following. Then write the finished questions.
4. they + past + have + part. + finish
5. we + pres. + must + wait
6. Lou + past + be + ing + admire + the + flower + plural
7. the + cat + pres. + tease + the + dog
8. the + parent + plural + pres. + visit + the + school
9. the + teacher + plural + pres. + be + early

Negative Questions and Contractions

All of the "yes/no" questions you made on page 66 were affirmative ones. But questions can also be negative. We make a question negative by simply adding **not** after the tense-modal, tense-**have,** tense-**be,** or tense-**do:**

   a. <u>past</u> + <u>do</u> + <u>he</u> + <u>win</u> (Did he win?)
   b. <u>past</u> + <u>do</u> + <u>not</u> + <u>he</u> + <u>win</u> (Didn't he win?)

▶ Notice that in the finished sentence for the **b** string above we used **didn't** instead of **did not.** The word **didn't** is a contraction, or shortened form, of **did not.** Note the apostrophe in **didn't.** What does it take the place of?

You probably know the following common contractions with **not,** but review them carefully.

Do: do not → **don't**   does not → **doesn't**
            did not → **didn't**

Modals: cannot → **can't**   could not → **couldn't**
            will not → **won't**   would not → **wouldn't**
            must not → **mustn't**   should not → **shouldn't**
            might not → **mightn't**

Have: have not → **haven't**   has not → **hasn't**
            had not → **hadn't**

Be: is not → **isn't**   are not → **aren't**
            was not → **wasn't**   were not → **weren't**

The usual contraction of **am** and **not** is **ain't,** which of course is not generally used in writing. To contract a sentence with **am not,** we join the subject and **am:**

        I am not going.   **I'm** not going.

Instead of using **isn't** and **aren't,** we can contract **is** and **are** with the subject, the way we contracted **I** and **am:**

        He's not going.   **We're** not going.

■ Write negative questions for the following, using contractions.

   1. Has she arrived?
   2. Are the boys ready?
   3. Can they answer the question?
   4. Should we help?
   5. Were the goldfish hungry?
   6. Does Alice live there?

Creatures and Their Territories

In his remarkable book, *The Territorial Imperative,* Robert Ardrey reports that animals stake out territories, which they defend against intrusion and return to again and again during mating season. This territorial behavior, he argues, is not confined to the lower animals, but may be observed in human conduct as well. Here is an excerpt from the book that describes the territorial behavior of robins and of a kind of fish called the three-spined stickleback. **Lack** is David Lack, an English scientist. Read the excerpt carefully.

The robin is one of the most enthusiastic of territorial creatures. (And as an American I must point out with territorial deflation that what we call a robin is a thrush with a red breast.) Besides his enthusiasm for exclusive property, the English robin has an equal enthusiasm for battle. Lack built a huge aviary thirty feet long with the plan of trapping birds and placing them in the aviary where he could watch them work out their social arrangements. But the plan developed complications. The aviary allowed a beaten bird no room for escape, and one male killed four other males in just four days. While it is possible that the murderer may have had a bad family background, suffered a deprived youth, or been a victim

of propaganda, it seems on the surface more likely that he enjoyed nothing more than a good fight. . . .

Trapping robins, in truth, was far easier than knowing what to do with them. A cock stakes out his borders on a lawn. From then on he has such an excessive curiosity concerning any foreign object lying about on his property that, should it be a trap, he will promptly find himself inside it. Lack had only to put out the most conspicuous trap available, and he would have a robin within two hours. One cock became a nuisance. He came to like traps. Trying to trap his mate, Lack had to let out the cock seven times on one particular day, eight times the next.

Like most birds, the robin sings only within his borders, where he pours out his defense and defiance. As in most species, the song is usually enough to keep away intruders. Should song fail, then the cock is ready for battle, but his opponent must be a robin. By experiment Lack discovered that it was an intruder's red breast that inflamed the proprietor's rage. He would ignore or merely investigate a variety of stuffed birds placed on his lawn; a mere tuft of red feathers was enough to bring on warfare. But since battle is preceded by one last attempt of the proprietor to discourage intrusion by peaceful means, Lack had to witness a scene of fair absurdity: his cock robins, red breasts puffed out like toy balloons, turning from side to side through an arc of 180 degrees while they displayed their frightening frontside to a bunch of red feathers a few inches away.

Niko Tinbergen had a comparable experience with his three-spined sticklebacks, the same creatures who stand on their heads in the water and dig holes in the sand during border disputes. When the breeding season arrives, the male stickleback stakes out a territory and develops a red underside and a furious disposition. He too will attack anything red. In his laboratory Tinbergen had some twenty aquaria lined up along windowsills facing the street, all loaded with three-spined sticklebacks shielded from each other's view

but yearning for mortal enemies. One day, to the scientist's astonishment, every male dashed to the window side of his tank, dorsal spines raised for action. One of Britain's red postal vans had passed in the street outside.

There is a considerable difference, however, between robins and three-spined sticklebacks: robins do not confine either their red breasts or their fiery belligerence to the breeding season, and neither do they confine them to the male. The hen has a red breast too, and in the autumn may stake out a territory of her own, sing on it, and respond to any intrusion with energy equal to the cock's. One autumn morning David Lack put a stuffed robin on the end of a six-foot stake and planted it within the borders of a notably fierce hen. For forty minutes she postured and sang and flew at the insolent specimen, pecking it again and again. Then the breakfast gong rang and Lack's appetite overcame

his scientific curiosity. He pulled up his stake and went into the house. Fortunately, he looked back. The hen was still attacking the place in the air where the stuffed robin had been. And she continued her attacks, violently pecking the air but with each attack striking an imaginary target that sank lower until at last it was only three feet off the ground. I do not believe that any reputable scientist has ever attempted an explanation for this one.

The Robins and Sticklebacks

► **Inflation** means blowing up something, as a balloon. What would **deflation** mean? The author says he is an American. Why does he point out **with territorial deflation** that Americans call the robin by the wrong name?

► What is **exclusive** property? Look up **exclusive,** if necessary.

► The Latin word for bird is **avis.** Figure out from the context — the other words with which it is used — what an aviary is. What are **complications?**

► In human society, anti-social conduct may be blamed on a criminal's family, his lack of early opportunity, or his exposure as a child to crime movies or violent TV shows. Is the author serious in giving these as possible causes for the violence of the cock robin that killed four other males?

► In the second paragraph, the author says that a cock robin **stakes out his borders.** Does he mean that the robin drives stakes at the borders of his territory, or simply that the robin decides where his territory ends? What is **excessive** curiosity?

► Is a foreign object one that comes from another country, like France, or simply an object that doesn't belong where it is?

► What is a **conspicuous** trap? See a dictionary if necessary.

► In the third paragraph, the author says the robin pours out his defense and defiance. What does the expression **pours out** mean here?

► What is meant by the **proprietor?** What is the robin the proprietor of? What does **inflame the proprietor's rage** mean?

▶ In the third paragraph, find a single sentence that expresses about the same ideas as this group of sentences:

> He would pay no attention to stuffed birds. Or he would do nothing more than investigate stuffed birds. There were several kinds of stuffed birds. Somebody placed the stuffed birds on his lawn. Something was enough to bring on warfare. Nothing more than a tuft of red feathers was enough.

In the single sentence from the paragraph, what word means **pay no attention to?** What word means **do nothing more than?** What word means **several kinds?** What words mean **nothing more than?**

▶ **Pre** means before and **cede** comes from a Latin verb meaning **to go.** So what does **preceded** mean?

▶ Does **180 degrees** in the third paragraph mean temperature or half of the 360 divisions of a circle?

▶ The fourth paragraph mentions a man named Niko Tinbergen. Read the paragraph again, then answer these questions:
  a. What was his occupation?
  b. In what kind of place did he do his work?
  c. In what country did he work?

▶ What word in the fourth paragraph comes from the Latin work **aqua,** meaning water?

▶ You learned earlier that **mortis** is a Latin word meaning death. What would a **mortal enemy** be?

▶ The fourth paragraph gives you clues by which you can figure out what **dorsal** means. How many spines, or hard pointed outgrowths, does the stickleback have? From the name **stickleback,** where would you guess these outgrowths are located? The author says that the fish had their **dorsal spines** raised for action. Then what do you think **dorsal** means?

▶ In the last paragraph, what is **fiery belligerence?** (The Latin word for war is **bellum.**)

▶ What does **postured** mean?

▶ Describe the position of the stuffed robin. Did David Lack leave the stuffed robin where it was when he went in for breakfast? Did the hen robin attack an imaginary target that was on the ground or in the air?

You have learned that for every statement there is a matching question that can be answered by **yes** or **no.** When somebody asks you, "Is Betty here?" he is asking you to say whether something is so or not. You say **yes** if it is and **no** if it isn't.

Not all questions ask whether something is so or not. For example, neither **yes** nor **no** is a possible answer to the question "Where is Billy?"

When somebody asks you "Where is Billy?" he is asking you to fill the blank in a statement like "Billy is   (somewhere) ." The information he wants is an adverbial of place like **outside** or **in the house** to replace the (somewhere):

Billy is   outside .

Billy is   in the house .

▶ Questions like "Where is Billy?" are related to statements with **be,** such as the following that contain adverbials of place. Tell what the adverbials of place are in these statements:

1. John is outside.
2. Mary is on the playground.
3. Mr. Wheeler is in the car.
4. The girls are upstairs.

We write "where" questions to match these by using **where** at the beginning, followed by the form of **be** and then the subject:

Be: a. John is outside.

      b. Where is John?

"Where" questions to match statements with modals and **have** are written in the same way. **Where** comes first, then the modal or **have,** then the subject. The adverbial of place, of course, does not appear in the question.

Modal: a. John will be at the station.

       b. Where will John be?

 Have: a. Mary had lived in Dallas.

       b. Where had Mary lived?

▶ Make "where" questions to match these:

5. Edna has been in Boston.
6. They should put the sofa in the living room.
7. The gorilla was in the arena.

You see that we make "where" questions much as we do "yes/no" questions. In both kinds we change the places of the subject and a following tense-modal, tense-**have,** or tense-**be.** But in the "where" question, we put in **where** at the beginning and leave off the adverbial of place at the end:

Be: a. John + pres. + be + here
       b. where + pres. + be + John

Modal: a. the + zebra + past + can + stay + in + the + corral
       b. where + past + can + the + zebra + stay

Have: a. Mary + past + have + part. + go + home
       b. where + past + have + Mary + part. + go

■ 8. Write the finished forms of the statements and questions above.

When the tense is followed by a verb instead of by a modal, **have,** or be, we switch just the subject and the tense, as we do in a "yes/no" question, and put **do** after the tense morpheme so that there will be something to carry the tense:

Verb: a. Jane + past + live + in + Washington
       b. where + past + do + Jane + live

■ 9. Write the finished statement and question for the two strings above.

■ Write "where" questions to match these statements:
10. Billy lives in Buffalo.
11. They swim in the pool.
12. The baskets are near the door.
13. Jane could be at the library.
14. Mrs. Daniels sat in the second row.
15. The boys have met at the drugstore.

Adverbials of Time and "When" Questions

▶ The adverbial of place is just one of a number of kinds of adverbials. Another kind is the **adverbial of time.** An adverbial of time tells **when** something was or happened. It may be an adverb — one word — like **yesterday.** Can you think of another example?

▶ It may be a prepositional phrase like **in the morning, on Tuesday, before noon.** Give another example.

Even certain noun phrases may function as adverbials of time. In "Henry will see us this afternoon," the adverbial of time is the noun phrase **this afternoon.** The word **this** is a common determiner in noun phrases, like **this afternoon,** that function as adverbials of time.

▶ Find the adverbials of time in the following:
1. Max will leave tomorrow.
2. They work in the morning.
3. We are going this week.
4. They met on Tuesday.
5. We must speak to him before noon.

Sentences that contain adverbials of time answer questions that begin with **when.** If somebody asks "When did Billy leave?" he is asking for information to fill the blank in a statement like "Billy left ___(sometime)___." The information he wants is an adverbial of time like **yesterday** or **before lunch.**

Billy left **before lunch.**

We write "when" questions exactly as we do "where" questions, except that **when** relates to time and **where** relates to place. We put **when** at the beginning, switch the subject with a tense-modal, tense-**have,** tense-**be,** or just tense with **do** added, and omit the adverbial of time:

Verb: a. <u>he</u> + <u>past</u> + <u>go</u> + <u>yesterday</u>
          b. <u>when</u> + <u>past</u> + <u>do</u> + <u>he</u> + <u>go</u>
Modal: a. <u>she</u> + <u>pres</u>. + <u>will</u> + <u>go</u> + <u>tomorrow</u>
          b. <u>when</u> + <u>pres</u>. + <u>will</u> + <u>she</u> + <u>go</u>

■ Write strings for "when" questions to match the following strings for statements with adverbials of time. Then write the finished questions.
6. <u>Ed</u> + <u>past</u> + <u>be</u> + <u>ing</u> + <u>work</u> + <u>yesterday</u>
7. <u>Ed</u> + <u>past</u> + <u>have</u> + <u>part</u>. + <u>work</u> + <u>in</u> + <u>the</u> + <u>morning</u>
8. <u>Ed</u> + <u>past</u> + <u>work</u> + <u>this</u> + <u>afternoon</u>
9. <u>they</u> + <u>pres</u>. + <u>will</u> + <u>help</u> + <u>us</u> + <u>today</u>
10. <u>They</u> + <u>past</u> + <u>meet</u> + <u>on</u> + <u>Friday</u>
11. <u>I</u> + <u>past</u> + <u>shall</u> + <u>arrive</u> + <u>at</u> + <u>ten</u>
12. <u>Sally</u> + <u>past</u> + <u>dust</u> + <u>the</u> + <u>piano</u> + <u>last</u> + <u>week</u>
13. <u>Bob</u> + <u>pres</u>. + <u>must</u> + <u>be</u> + <u>here</u> + <u>tonight</u>
14. Write "when" questions to match the statements in 1–5.

George Parrish Jr.

A Poem

Before there were clocks and watches — and even afterwards sometimes — people measured hours by the time it took sand to run from one half of a glass through a hole to the other half. We look through such an hourglass in the illustration opposite. The famous American poet, Henry Wadsworth Longfellow, had an hourglass with sand brought from the Arabian Desert. In this poem he imagines the things that the desert sand may have seen. (One might add to the list the Statue of Ozymandias.)

Sand of the Desert in an Hourglass

A handful of red sand, from the hot clime
    Of Arab deserts brought,
Within this glass becomes the spy of Time,
    The minister of Thought.

How many weary centuries has it been
    About these deserts blown!
How many strange vicissitudes has seen,
    How many histories known!

Perhaps the camels of the Ishmaelite
    Trampled and passed it o'er,
When into Egypt from the Patriarch's sight
    His favorite son they bore.

Perhaps the feet of Moses, burnt and bare,
    Crushed it beneath their tread;
Or Pharaoh's flashing wheels into the air
    Scattered it as they sped;

Or Mary, with the Christ of Nazareth
    Held close in her caress,
Whose pilgrimage of hope and love and faith
    Illumed the wilderness.

Or anchorites beneath Engaddi's palms
    Pacing the Dead Sea beach,
And singing slow their old Armenian psalms
    In half-articulate speech;

Or caravans, that from Bassora's gate
    With westward steps depart;
Or Mecca's pilgrims, confident of Fate,
    And resolute in heart!

These have passed over it, or may have passed!
    Now in this crystal tower
Imprisoned by some curious hand at last,
    It counts the passing hour.

And as I gaze, these narrow walls expand:
    Before my dreamy eye
Stretches the desert, with its shifting sand,
    Its unimpeded sky.

And borne aloft by the sustaining blast,
    This little golden thread
Dilates into a column high and vast,
    A form of fear and dread.

And onward, and across the setting sun,
    Across the boundless plain,
The column and its broader shadow run,
    Till thought pursues in vain.

The vision vanishes!   These walls again
    Shut out the lurid sun,
Shut out the hot, immeasurable plain,
    The half-hour's sand is run!

Sand of the Desert in an Hourglass

▶ The Arab deserts are in such countries as Egypt, Saudi Arabia, Libya. Locate these on a map or on a globe. **Clime** is a poetic word. What is the more usual one?

▶ Longfellow calls the sand the **spy of Time** — it witnessed all the events of history. One meaning of **minister** is servant or agent. What might **minister of thought** mean?

Vicissitudes means changes, often painful ones.

The Ishmaelites were descendants of Ishmael, who was banished from his home. The Bible tells that a caravan of Ishmaelites took Joseph, son of the Patriarch Jacob, to Egypt.

▶ Who was **Moses,** and what did he have to do with Egypt? Why would his feet be burnt and bare?   Look up **Pharaoh.**

▶ What did Mary and Christ of Nazareth have to do with Egypt? **Illumed** is another poetic word. What does it mean? What is the more usual form?

▶ **Anchorites** are religious people who have withdrawn from the world. Where is the Dead Sea? What are the anchorites said to be doing there? What is a **psalm?** What does **articulate** mean? Look up the word in a dictionary.

▶ What is a **caravan?** **Mecca** is the holy Mohammedan city in Saudi Arabia. Mohammedans hope to go there as **pilgrims** at least once in their lifetime. Look up **pilgrims.**

▶ What is the crystal tower mentioned in the eighth stanza? What words in this stanza show that the poet is again speaking of the sand as if it were a person?

▶ In the next stanza, find the subject of the verb **stretches.** It is not in the usual subject position. What does **impede** mean? What is meant by **unimpeded sky?**

▶ What is the **golden thread** mentioned in the third stanza from the end? What does it seem to the poet to become? What does **dilate** mean? What does the poet seem to see happening as described in the next to the last stanza?

▶ When does the vision vanish? What do the walls of his room shut out? What does **lurid** mean?

■ A Report to Write

The commerce that crossed the Arabian deserts for thousands of years moved chiefly by caravan. Even today the caravan is an important means of travel, even though it may be made up of trucks instead of camels.

Look up **caravan** in an encyclopedia or other source of information in the library. Find what caravans are, what kinds of goods they have carried, what routes they have followed, why they were necessary. Write your information as a report.

The Dead Sea, on the boundary between Israel and Jordan, lies 1,300 feet below sea level, and in places the extremely salty water is more than 1,300 feet deep. This north-south lake, 45 miles long and up to 10 miles wide, is situated in a deep, rock-walled canyon. It is fed from the north by the waters of the Jordan River, but has no corresponding outlet, the valley that continues to the south being a bone-dry trough called Wadi Arabia. Evaporation accounts for the heavy concentration of salts in the water which, like the Great Salt Lake in Utah, is a source of valuable minerals.

Writing a Caption

■ A caption gives information about an illustration in very condensed form. Study the caption under the picture above. Then copy single sentences from the caption that say about the same thing as each group of sentences that follows:

1. The lake is situated in a canyon. The canyon is deep. The canyon has rock walls. The lake lies in a north-south direction. The lake is 45 miles long. The lake is up to 10 miles wide.

2. The waters of the Jordan River feed the lake from the north. The lake has no outlet that corresponds to the Jordan River. A valley continues to the south. It is a trough. It is bone-dry. It is called Wadi Arabia.

3. There is a heavy concentration of salts in the water. Evaporation accounts for this. The water is a source of minerals. The minerals are valuable. The water is like the Great Salt Lake in Utah.

■ Facts about the picture of Mecca above are provided here in the form of brief statements. Write a caption for the picture, drawing on this information, but use only a few sentences that present the facts in condensed form.

Mecca is a city. It is in Saudi Arabia. Mohammed was born in Mecca. Mohammed was a Prophet. He founded a religion. The religion is called Islam. Believers in Islam are called Moslems. Mecca is a holy city to Moslems. A mosque stands in the center of Mecca. The Kaaba is inside the mosque. The Kaaba is a small building. The Kaaba contains an object. The object is The Black Stone. The Black Stone is holy to Moslems. Moslems pray five times every day. They face the Kaaba in Mecca during the prayer. A Moslem must make one pilgrimage during his lifetime. He must go to Mecca. Over 150,000 Moslems visit Mecca in some years. Nonbelievers cannot enter Mecca.

Adverbials of Manner and "How" Questions

You know that we can make "where" questions to match statements containing adverbials of place and "when" questions to match those with adverbials of time. A sentence containing both an adverbial of place and an adverbial of time can have both a matching "where" question and a matching "when" question:

    a. Mr. Peebles was in the garage this morning.

    b. When was Mr. Peebles in the garage?

    c. Where was Mr. Peebles this morning?

▶ Which adverbial in **a** was left out of the "when" question?

▶ Which adverbial in **a** was left out of the "where" question?

■ Write two different **wh** questions for each of the following statements.

    1. Jack was here yesterday.

    2. Ned should be in school now.

    3. Lavia lived in Chicago last year.

    4. Clarke left the letter in the box this morning.

Another kind of adverbial is called the **adverbial of manner.** It is usually an adverb — one word like **happily, thoroughly, slowly** — and it tells the way something is done. A few adverbs of manner do not end in **ly.** Sometimes prepositional phrases are used as adverbials of manner.

▶ Point out the adverbials of manner in the following:

    5. The speaker answered the questions patiently.

    6. Miss McHenry was breathing deeply.

    7. Mr. Grandison had fought with courage.

    8. Abe works well.

    9. Dan hit it hard.

    10. Nelda replied in an impatient manner.

    11. This wood burns slowly.

    12. The girl smiled weakly.

Sentences that contain adverbials of manner answer questions that begin with **how.** If somebody asks "How did Billy play?", he is asking for information to fill the blank in a statement like "Billy played ___(in some way)___ ." The information he wants is an adverbial of manner like **clumsily:**

        Billy played ___clumsily___ .

The process of making "how" questions is like that of making "where" and "when" questions. We put **how** at the beginning, omit the adverbial of manner, and change the positions of the subject and a following tense-modal, tense-**have,** tense-**be,** or just tense. If we switch just tense, then of course we put in **do** to carry the tense:

    Be: a. she + past + be + ing + breathe + deeply
           b. how + past + be + she + ing + breathe
  Verb: a. she + past + breathe + deeply
          b. how + past + do + she + breathe

■ Write question strings with **how** to match the following strings that contain adverbials of manner. Then write the finished questions.

    13. they + past + work + carefully
    14. he + past + be + ing + play + beautifully
    15. she + past + will + study + hard
    16. they + pres. + have + part. + listen + thoughtfully
    17. Peter + pres. + dress + neatly

■ 18. Write "how" questions to match the statements numbered 5–12 on page 82.

Adjectives and "How" Questions

We may also make "how" questions that can be answered by statements containing forms of **be** and verbs like **seem, look, taste, feel,** followed by adjectives:

              a. The plan looks good.
              b. How does the plan look?

■ Make "how" questions to match the following:
    19. Dave looks well.
    20. The pie was delicious.
    21. The natives seemed friendly.
    22. The idea sounded fine to Jim.
    23. The milk smelled sour.

In Sentence 21 above, **friendly,** though it ends in **ly,** is an adjective. The ending **ly** is used not only to make adverbs of manner from adjectives but also to make adjectives from certain nouns as in **friendly, costly, kingly, leisurely.**

Long ago you learned to use the word **very** as a test for adjectives. Use the **very** test to tell which complement in the sentences below is an adjective:

a. She is a girl.

b. She is pretty.

▶ The word **very** is an adverb, and one thing that adverbs may do is go with adjectives: **very pretty, very skillful, very hungry.** What kind of word does **very** go with in the following sentence?

He played very skillfully.

As you see, we may use **very** not only with adjectives but also with certain other adverbs.

▶ Another thing that is true about adverbs is that some of them may be repeated. Study the following sentences:

c. He drove very cautiously.

d. He drove very, very cautiously.

Which sentence contains three adverbs? What adverb is repeated? Which sentence makes his driving seem more cautious, **c** or **d?**

The word **very** is one of a group of adverbs that we call **intensifiers.** To **intensify** means to give something more force or emphasis, just as **very** gives the adverb **cautiously** greater emphasis in Sentence **c.** But not all intensifiers increase the degree of emphasis. Study the following sentence:

Helen seemed somewhat surprised.

Here, the intensifier **somewhat** just tells what the speaker thinks about the degree to which Helen appeared surprised. All of the intensifiers give the speaker's judgment about the degree of some quality, manner of action, amount, or number.

■ Find the intensifier in each of the following sentences and tell what kind of word it goes with, adjective or adverb:

1. The train went very slowly.
2. Jerry looked extremely tired.
3. Ruth seemed quite happy.
4. The time passed rather quickly.
5. The present didn't cost very much money.
6. There are very many acorns this year.

The word **how,** which you have been using as the first word of questions that go with adverbials of manner, is an adverb. We use it to ask questions about the way something is done, or the way something looks or tastes or feels, as you have seen. We also use **how** to ask questions about the degree of intensity of a quality or way of doing something:

e. How slowly did the train go?

f. How happy did Ruth seem?

Questions like **e** and **f** ask someone to fill the blanks in sentences like the following:

The train went ___?___ slowly.

Ruth seemed ___?___ happy.

► Find two sentences on page 84 that are answers to **e** and **f,** and tell what intensifiers fill the blanks.

The adjectives **many** and **few** are used with plural count nouns like **acorns** or **visitors** to give the speaker's judgment about the size of the number: **many acorns, few visitors.** The adjectives **much** and **little** are used with noncount nouns like **money** or **snow** to give a judgment about the size of the amount: **much money, little snow.** We use **how** to ask questions about the size of the number or amount described as **many, few, much,** or **little.**

g. How many acorns are there this year?

h. How much money did the present cost?

Questions like **g** and **h** ask someone to fill the blanks in such statements as the following:

There are ___?___ many acorns this year.

The present didn't cost ___?___ much money.

► Find sentences on page 84 that answer **g** and **h** above.

► For each incomplete statement below, write a "how" question. Then copy the incomplete statement and use an intensifier to fill the blank:

7. The man stuttered ___?___ badly.

8. The wolfhound seemed ___?___ hungry.

9. There are ___?___ many squirrels this year.

10. I spent ___?___ much money.

Instead of questions like "How little is left?", we usually ask "How much is left?" The answer is "Very little is left."

1. Make adverbs of manner of the following adjectives by adding **ly,** and use each adverb in the appropriate sentence. If you make mistakes, study pages 63, 82–83.

manual   visual   mortal   annual

a. During fog, pilots cannot steer _____.
b. Cars without automatic transmissions are shifted _____.
c. We celebrate our birthdays _____.
d. The man injured _____ in the accident died this morning.

2. Transform the following strings into negatives by inserting **not** in the proper place, and including **do** to carry the tense when necessary. If you make mistakes, study pages 64–65.

a. Al + past + shall + go + with + us
b. I + pres. + have + part. + find + it
c. Max + pres. + like + milk
d. the + kitten + plural + pres. + be + ing + purr

3. Write "yes/no" questions to match the following strings:

a. they + past + have + part. + eat
b. we + pres. + need + a + guide
c. the + runner + past + be + safe
d. Jack + past + can + help + us

4. Write negative question strings for the following affirmative strings. Then write the finished negative questions, using contractions. If you make mistakes, study pages 66–67.

a. pres. + be + you + hungry
b. pres. + can + Ellie + whistle
c. pres. + do + the + doctor + make + house + call + plural
d. pres. + have + the + train + part. + arrive

5. Write "where" question strings that match the following statement strings. Then write the finished "where" questions. If you make mistakes, study pages 73–74.

a. Bill + pres. + live + in + Detroit
b. the + pupil + plural + pres. + must + stay + in + the + room
c. the + pet + plural + pres. + be + in + the + window
d. Rover + pres. + have + part. + bury + his + bone + in + the + garden

6. Write "when" question strings to match the statement strings below. Then write the finished "when" questions. If you make mistakes, study pages 74–75.
   a. the + girl + past + take + the + cart + yesterday
   b. the + dog + plural + past + be + ing + bark + this + morning
   c. Mel + pres. + will + leave + tonight
   d. the + bus + past + have + part. + arrive + at + noon
   e. Alice + past + shall + have + part. + leave + before + noon

7. Write question strings with **how** to match the statement strings below. Then write the finished "how" questions. If you make mistakes, study pages 82–83.
   a. they + past + go + gladly
   b. John + pres. + have + part. + work + efficiently
   c. the + furnace + past + shall + run + quietly
   d. Billy + pres. + be + ing + play + skillfully
   e. the + principal + past + answer + question + plural + with + patience
   f. she + past + have + part. + sing + well

8. Write "where," "when," or "how" questions to match the following statements, using **where** if the statement contains an adverbial of place, **when** if it contains an adverbial of time, and **how** if it contains an adverbial of manner. Write just the finished questions. If you make mistakes, study pages 73–75, 82–83.
   a. Nelda was working at midnight.
   b. He should do it quietly.
   c. They swam in the creek.
   d. She hid the watch under a pillow.
   e. Jim had finished at ten.
   f. The choir sang sweetly.
   g. The check came yesterday morning.
   h. The monster was in a cave.
   i. The engine is running smoothly.
   j. We could build the hut there.
   k. George has been waiting outside.
   l. Edna would speak cleverly.
   m. The carpenter can come next week.
   n. Snow has fallen north of here.

PART

4

A Poem

Ascent to the Sierras

Beyond the great valley an odd instinctive rising
Begins to possess the ground, the flatness gathers to little
    humps and barrows, low aimless ridges,
A sudden violence of rock crowns them.   The crowded
    orchards end, they have come to a stone knife;
The farms are finished; the sudden foot of the sierra.   Hill
    over hill, snow-ridge beyond mountain gather
The blue air of their height about them.

    Here at the foot of the pass
The fierce clans of the mountain you'd think for
    thousands of years,
Men with harsh mouths and eyes like eagles' hunger,
Have gathered among these rocks at the dead hour
Of the morning star and the stars waning
To raid the plain and at moonrise returning driven
Their scared booty to the highlands, the tossing horns
And glazed eyes in the light of torches.   The men have
    looked back
Standing above these rock-heads to bark laughter
At the burning granaries and the farms and the town
That sow the dark flat land with terrible rubies . . .
Lighting the dead . . .
    It is not true: from this land
The curse was lifted; the highlands have kept peace with
    the valleys; no blood in the sod; there is no old sword
Keeping grim rust, no primal sorrow.   The people are all
    one people, their homes never knew harrying;
The tribes before them were acorn-eaters, harmless as deer.
    Oh fortunate earth; you must find someone
To make you bitter music; how else will you take bonds
    of the future, against the wolf in men's hearts?

ROBINSON JEFFERS

89

Ascent to the Sierras

The Sierras are high mountains in our far West.

▶ An **instinctive** rising is a rising that seems to come from within, as though the land were alive. What crowns the little humps and barrows, and the low ridges? What would **aimless** ridges be?

▶ What lies at the end of the orchards, as though suddenly they have been cut off?

▶ How does the poet describe the distant height of hill, mountain, and snow-ridge?

▶ In many parts of the world violence and pillage have marked the lands where mountains and plains meet. In the second line of the second stanza the poet inserts the words **you'd think** after the subject, **the fierce clans of the mountain.** Why would you think such fierce clans would be found here?

▶ What were the eyes of the fierce mountain men like? What adjective does the poet use to describe their mouths?

▶ At what time of day did the clansmen gather to raid the plain? At what time of day did they return?

▶ The subject of the first sentence of the second stanza is very complicated: **the fierce clans of the mountain, men with harsh mouths and eyes like eagles' hunger.** The main things that are said about the subject are these: **have gathered to raid the plain and have driven their scared booty to the highlands.** Where have the clans gathered? What do you think their "scared booty" must have been? What other details are given in this long and complicated sentence?

▶ What were the **terrible rubies** with which they sowed the plain?

▶ Did all this ever actually happen in our Sierra country? What does the poet mean by **the curse was lifted?**

▶ Look up **primal** and **harry.**

▶ To take a bond of someone is to require a sum of money as a guarantee. To **take bonds of the future** would be to require some guarantee from the future. Against what would the fortunate earth want a guarantee? What does **the wolf in men's hearts** mean?

▶ Do you think that the poet fears that our own land may not always be safe from violence and pillage?

▶ "Ascent to the Sierras" is a great description of a scene in poetic form, although this is not the poem's only claim to distinction. Go back to the poem and pick out some expressions that seem to you to make the scene real.

Here is a description in prose of the Tisisat Falls, a little-known waterfall on the Blue Nile in Africa:

> . . . Looking down from the top one sees far below a narrow gorge filled with racing water, and it twists and turns until it is finally lost to sight in the surrounding cliffs. The spray flung up from this gorge creates a perpetual soft rain which is blown up the hillside opposite, and here a forest of wet green reeds keeps waving from side to side like seaweed at the bottom of the sea. To stand there just for five minutes means that you will be wet to the skin. For the newcomer it is an alarming sort of place, and he will see with surprise flocks of little black birds with pointed pinkish wings flying directly into the spray and landing on the slippery rocks at the very lip where the water makes its frightful downward plunge. Unconcerned they fly off again through a rainbow which is nearly circular and which hangs in the spray like a whirling firework.

▶ 1. Much of the vividness of this description depends on words that indicate movement. The water is **racing.** It **twists** and **turns.** Spray is **flung** up. Give other examples.

▶ 2. The wet green reeds keep waving from side to side **like seaweed at the bottom of the sea.** A comparison like this one is called a **simile.** Find another simile in the description.

▶ 3. Find all the adjectives you can which describe size or shape. Find all the expressions that appeal to the sense of sight. Find those that appeal to the sense of touch.

■ 4. Choose a scene that you are familiar with and that involves movement: a horse or car race, a storm, the surf, a freight train rounding a curve. Write a paragraph of description.

One of the morphemes which you have used to change words from one class, such as nouns, to another, such as adjectives, is usually spelled **al.** You have learned that the **al** may be added to English nouns, such as **person,** and also to words which had the form of nouns in another language, but are not ordinarily nouns in modern English: **totus + al → total.**

▶ We add **al** to concrete nouns, nouns which refer to things that actually exist in the world of real things, such as **tide, section, manus** (hand). We also add **al** to abstract nouns, nouns that refer to qualities like the quality of intellect, **mentis** (mind); or to conditions or states, like the state of death, **mortis.** What are the adjectives that refer to the quality of intellect and to the condition of death? What adjective refers to something done by hand?

■ Decide whether each of the following adjectives was made from a concrete or an abstract noun. If you need to, look at the meanings of the Latin nouns on pages 51 and 63. Write each adjective under either the heading concrete or abstract.

vital   dental   rural   social   normal   total

▶ One of the morphemes which makes nouns from other words is usually spelled **ity.** Try making nouns by adding **ity** to the six adjectives above: **vital, dental, rural, social, normal, total.** Then look up the six words that you have made by combining adjectives and **ity** and see which of them are actually English nouns.

▶ The ending **ity** is used to make abstract nouns, not concrete ones. Did you find that **vitality, normality,** and **totality** are actual English nouns? Are these three nouns concrete or abstract?

■ Add **ity** to as many of the following adjectives as you can, being sure that each result is an abstract noun, one that refers to a quality, state, or condition. Use a dictionary to make sure that your work results in actual nouns.

mental   vocal   oral   mortal   manual   local
moral   liberal   postal   original   tribal   final

In the **ity** words, can you hear the sound /a/ in the **al** syllable?

▶ 1. What kind of adverbial is there in the following statement?

They work in the city.

Do you think that the adverbial of place is a necessary complement in this sentence, or could we remove it and still have a good English sentence? Let's try it:

They work.

Is "They work" a good English sentence? Then is the adverbial of place **in the city** simply additional information?

▶ 2. What kind of adverbial do you find in the following statement?

He broke a window this morning.

Let's remove the adverbial of time and see whether we have a good sentence left. Is "He broke a window" a good English sentence? Then is the adverbial of time a necessary complement, or simply additional information?

▶ 3. You have removed an adverbial of place and an adverbial of time from sentences without destroying the sentences. What kind of adverbial does the following sentence contain?

She cried softly.

If we remove the adverbial of manner, we have left "She cried." Is this a good sentence? Then is the adverbial of manner, like the other two adverbials, simply additional information rather than a necessary part of the sentence?

▶ 4. Can we think of all adverbials as simply additional information in all sentences in which they occur? What is the adverbial in the following sentence?

The boys were in a boat.

Does the verb phrase begin with a verb or a form of **be?** What kind of adverbial is **in a boat?** Can we remove the adverbial of place and still have a good sentence? Let's try it.

The boys were

Is this a good sentence? Then is the adverbial of place **in a boat** simply additional information, or is it a necessary complement? Would you say that except for adverbials of place after **be,** adverbials seem to be just additional information?

▶ Study the following statements and find the objects of the verbs:

John washed the car.

John was washing the dog.

Are the noun phrases, **the car** and **the dog,** human or non-human — that is, do they refer to persons or don't they?

When someone asks you a question like "What did John wash?" he is asking you to fill the blank in a statement like "John washed ___(something)___ ." The information he wants is a nonhuman noun phrase like **the car** or **the dog,** that functions as the object of a verb like **wash:**

John washed **the car.**

John was washing **the dog.**

The "wh" word **what** is used to ask questions that can be answered by a nonhuman noun phrase.

We write "wh" questions with **what** in just the same way that we write them with **where, when,** and **how.** We write the "wh" word first; we reverse the subject with a tense-**modal,** tense-**have,** tense-**be,** or tense. The question does not contain the noun phrase object that appears in the matching statement.

Verb: a. John + past + wash + the + car

  b. What + past + do + John + wash

  Be: a. John + past + be + ing + wash + the + dog

  b. What + past + be + John + ing + wash

■ Write question strings with **what** to match the following statement strings. Then write the finished questions.

1. Minnie + pres. + be + ing + study + history
2. Joan + past + clean + the + kitchen
3. Jane + pres. + have + part + see + the + play
4. Alice + pres. + must + read + the + poem

■ Make questions with **what** to match the following statements:

5. Mike is reading a book.
6. Sylvia will wear a new dress.
7. The man ordered a steak.
8. They have brought a parrot.
9. Daniel drank the orange juice.
10. Millie should study geography.

"Wh" Questions with "Whom" and "What"

▶ Find the object of the verb in this sentence:

John saw the girl.

Is the noun phrase **the girl** human or nonhuman — that is, does it refer to a person or doesn't it?

When someone asks you a question like "Whom did John see?" he is asking you to fill the blank in a statement like "John saw ___(somebody)___." The information he wants is a human noun phrase, like **the girl** or **Mary,** that functions as the object of a verb like **see.**

When we ask questions that can be answered by human noun phrases, we use **who** or **whom** instead of **what.** **Whom** is the object form of **who,** as **him** is the object form of **he,** and **them** is the object form of **they.** That is why in writing we generally use **whom** in the question when we are asking for an answer that will have a human noun phrase as object. In speaking, we sometimes use **who** instead. Here is another example:

a. Alice was helping Bill.
b. Whom was Alice helping?

■ Write similar questions to match the following incomplete statements, using **whom.** Then complete the statements, supplying human noun phrases to replace ___(somebody)___.

1. He had insulted ___(somebody)___.
2. Dr. Marples chose ___(somebody)___.
3. The police are questioning ___(somebody)___.
4. Mike should ask ___(somebody)___.

■ Write questions with **what** or **whom** to match the following statements. Use **whom** if the object is a human noun phrase. Use **what** if the object is nonhuman.

5. Sam caught a fish.
6. We should invite Barbara.
7. He asked a clerk.
8. The children found a cigar box.
9. The bear had climbed a tree.
10. They rescued Mr. Gordon.
11. The teacher scolded a third grader.
12. The soldier helped a lady.
13. Miss Martin consulted the computer tape.

A Myth

In 1903, two American brothers, Orville and Wilbur Wright, made the first flight in an airplane. But they weren't the first to dream of flying. Read the following story of fliers who tried their wings more than two thousand years ago.

Daedalus and Icarus

Daedalus was an architect employed by the King of Crete. He was an extraordinarily clever architect, and he built for the King a wonderful labyrinth in which people might wander lost for days unless they knew the secret plan of it. But kings are ever fickle, and one day Daedalus fell into the King's disfavor. He was put into prison, along with his son Icarus. Through his ingenuity, Daedalus managed to escape from prison and flee, taking the boy with him. But they were not able to leave the island of Crete. Every ship was watched, and there was no way for them to cross the seas.

"If only we were birds," Daedalus said to his son, "we could fly away to freedom." Then, thoughtfully, he said to himself, "If birds can fly, why cannot men, who are much cleverer than birds?"

His active imagination went to work at once. He knew that birds flew by means of feathered wings, so he decided to construct such wings. First he obtained a large number of feathers, mostly from birds of considerable size, like eagles. These he fashioned into wings, sewing them together with thread and then fixing them with wax. When he had made a pair of wings, he went to a deserted beach to try them out.

His first efforts were unsuccessful. He ran along the beach and launched himself into the air, flapping the wings, but was unable to stay aloft for more than a few yards. He decided that the elevation of the wings was wrong, and he patiently went to work to alter it. The next time he flew more than a hundred yards. He made a few more adjustments in the shape and contour of the wings and tried again. This time the result was all that he desired. He soared into the air and moved forward almost effortlessly, rising to a height of a thousand feet and swooping and gliding as he pleased. He obtained as he flew some marvelous views of the island of Crete.

After landing, Daedalus set instantly about making a similar pair of wings for his son Icarus, fashioning them in exactly the same way but on a smaller scale, for Icarus was not yet full grown. When the wings were finished, he fastened them to his son's shoulders and explained the principles of flight. After Icarus had made several trials from the beach, performing them creditably, they were ready to escape.

Daedalus briefed his son before departure. "The important thing, my boy," he said, "is to maintain the right altitude — let us say between seven hundred and a thousand feet. If we fly lower than that, the fog and dew will dampen the feathers and make them heavy. At higher altitudes, the fierce rays of the sun

will melt the wax which binds the feathers together. In either case we would fall to our death. Follow me, and do as I do."

Icarus promised to obey, and they took off, rising above the island and moving out over the sea. At first Icarus followed his father carefully, flying just below him and to the right. But, alas, wings are intoxicating things. Soon Icarus was not content to follow his father's sober and prudent plan of flight. Thus, he thought to himself, might a poor cart bounce along a road on the plain.

Seized suddenly by an impulse to try his wings to the utmost, Icarus swooped past his father and went into a series of loops and rolls. Emerging from these easily, he decided that his father, though a clever man, was overly cautious: It took youth and courage to show what wings could do. Above all, he wanted to fly high, as far above the earth as possible.

Of a sudden, while his father watched with dismay, Icarus went into a steep climb. He soared ever upward, feeling the fierce exhilaration of complete liberation from the earth. But it was as Daedalus had said. As he drew nearer the sun, the heat grew more intense and melted the wax that bound the feathers together. One by one they fell off and dropped away. Soon Icarus could fly no more. He tried bravely to beat the feathers that remained to him, but in vain. He lost his forward motion, spun, and plummeted into the sea.

Daedalus circled again and again the spot where Icarus had fallen, but there was no sign of the boy, only a few feathers floating on the waves. The grief-stricken father flew on to land, and offered up his wings at the temple of Apollo, with prayers for his lost son. Daedalus never flew again.

Daedalus and Icarus

▶ Crete is in the Mediterranean Sea. Find it on a map or a globe. What is an **architect?**

Labyrinth was originally a proper noun — the name of the maze Daedalus was supposed to have built in Crete. Now it means a maze, or anything hard to find one's way through.

▶ What does "kings are ever fickle" mean? Look up **ingenuity.** Why were Daedalus and Icarus unable to leave Crete?

▶ What gave Daedalus the idea of flying? How did he make his wings? Describe his first efforts to fly. What is meant by **elevation** and by **contour?** See a dictionary.

▶ What is a **smaller scale?** Why were Icarus' wings made on a smaller scale? What does **creditably** mean? What did Icarus do creditably?

▶ What is **altitude?** What did Daedalus fear would happen if they flew at too low an altitude? at too high an altitude?

▶ How did Icarus fly at first? What is meant by "wings are intoxicating things"? To what did Icarus compare the way they were flying?

▶ What was the impulse that seized Icarus? Look up **impulse.** Describe what he did. What does **plummet** mean? What happened to Icarus?

▶ What did Daedalus do with his wings? Who was Apollo?

The story of *Daedalus and Icarus* is based on an ancient myth which has been rewritten in modern language. Here are the first two paragraphs of another story based on a myth. Study them.

Echo

A maiden named Echo was one of the loveliest of the nymphs that served the Greek goddess Diana. Beautiful though she was, her tongue was never still. She talked continually even in the presence of Juno, the Queen of the gods. No reproof could silence the running chatter that fell about Echo from morning until night like the sound of falling water.

At length, when all other measures had failed to silence the vivacious nymph, Juno took from her the ability to speak in her own words. She could only repeat the last part of another's sentence.

▶ 1. What simile can you find in the first paragraph?

▶ 2. What single sentence above expresses the following ideas? Running chatter fell about Echo from morning until night. It was like the sound of falling water. No reproof could silence it.

■ 3. The following brief statements contain all the information you need to write the last two paragraphs of the story. But you will need to write these paragraphs in your own words, using longer, more interesting sentences and deciding when you should begin the second of the two paragraphs.

The punishment began. Echo fell in love with Narcissus soon after this. Narcissus was young. Narcissus said something. Echo could only repeat after him the last part of this. She repeated senselessly. He spurned this maiden naturally. She was foolish. His scorn broke her heart. This was long ago. You may hear the voice of the nymph Echo even today. You may hear it in the wild cliffs of the mountains. The voice repeats something again and again. Sounds come her way. The voice repeats the last part of every sound.

In English there are base morphemes, like <u>sing</u> and <u>bad</u>, and morphemes that we add to base words. The morphemes that we add are of two kinds: **inflectional** and **derivational.**

There are only eight inflectional morphemes in English, and if you have studied earlier books in this series you are familiar with all of them. Four of the eight inflectional morphemes are added to verbs: <u>present</u>, <u>past</u>, <u>ing</u>, and <u>part</u>. Two, <u>plural</u> and <u>possessive</u>, are added to noun phrases. The remaining two inflectional morphemes are the two morphemes of comparison: <u>comparative</u> and <u>superlative</u>.

You have seen that when we add the morpheme spelled **ity** to adjectives that end in **al,** we form abstract nouns — nouns that refer to a quality, state, or condition:

<u>mental</u> + <u>ity</u> → **mentality**   <u>vital</u> + <u>ity</u> → **vitality**

Compare the respellings of **mental** and **mentality, vital** and **vitality:**

mental (men′təl)   mentality (men·tal′ə·tē)
vital (vit′əl)   vitality (vi·tal′ə·tē)

► What syllable in **mental** and **vital** is accented? What is the vowel sound in the syllable with weak stress in each word?

► When you add **ity** to **mental** and **vital,** what syllable is accented? What is the vowel sound in the accented syllable? Do you see that adding **ity** to words like **mental** and **vital** helps you spell the **əl** syllable because you can hear the / a / sound?

We can add **ity** to other adjectives, also, to make abstract nouns. Study the following:

<u>rapid</u> + <u>ity</u> → **rapidity**   <u>frigid</u> + <u>ity</u> → **frigidity**

Which syllable in **rapid** and **frigid** is accented?

Even though many people pronounce the **id** in **rapid** and **frigid** as / id /, many others use the schwa sound:

rapid (rap′əd)   **frigid** (frig′əd)

When we add **ity** to words like **rapid** and **frigid,** what happens to the accent? Study the following respellings.

rapidity (ra·pid′ə·tē)   **frigidity** (fri·jid′ə·tē)

Add **ity** to the following adjectives as an aid to remembering the spelling of the **id** syllable:

stupid   solid   valid   timid   acid

101

Adding Adverbials to Sentences

You have seen that adverbials of place, time and manner may be simply additional information in sentences with verbs. In sentences with forms of **be,** adverbials of place are true complements, necessary to the sentence.

▶ 1. If an adverbial in a sentence is additional information, then the sentence must contain at least two ideas — one expressed by the basic sentence, the other expressed by the adverbial. Do you think the idea of the basic sentence and the idea of the adverbial could be expressed in two separate sentences?

▶ Study the following affirmative statement:

    a. The snow began.

Is this a good basic English sentence?

Suppose that we have this additional information about the beginning of the snow:

    b. It happened silently.

We can add the additional information in Sentence **b** to Sentence **a,** and then **a** will express all the meaning of both **a** and **b.** We will put the symbol S at the end of Sentence **a** to show that we will put the meaning of another sentence at that place in Sentence **a.** Then we will reduce Sentence **b** to the adverbial of manner **silently,** and insert, or embed, **silently** in Sentence **a,** replacing the S:

    a. The snow began + S. ⎫
                     ⎬ →
    b. It happened silently. ⎭

    c. The snow began silently.

2. Here is an example with an adverbial of place:

    a. The snow began + S. ⎫
                     ⎬ →
    b. It happened in the hills. ⎭

    c. The snow began in the hills.

Here is an example with an adverbial of time:

    a. The snow began + S. ⎫
                     ⎬ →
    b. It happened at midnight. ⎭

▶ What will the **c** sentence be?

◼ Write **c** sentences for the following:

3. a. The sun set + S.

    b. It happened with a burst of color.

4. a. The team passed + S.

    b. It happened ten minutes ago.

5. a. They launched the rocket + S
   b. It happened at Cape Kennedy.
6. a. A ship entered the harbor + S
   b. It happened before daylight.
7. a. The flood washed out the road + S
   b. It happened above the bridge.
8. a. The clouds gathered + S
   b. It happened threateningly.

▶ 9. It is possible to add more than one adverbial to the same **a** sentence. Study the following:

   a. The circus arrived + S
   b. It happened noisily.

What kind of adverbial does the **b** sentence contain? What will the **c** sentence be?

▶ 10. Now use the **c** sentence from 9 above as the **a** sentence, with a new **b** sentence:

   a. The circus arrived noisily + S
   b. It happened at the fairgrounds.

What kind of adverbial does the **a** sentence contain? What kind does the **b** sentence contain? What will the **c** sentence be?

▶ 11. Now we will use the **c** sentence from 10 above as the **a** sentence, again with a new **b** sentence.

   a. The circus arrived noisily at the fairgrounds + S
   b. It happened after midnight.

What two kinds of adverbials does this **a** sentence contain? What kind does the new **b** sentence contain? What will the **c** sentence be this time?

■ The following **a** sentences contain one or more adverbials. Embed the **b** sentences in them by using the adverbial in Sentence **b** to replace the symbol **S**. Write the **c** sentences.

12. a. A storm blocked the roads in the hills + S
    b. It happened suddenly.
13. a. A rocket flared brilliantly + S
    b. It happened above the stadium.
14. a. An accident wrecked the elevator in the mine completely + S
    b. It happened last night.
15. a. The workman touched the wire in the lamp + S.
    b. It happened accidentally.

103

You have seen that we can ask questions with **what** and **whom,** expecting a reply like "He raised goldfish" or "She met my father." When the noun phrase object is nonhuman, we use **what:** "What did he raise?" When the object is human, we use the object form of **who:** "Whom did she meet?"

We can also make questions that can be answered by noun phrases functioning as subjects of questions.

When someone asks you a question like "What dug up our tulips?" he is asking you to fill the blank in a statement like "___(Something)___ dug up our tulips." The information he wants is a nonhuman noun phrase like **dogs** that functions as subject:

Dogs dug up our tulips.

We know that the noun phrase is nonhuman because **what** matches nonhuman noun phrases.

► When someone asks you "Who threw a snowball?" he expects you to replace **somebody** in a statement like "___(Somebody)___ threw a snowball." The information he wants is a human noun phrase like **Eddie** or **those fellows.** Why does the question begin with **who** instead of **what?** Why does it begin with **who,** not **whom?**

► Make questions to match the following incomplete statements, using **who.** Then complete the statements, supplying human noun phrases to replace ___(Somebody)___.

1. ___(Somebody)___ was picking roses.
2. ___(Somebody)___ might refuse the invitation.
3. ___(Somebody)___ sings loudly in the tub before breakfast.
4. ___(Somebody)___ has fixed the door handle.

■ Make questions to match the following statements, using **who** or **what** to replace the subject. You must first decide whether the noun phrase subject of the statement is human or nonhuman.

5. My sister saw the accident.
6. A rock hit David.
7. Miss Worble made the first speech.
8. An accident has happened in Springfield.
9. A child led them to the cave.

■ Write questions to match the following incomplete statements, using **who** or **whom.**

10. Mr. Johnson greeted ___(somebody)___ .
11. The audience cheered ___(somebody)___ .
12. ___(Somebody)___ brought a camera.
13. ___(Somebody)___ is cooking hamburgers.
14. Jack had told ___(somebody)___ .
15. ___(Somebody)___ lives in that shack.
16. ___(Somebody)___ has met the newcomer.
17. Miss Whipple introduced ___(somebody)___ to the class.

■ Write questions to match the following incomplete statements using **what, who,** or **whom.**

18. ___(Something)___ made tracks on the back porch.
19. ___(Somebody)___ opened the back door.
20. He called ___(somebody)___ on the telephone.
21. She planted ___(something)___ in her garden.
22. ___(Something)___ makes a banging noise.
23. ___(Somebody)___ ran over the baby's ball.
24. John gave ___(something)___ to your sister.
25. Mr. Carter asked ___(somebody)___ for help.
26. Miss Burrows liked ___(somebody)___ .
27. ___(Something)___ makes tunnels in the lawn.

■ Write questions that can be answered by the noun phrases in heavy black type in the following statements. You will use **what, who,** or **whom** in each question.

28. The children asked **our teacher.**
29. **The children** asked our teacher.
30. The plumber repaired the **dishwasher.**
31. **The plumber** repaired the dishwasher.
32. Our dog bit **the mailman.**
33. **Our dog** bit the mailman.
34. The geese gobbled **the grain.**
35. **The geese** gobbled the grain.
36. **Mr. Atkins** resisted arrest.
37. Mr. Atkins resisted **arrest.**
38. The monkey obeys **the zookeeper** at the zoo.
39. **The monkey** obeys the zookeeper at the zoo.
40. **Mr. Jeffers** works at the zoo.

A Poem

"Ascent to the Sierras," on page 89, calls our West a fortunate land because no fierce mountain clans have ever raided the peaceful valleys. Here is a poem which takes the side of the mountain clan, and boasts about a raid on a valley.

The War Song of Dinas Vawr

The mountain sheep are sweeter,
But the valley sheep are fatter;
We therefore deemed it meeter
To carry off the latter.
We made an expedition;
We met an host and quelled it;
We forced a strong position,
And killed the men who held it.

On Dyfed's richest valley,
Where herds of kine were browsing,
We made a mighty sally,
To furnish our carousing.
Fierce warriors rushed to meet us;
We met them, and o'erthrew them:
They struggled hard to beat us;
But we conquered them, and slew them.

As we drove our prize at leisure,
The king marched forth to catch us:
His rage surpassed all measure,
But his people could not match us.
He fled to his hall-pillars;
And, ere our force we led off,
Some sacked his house and cellars,
While others cut his head off.

We there, in strife bewildering,
Spilt blood enough to swim in:
We orphaned many children,
And widowed many women,
The eagles and the ravens
We glutted with our foemen;
The heroes and the cravens,
The spearmen and the bowmen.

We brought away from battle,
And much their land bemoaned them,
Two thousand head of cattle
And the head of him who owned them:
Ednyfed, King of Dyfed,
His head was borne before us;
His wine and beasts supplied our feasts,
And his overthrow, our chorus.

THOMAS LOVE PEACOCK

Dinas Vawr was a minor Welsh king who lived in the days of King Arthur. Thomas Love Peacock wrote this war song to express in a subtly comic way the savagery, boastfulness, and folly of military glory.

► The word **meeter** in the third line of the poem is the comparative form of the adjective **meet,** which means proper or suitable. What does **deem** mean? Which kind of sheep did they judge it more suitable to carry off?

► **Kine** is an ancient word for cattle. What is a **sally?** What is meant by the expression **to furnish our carousing?**

► The first line of the third stanza ends with the word **leisure.** What is the word that is supposed to rhyme with **leisure?** Peacock was an Englishman. How do you think the English pronounce **leisure?**

► What was the prize they drove off? What does **ere** mean in the sixth line of the third stanza? What does the verb **sack** mean? Guess. Then look up the word to check your guess.

► **Glutted** means overfed, or gorged. What are **cravens?** What weapons were used in the fighting?

► In the last stanza, what does **bemoaned** mean?

► What does the word **borne** mean? What does its homophone **born** mean? Notice the difference in spelling.

► The last line says that the overthrow of King Ednyfed supplied our chorus. Does the verb **supplied** appear in the last line? What does the last line mean?

Rhyme and Stress

To show a rhyme scheme, we can use letters for words that rhyme. Here are the rhyming words of the first stanza. The rhyming words in each pair are given the same letter.

Line 1	sweeter	a
Line 2	fatter	b
Line 3	meeter	a
Line 4	latter	b
Line 5	expedition	c
Line 6	quelled it	d

| Line 7 | position | c |
| Line 8 | held it | d |

■ Write a similar rhyming scheme for the second stanza, lines 9–16. Begin with the letter **a** again for the first pair of rhyming words in Stanza 2.

► As you see, the rhyme scheme of the first two stanzas is perfectly regular — every other line rhymes. Is this true of the third stanza? What two lines in Stanza 3 don't actually rhyme? Do **pillars** and **cellars** sound somewhat alike, even though they don't actually rhyme?

► What are the actual rhyming words in the fourth stanza?

► The last stanza begins with the **a b a b** pattern, but the last four lines depart from it. Two of the last four lines contain **internal** rhymes — that is, a sound within the line rhymes with the sound at the end of it. What are these two internal rhymes? What word within the sixth line rhymes with two words in the fifth line?

► In this poem, the syllables usually come in pairs. Each syllable with weak stress, except the last syllable in each line, is usually followed by a syllable with first stress. Here are the first two lines, marked to show the first stresses:

The móuntain shéep are swéeter

But the válley shéep are fátter

What syllable with first stress has two weakly stressed syllables before it instead of one? Copy the rest of the first stanza, line by line, and mark the syllables to show stress.

► Each group of syllables in poems that include a syllable with first stress is called a **foot.** Count the number of stress marks in each line. How many feet are there in each line?

► "The War Song of Dinas Vawr" has a real swing to it, partly because of a rhyming trick the poet uses. Notice the last foot in each line. Does the rhyme occur in the stressed syllable? Does the weakly stressed syllable at the end of each line have exactly the same sound as the syllable at the end of the rhyming line? This and other tricks of rhyme and rhythm enable the poet to get a slightly comic effect. Note that sometimes he uses two words for his rhymes: **quelled it, held it,** for example. Find other examples of two-word rhymes.

REVIEW: "Wh" Questions

▶ You know that questions with **where** match statements with adverbials of place and those with **when** match statements with adverbials of time. What kind of adverbials do we find in statements that match "how" questions?

Questions that begin with **where** and **when** are called "wh" **questions.** "How" questions are also called "wh" **questions,** even though **how** begins just with **h,** not **wh.**

It is possible to have a single statement that will match all three kinds of "wh" questions with adverbials. Such a statement must contain an adverbial of place, an adverbial of time, and an adverbial of manner:

Statement: The baby played there happily this morning.
Question a: Where did the baby play happily this morning?
Question b: When did the baby play there happily?
Question c: How did the baby play there this morning?

▶ Make similar **a, b,** and **c** questions to match the following:
1. Ed ran upstairs angrily yesterday.
2. Sally sat silently in the corner after supper.

■ The following incomplete statements will answer "wh" questions when the blanks with ___(somewhere)___ , ___(sometime)___ , and ___(in some way)___ are filled with adverbials of place, time, and manner. Write the "wh" question that matches each incomplete statement. Then think of an appropriate adverbial and write a statement that answers the "wh" question.
3. The butcher put the meat ___(somewhere)___ .
4. The snake hissed ___(in some way)___ .
5. Mrs. Carlson wrecked the car ___(sometime)___ .
6. Benny told the story ___(in some way)___ .
7. The team won the game ___(sometime)___ .
8. The girls had a good time ___(somewhere)___ .
9. The carpenter cut his hand ___(in some way)___ .
10. The actor's costume arrived at the theater ___(sometime)___ .
11. Alice danced across the stage ___(in some way)___ .
12. Mr. Whiting worked ___(somewhere)___ this morning.
13. The bear slept snugly ___(somewhere)___ all winter.
14. The bear slept ___(in some way)___ in its den all winter.
15. The bear slept snugly in its den ___(sometime)___ .

110

▶ You know that questions with **what, who,** and **whom** match statements with noun phrases. Tell which of these words ask for human and which for nonhuman noun phrases as answers. Then which words ask for noun phrases that function as subject and which for noun phrases in the object function. Which of these three words asks for either a subject or an object function in the noun phrase that answers the question?

■ Write a question to match each incomplete statement below. Then rewrite the statement supplying an appropriate noun phrase to answer the question.

    16.   (Somebody)   opened the sardines.
    17. The teacher assigned   (something)   as homework.
    18. Mollie met   (somebody)   in the park.
    19.   (Something)   was hiding under the porch.
    20. Mr. Wallace married   (somebody)   in Chicago last winter.

■ Write questions that can be answered by the noun phrases or the adverbials in heavy black type in the following statements. You will use all the "wh" question words you have studied: **where, when, how, what, who,** and **whom.**

    21. Max is **in the kitchen.**
    22. Sally left town **this morning.**
    23. Mrs. Field bought **a rug.**
    24. We should ask **Harry Shaw.**
    25. Al did his part **well.**
    26. **The Governor** is going to speak.
    27. They saw **an Englishman.**
    28. Everybody went **to the ball game.**
    29. **Herbert** bought the houseboat yesterday.

■ Write a question to match each incomplete statement below. Then rewrite the statement, supplying an appropriate adverbial or noun phrase to answer the question.

    30.   (Something)   eats the lilies in our garden.
    31. The turkeys live   (somewhere) .
    32.   (Somebody)   teaches French at Fillmore High.
    33. The team played   (in some way)   last week.
    34. The principal called   (somebody)   to his office.
    35. The bell in the tower rings very loudly   (sometimes) .
    36. Mrs. Whiteside threw   (something)   into the pond.

When we write a sentence, we usually don't stop to think about the names of the structures we will use, like noun phrase or verb phrase. Even so, underneath the words we use lie the grammatical structures of English.

Let's write a simple, affirmative statement, not by starting with the words we will use but by starting with the basic structures beneath the surface. The two basic structures we will start with are a noun phrase and a verb phrase:

$$NP \quad + \quad VP$$

There are four kinds of noun phrases that we can choose a subject from, and many different kinds of verb phrases. Let's choose a determiner + common noun for NP, and a VP made up of tense, verb, and NP functioning as object. We can add these decisions to our basic NP and VP structures:

Next, we need to make some additional decisions.

For determiner, we might decide on an **article.**

For common noun, we could choose a **count noun, singular,** and one that refers to a **human.**

For a verb, we have already chosen the kind called **transitive,** because we have put an NP object after it. A transitive verb is one that takes noun phrase as object.

For our final NP, let's choose a **proper noun** that is the name of a person.

We can add all this information to our basic NP and VP:

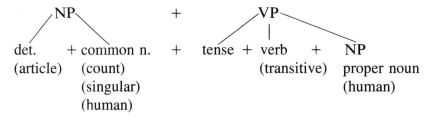

Now we are at the place where we usually start when we write such a sentence. We are ready to choose exactly what we will say. Let's make the choice just for the sake of this exercise, as shown on page 113.

det. (article): the
common n. (count, singular, human): man
tense (present or past): past
verb (transitive): help
NP, proper noun (human): Henry

We now have the following string of morphemes:

the + man + past + help + Henry

■ 1. Write a statement, using this morpheme string.

■ 2. Suppose you had started off to ask an affirmative question that could be answered **yes** or **no.** What "yes/no" question matches this affirmative statement? Write the question.

■ 3. Suppose that you had started off to write a negative statement. Write the negative statement.

■ 4. Write a negative "yes/no" question that matches the negative statement you wrote in 3. Use a contraction.

■ 5. Write two "wh" questions that match the statement in 1, using **who** for one and **whom** for the other.

■ 6. Now, make an original final choice of morphemes that meets all the requirements of the decisions at the bottom of page 112. That is, choose an article, but not **the.** Choose a common n. that is count, singular, and human, but don't use **man.** Which tense will you have to choose to be different? Choose a different verb that will take an object. Choose the name of a different person. Then write all five kinds of sentences, using your choices.

■ 7. Here is another chart of information that can be used to make final choices of morphemes for a morpheme string:

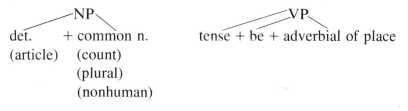

det.   + common n.   tense + be + adverbial of place
(article)   (count)
             (plural)
             (nonhuman)

Make your own choices of morphemes. Then write:
a. an affirmative statement
b. a negative statement
c. a "yes/no" question that matches **a**
d. a "yes/no" question that matches **b**
e. a "wh" question

1. Write adjectives by adding the adjective-making morpheme spelled **al** to the following. If you make mistakes, study pages 63, 92.

manus al   totus al   vita al

2. Write abstract nouns by adding the morpheme spelled <u>ity</u> to as many of the following adjectives as you can. Be sure that each word you write is an actual English noun. If you cannot make an actual word this way, do not write anything. If you make mistakes, study pages 92, 101.

<u>manual</u> <u>ity</u>   <u>vital</u> <u>ity</u>   <u>total</u> <u>ity</u>
<u>solid</u> <u>ity</u>   <u>valid</u> <u>ity</u>   <u>timid</u> <u>ity</u>

3. The following sentences contain adverbials. If the adverbial simply gives additional information, drop it and write the sentence that remains. If the adverbial is a necessary complement, write the whole sentence and underline the adverbial. If you make mistakes, study page 93.

a. The children were inside.

b. The team played baseball in the park.

c. The actor played the part last year.

d. Jane was on the merry-go-round.

4. Write questions with **what** or **whom** to match the following statements. Use **whom** if the object is a human noun phrase. Use **what** if the object is nonhuman. If you make mistakes, study pages 94–95.

a. Tom dropped the vase.

b. Mr. White knows our teacher.

c. We might ask Miss Wilson.

d. The coach had benched the quarterback.

e. Bill called the cat.

5. Write questions to match the following incomplete statements, using **who** or **whom.** If you make mistakes, study pages 104–05.

a. The policeman arrested __(somebody)__ .

b. __(Somebody)__ has set the table.

c. __(Somebody)__ was behind the door.

d. Jean dislikes __(somebody)__ .

e. John brought __(somebody)__ to the party.

6. Write questions to match the following incomplete statements, using **what, who,** or **whom.** If you make mistakes, study pages 94–95, 104–05.

   a. They bought ___(something)___ at the hardware store.

   b. ___(Somebody)___ placed a long distance call.

   c. Bob saw ___(somebody)___ at the window.

   d. ___(Something)___ made these tracks in the snow.

   e. ___(Somebody)___ put my books under the desk.

   f. Mr. Whitcomb called ___(somebody)___ to his office.

   g. We should get ___(something)___ for Uncle Bill.

7. Convert the **b** sentences into adverbials and embed the adverbials in the **a** sentences to replace the symbol S. If you make mistakes, study pages 93, 102–03.

   (1) a. They reported a flying saucer + S

      b. It happened near Omaha.

   (2) a. Bob skated on the lake + S

      b. It happened last week.

   (3) a. The fire destroyed the barn + S

      b. It happened quickly.

   (4) a. The hailstorm flattened the hay in the meadow + S

      b. It happened yesterday.

   (5) a. The star shone brightly + S

      b. It happened near the horizon.

8. Write questions that can be answered by the noun phrases or adverbials in heavy black type in the following statements. You will use all the "wh" question words you have studied: **where, when, how, what, who, whom.** If you make mistakes, study pages 110–11.

   a. Jimmy limped **painfully** in the gym this morning.

   b. Jimmy limped painfully in the gym **this morning.**

   c. Jimmy limped painfully **in the gym** this morning.

   d. Janet caught **a trout** in the brook.

   e. Mr. Willis telephoned **Mr. Warren.**

   f. **Miss Sands** voted for the losing candidate.

   g. **A sparrow** dashed against the window.

   h. They left **some food** in the refrigerator last night.

   i. They left some food **in the refrigerator** last night.

   j. They left some food in the refrigerator **last night.**

   k. **This test** was fun.

PART

5

A Nonsense Poem

This famous poem by Lewis Carroll doesn't mean much, but it teaches us a good deal about how our language works.

Jabberwocky

'Twas brillig, and the slithy toves
Did gyre and gimble in the wabe:
All mimsy were the borogoves,
And the mome raths outgrabe.

"Beware the Jabberwock, my son!
The jaws that bite, the claws that catch!
Beware the Jubjub bird, and shun
The frumious Bandersnatch!"

He took his vorpal sword in hand:
Long time the manxome foe he sought —
So rested he by the Tumtum tree,
And stood awhile in thought.

And, as in uffish thought he stood,
The Jabberwock, with eyes of flame,
Came whiffling through the tulgey wood,
And burbled as it came!

One, two!   One, two!   And through and through
The vorpal blade went snicker-snack!
He left it dead, and with its head
He went galumphing back.

"And hast thou slain the Jabberwock?
Come to my arms, my beamish boy!
O frabjous day! Callooh! Callay!"
He chortled in his joy.

'Twas brillig, and the slithy toves
Did gyre and gimble in the wabe:
All mimsy were the borogoves,
And the mome raths outgrabe.

Word Classes

The words we use in our sentences can mostly be sorted into large groups, or **word classes.** We give names to these groups: **noun, verb, adjective, adverb.** When we say that two words belong to the same class — say the class of nouns — we are saying that they are in some way alike, and are different from other words that are not nouns.

▶ Let us consider some of the ways in which nouns are alike. What are the nouns in the subjects of the following sentences?

    a. A boy was near the teacher.

    b. A chalkboard was near the teacher.

▶ In what way are **boy** and **chalkboard** alike? They aren't at all alike in sound; they have almost no sounds in common. They certainly aren't alike in meaning. How are they alike, then, and why are they both members of the same word class?

▶ They are alike in the ways in which they fit into the grammar of the sentence. For instance, they both are part of a subject, and the same sort of subject — a noun phrase made up of determiner + noun. What determiner comes before **boy** and **chalkboard?** What kind of determiner is it?

▶ They are also alike in their position in the sentence. They are alike in what follows them, as well as in what goes before. What word follows **boy** and **chalkboard?** What is this word a form of?

▶ Of course they are still followed by a form of **be** in these sentences:

    c. A boy is near the teacher.

    d. A chalkboard is near the teacher.

What form of **be** follows the noun in **c** and **d?**

A following form of **be** helps to mark a noun as a noun. So does a following verb:

    e. A boy stood near the teacher.

    f. A chalkboard stood near the teacher.

▶ What is the following verb in **e** and **f?**

▶ What is the noun in the subject of the following sentence?

    g. A tove stood near the teacher.

How do you know it is a noun?

► Of course we recognize nouns and noun phrases in functions other than that of subject. What are the nouns in the predicates of the following sentences?

    h. A boy stood near the chalkboard.

    i. A boy stood near the teacher.

    j. A boy stood near the tove.

Again we recognize the nouns partly by the determiners that come before them. What determiner comes before the nouns in the predicates of Sentences **h, i,** and **j?** What kind of determiner is it?

We also recognize the nouns by the preposition that precedes them. We expect noun phrases to follow prepositions. What is the preposition that precedes these noun phrases?

► We recognize nouns in other ways. For instance, some nouns form plurals. What are the plurals of the nouns in the predicates of **h, i,** and **j?** But words that are not nouns do not form plurals. There is no plural of **near, the, beautiful,** or **stood.**

► We recognize verbs in different but similar ways. What are the verbs in the following sentences?

    k. A girl painted a picture.

    l. A girl knocked on the door.

    m. A girl outgrabed something.

Again, we don't recognize verbs by their meanings. The verb **painted** doesn't have at all the same meaning as **knocked,** and **outgrabed** doesn't mean anything at all.

► We recognize verbs partly by their position — what comes before and after them in the sentence. What noun phrase comes before the verbs in **k, l,** and **m?** Two of these sentences are followed by noun phrases functioning as objects. Which ones? One is followed by a prepositional phrase. Which one?

► Just as nouns are alike because they express number — singular and plural — so verbs are alike because they express tense — past and present. What is the tense of the verbs in **k, l,** and **m?** How is this tense expressed?

► What is the tense of the verbs in these sentences?

    n. The boys galumph in the woods.

    o. He galumphs too.

Lewis Carroll's "Jabberwocky" is useful in helping us to understand the mechanism of our language, and particularly the system by which we recognize word classes.

Look again at the first stanza:

> 'Twas brillig, and the slithy toves
> Did gyre and gimble in the wabe:
> All mimsy were the borogoves,
> And the mome raths outgrabe.

► The first word is a contraction, a rather old-fashioned one. What two words does it contain? Which of the words is a form of **be?**

In *Through the Looking-Glass* by Lewis Carroll, there is an explanation of the meaning of some of the words in "Jabberwocky." The meaning of **brillig** is given as "four o'clock in the afternoon — the time when you begin broiling things for dinner." So what kind of word is **brillig?**

When the personal pronoun **it** is followed by a form of **be,** we expect the complement to be an adverbial of place, an adjective, or a noun phrase, but not an adverb of time. Since **brillig** is an adverb of time, according to the author of the poem, the **it** of **'twas** must be the word we use in sentences like "It was raining," or "It was midnight." This **it** is not the personal pronoun, but just an **it.**

► The first line ends "and the slithy toves." Of course, we know that **toves** is a noun. What is it in the word **toves** that tells us this? What kind of word follows **toves?** Is the noun **toves** part of a noun phrase subject? What is the predicate if "the slithy toves" is the subject?

► What kind of word do you think **slithy** is?

► We know that an adjective can occur between a determiner and a noun: "the slithy toves." The noun is **toves,** the determiner is **the,** so could **slithy** be an adjective? Nouns can occur there too, of course: "the tree toads." However, we have another clue here: many adjectives end in **y: slimy, funny, pretty.** Give two more.

The second line is this:

> Did gyre and gimble in the wabe:

► What word class do **gyre** and **gimble** belong to? You probably said **verb** straight off, and this is right. We know that they are verbs by their position, even though the position is a somewhat old-fashioned one. We now use **do (does, did)** directly before a verb only when we want to emphasize that something is true: "He **did** study the lesson." But in older English people used **do** without emphasis even in affirmative statements, as here. Anyway, there is no other possibility, and the line must have the form of "Did croak and tumble in the swamp." Give two other real verbs that might replace the made-up verbs **gyre** and **gimble.**

► What word class do you think **wabe,** at the end of the second line, belongs to? Give two clues that would help you to decide this.

► The third line is not in the usual order:

All mimsy were the borogoves.

The borogoves would come first in ordinary prose. What kind of structure is **the borogoves?** What word class does **borogoves** belong to? How do you know? What word class do you think **mimsy** belongs to? Give your reasons.

► The word **rath,** in the fourth line, means a sort of green pig, according to *Through the Looking-Glass.* What word class do you think **mome** must belong to?

Substituting for Nonsense Words

■ Decide what word class each nonsense word belongs to in the sentences below. Rewrite each sentence, substituting for each nonsense word a real noun, adjective, adverb, or verb.

1. A weazy lumer didn't gart his kerls.
2. The worb gorned sharly at the turper.
3. A momb firned the groot.
4. A reft coaned our crasp notremly.
5. Did the mank dit the warfle?
6. She whammened the shallen toamly in a gurse.
7. The author wozens the marplet oberly.
8. An asty opernick bilted some camberns.
9. He torples cubbens under the crompitch.

Relative Clauses

1. You remember that one way of expanding a noun phrase is to apply the possessive morpheme, poss., to the noun in the subject of a "have" sentence. We then rewrite the "have" sentence as a possessive noun phrase:

The cowboy has a horse. → the cowboy's horse

The possessive noun phrase that results is used to replace a noun phrase in another sentence:

a. The horse is a pinto. → NP + is a pinto.
b. The cowboy has a horse. → the cowboy's horse $\Big\} \rightarrow$
c. The cowboy's horse is a pinto.

This is called the **possessive transformation.**

2. Another way to expand a noun phrase is to change a simple sentence like "The man bought the car" to a noun phrase that contains a relative clause:

the man who bought the car

▶ The word **who** is a **relative pronoun,** and the group of words **who bought the car** is called a **relative clause.** Where did we put the relative pronoun **who** in this sentence to make a relative clause? A relative clause contains a relative pronoun plus the verb phrase predicate of a simple sentence.

We can then use the expanded noun phrase, **the man who bought the car,** to replace a noun phrase in another sentence, just the way we do with a possessive noun phrase:

a. The man couldn't pay for it. → NP + couldn't pay for it.
b. The man bought the car. → the man who bought the car. $\Big\} \rightarrow$
c. The man who bought the car couldn't pay for it.

▶ What is the function of the expanded noun phrase, **the man who bought the car,** in the transform, Sentence **c?**

▶ Tell what the relative clause is in each of the following transforms. Tell what the expanded noun phrase is:

3. People who are hungry will be fed.
4. The man who saw the accident reported it.
5. The girl who knows my sister told me.
6. Pupils who are late must go to the office.
7. Someone who understands cars should look at it.
8. The children who found the wallet returned it.
9. Everyone who knows Herb likes him.

As you have seen, a relative pronoun plus the verb phrase predicate of a sentence like "The man bought the car" makes a relative clause: **who bought the car.**

▶ A clause is a structure that has a subject and a predicate, but it may or may not be a sentence. The relative pronoun **who** functions as subject of the relative clause **who bought the car.** What word in the relative clause expresses tense? What is the tense?

A relative clause, like **who bought the car,** is not a sentence. The relative pronoun **who** makes it just part of a sentence, not a sentence by itself. We do not put a capital letter at the beginning of it and a period at the end.

▶ Is an expanded noun phrase, like "the man who bought the car," a sentence? Is a transform like "The man who bought the car couldn't pay for it" a sentence? What is the subject of this sentence?

■ Tell whether the subject of each of the following simple sentences is human or nonhuman. Then write an expanded noun phrase from the sentence by making a relative clause from the verb phrase predicate. Use the relative pronoun **who.**

10. The child found the money.
11. A man works in the park.
12. Somebody knows Jack.
13. People live in Menlo Park.
14. The lady runs the library.
15. The man caught the horse.

When the relative pronoun refers to a human subject of a sentence, we may use **who.** But we may also use the relative pronoun **that,** as in the following:

The man bought the car. → the man that bought the car

■ Write expanded noun phrases from the following sentences with human noun phrase subjects. Use the relative pronoun **that.**

16. A boy was lost in the park.
17. Players are late for practice.
18. People bought the land.
19. Everybody saw it.
20. The doctor set the bone.

An Adventure

Read this account from the autobiography of one of America's well-known heroes, Davy Crockett.

Barking up the Wrong Tree

One night there fell a heavy rain, and it turned to a sleet. In the morning all hands turned out hunting. My young man, and a brother-in-law who had lately settled close by me, went down the river to hunt for turkeys; but I was for larger game. So I started to go up above the harricane, determined to have a bear. I had two pretty good dogs and an old hound, all of which I took along.

I had gone about six miles up the river, and it was then about four miles across to the main Obion River. So I determined to strike across to that, as I had found nothing yet to kill. I got on to the river and turned down it, but the sleet was still getting worse and worse.

The bushes were all bent down and locked together with ice, so that it was almost impossible to get along.

In a little time my dogs started a large gang of old turkey gobblers, and I killed two of them, of the biggest sort. I shouldered them up and moved on until I got through the harricane. I was then so tired I laid my gobblers down to rest, as they were confounded heavy and I was mighty tired.

While I was resting, my old hound went to a log and smelt it a while, and then raised his eyes toward the sky and cried out. Away he went, and my other dogs with him. I shouldered up my turkeys again and followed on as hard as I could drive. They were soon out of sight, and in a very little time I heard them begin to bark. When I got to them, they were barking up a tree, but there was no game there. I concluded it had been a turkey, and that it had flown away.

When they saw me coming, away they went again; and, after a little time, began to bark as before. When I got near them, I found they were barking up the wrong tree again, as there was no game there. They served me in this way three or four times, until I was so mad that I determined, if I could get near enough, to shoot the old hound at least.

With this intention I pushed on the harder, till I came to the edge of an open parara. Looking on before my dogs, I saw about the biggest bear that ever was seen in America. He looked, at the distance he was from me, like a large black bull. My dogs were afraid to attack him. That was the reason they had stopped so often, that I might overtake them. They were now almost up with him.

I took my gobblers from my back and up in a sapling, and broke like a horse after my bear, for the sight of him had put new springs in me. I soon got near to them, but they were just getting into a dense thicket. I couldn't run through the thicket but had to pick my way along, and had close work even at that.

In a little time I saw the bear climbing up a large
black-oak tree, and I crawled on till I got within about
eighty yards of him. He was sitting with his breast
to me; and so I put fresh priming in my gun and fired
at him. At this he raised one of his paws and snorted
loudly. I loaded again as quick as I could, and fired
as near the same place in his breast as possible. At
the crack of my gun he came tumbling down; and the
moment he touched the ground I heard one of my
best dogs cry out.

I took my tomahawk in one hand and my big butcher
knife in the other, and ran up within four or five paces
of him. At this, he let my dog go and fixed his eyes
on me. I got back in all sorts of a hurry, for I knew
if he got hold of me, he would hug me altogether too
close for comfort. I went to my gun and hastily
loaded her again and shot him the third time, which
killed him good.

I now felt well satisfied that a dog might sometimes
be doing a good business, even when he seemed to be
barking up the wrong tree. We got our meat home,
and I had the pleasure to know that we now had plenty,
and that of the best. And I continued through the
winter to supply my family abundantly with bear meat
and venison from the woods.

► Did Davy Crockett hunt for sport or because he had to have food? What part of the story tells you?

► What does "I was for larger game" mean?

Harricane is a form of the word **hurricane.** Here it means a place where the trees have been blown down by a hurricane. The dead trees and their branches make such a place hard to travel through.

► What does **start** mean in "started a gang of turkey gobblers"? What does "shouldered them up" mean?

► Which dog first smelled the bear? How did he show that he did? What did the dogs do then? What did Crockett find when he first came up to them? What did he conclude?

► What does "served me in this way" mean? How did they serve him three or four times?

► **Parara** is a form of the word **prairie.** What is a prairie? Look in a dictionary if you don't know. Describe what Crockett saw when he came to the edge of the open parara.

► What is meant by "broke like a horse after my bear"? What had put new springs in him? What does that mean?

► Old guns had to be **primed.** That is, before a person shot them, he had to put some loose gunpowder where a spark would set fire to it and thus set off the explosion. How many times did Crockett have to shoot the bear? Tell what happened between the second and third shots. What is a **tomahawk?**

► What do we mean nowadays if we say that a person is barking up the wrong tree?

What Words Come From

The pioneers borrowed many words from the Indians they lived and fought with. One was **tomahawk.** This has nothing to do with **hawks.** It comes from the Indian word **tamahaken,** which meant something to cut with.

A few of many other words borrowed from Indian languages are **wampum, wigwam, moccasin, powwow.** Look these up in a dictionary to be sure you know what they mean.

Davy Crockett was best known for his part in the defense of the Alamo in the war between Texas and Mexico. Find out what else you can about him, by using encyclopedias and books on American history. There may be a biography of Colonel Crockett in your school or public library. Write a report telling of your findings.

To help you in preparing your report, you should take notes as you read about Crockett. For example, Crockett was a frontiersman, but also a politician. Here are some topics and an example of notes one might write down from reading about his political career.

Davy Crockett

Early Life

Political Career

 Elected to Tennessee legislature, 1821.

 Two terms in Congress, Washington, D.C. — 1827–31, 1833–35.

 Wit, frontier humor, shrewdness made him popular in Washington.

 Defeated for reelection in 1834.

The Alamo

If you organize your notes by topic, your paragraphing is pretty well taken care of. You may be able to present each topic in a single paragraph of your report. You might add to the three topics suggested above another one — a description of the kind of person he was.

More About Word Classes

We have used the poem "Jabberwocky" to see some of the ways to recognize different classes of words.

► The following sentence contains a noun, a verb, and an adjective. Only one of these is a real word. But you can tell which is the noun, which is the verb, and which is the adjective. Tell what words they are:

   Shun the frumious Bandersnatch.

▶ The following sentence contains a nonsense noun, adjective, verb, and adverb of manner.   Tell what words they are:

The Jabberwock whiffled frumiously through the tulgey wood.

There are four large word classes in English and many small ones.   The large ones are **nouns, verbs, adjectives,** and **adverbs.**

If a word belongs to one of the four large word classes, we can usually tell which one it belongs to by clues within the sentence or by the form of the word itself, even if we do not know what the word means.   But words that belong to the smaller word classes are usually more difficult to identify if they are not familiar.   Suppose we tried to put nonsense words in place of the other words in "Did gyre and gimble in the wabe"?

Moux gyre ruf gimble gorb teck wabe.

This doesn't mean anything at all to us.

▶ We recognize the smaller word classes because we usually learn their members one by one.   For instance, personal pronouns are a word class.   There are seven of them (in the subject form), including **I, you,** and **we,** and we have learned their use and meaning.   Name the other four.

▶ The indefinite pronouns are another small word class. There are twelve of them, including **somebody, everything, anyone.**   Name the other nine members of this word class. Every indefinite pronoun is a combination of **some, any, every,** or **no** with **body, one,** or **thing.**

▶ We regard the word **be** as a word class by itself.   There are five forms of **be** that show tense, including **am.**   What are the other four?

▶ The articles make up a small word class that includes **null** and **some.**   What are the other two articles?

We can invent new nouns, verbs, adjectives and adverbs of manner.   New words come into these large word classes every day.   But many of the smaller word classes are much more fixed.   Our language is constantly changing, but we don't change personal pronouns, prepositions, forms of **be** or question words like **where** or **when** very rapidly.   Such changes occur very slowly indeed.

When we change a sentence into an expanded noun phrase containing a relative clause, we do so in order to use the noun phrase in another sentence. Study the following example, which shows what we call the **relative clause transformation:**

   a. The boy rides it to school. → NP + rides it to school.
   b. The boy owns the horse. → the boy who owns the horse.   →
   c. The boy who owns the horse rides it to school.

▶ Which sentence was changed into an expanded noun phrase containing a relative clause, **a** or **b?** What is the relative clause that was used to expand the noun phrase? To what sentence was the expanded noun phrase added in order to make the transform, Sentence **c?** What symbol did the expanded noun phrase replace in Sentence **a?**

■ Make **c** sentences from the following by applying the relative clause transformation.

   1. a. The boy was a stranger. → NP + was a stranger.
      b. The boy ran. → the boy who ran   →
   2. a. The boy found it. → NP + found it.
      b. The boy lost his sweater. → the boy that lost his sweater.   →

■ Exercises 1 and 2 were almost completed for you. In the following, you must decide for yourself what noun phrase in **a** to replace with the expanded noun phrase made from **b.** Use either **who** or **that** as the relative pronoun.

   3. a. The lady teaches in our school.
      b. The lady lives next door.
   4. a. A man sent me the stamps.
      b. A man knows my father.

The expanded noun phrases in the examples above all function as subjects of the **c** sentences, but this is not the only function they could have. Study the following.

   a. I know the girl. → I know + NP
   b. The girl lost the money. → the girl who lost the money   →
   c. I know the girl who lost the money.

▶ What is the function of NP in Sentence **a?** What is the function of the expanded noun phrase, **the girl who lost the money,** in **c?**

130

■ Make **c** sentences of the following, and tell the function of the expanded noun phrase in each.

   5. a. I asked the lady.
      b. The lady runs the library.
   6. a. I know some people.
      b. Some people live in Boston.
   7. a. I met somebody.
      b. Somebody knows Jack.
   8. a. A man found the boy.
      b. The boy was lost in the park.

We have seen that either **who** or **that** can be used as the relative pronoun when the relative pronoun refers to a person — to a human noun phrase. But when the noun phrase to which the relative pronoun refers is nonhuman, **who** cannot be used, although **that** can be:

   a. We bought some furniture. → We bought + NP ⎫
   b. Some furniture was on sale. → some furniture that ⎬ →
      was on sale. ⎭
   c. We bought some furniture that was on sale.

Of course, we couldn't say, "We bought some furniture who was on sale." But we could use another relative pronoun, **which,** instead of **that:**

   We bought some furniture which was on sale.

In relative clauses of the sort we are studying now, it is more common to use **that** than **which.**

■ Write **c** sentences from the following pairs:

   9. a. The car belongs to Mr. Wheeler.
      b. The car broke down.
  10. a. He picked up a book.
      b. A book had fallen from the shelf.
  11. a. The dog growled at me.
      b. The dog sat on the sofa.
  12. a. Herb stepped on some marbles.
      b. Some marbles were lying on the floor.
  13. a. The road is very narrow.
      b. The road winds up the mountains.
  14. a. We met a cat.
      b. A cat looked hungry.
  15. a. They put on the suits.
      b. The suits were dropped from a helicopter.

The relative clause transformation is one of many ways to combine short, choppy sentences into longer, smoother ones. Here is an example — a sentence that contains two relative clauses:

> Even the **old men** who could no longer venture out to sea became links in the long chain of people who were hauling nets.

The first relative clause is one that goes back to a sentence like this:

> The old men could no longer venture out to sea.

▶ What is the relative clause?

▶ The expanded noun phrase "the old men who could no longer venture out to sea," to which the word **even** has been added, functions as subject of the entire sentence. Now find the second relative clause, which goes back to a sentence like this one:

> People were hauling nets.

What is the expanded noun phrase?

The following sentence contains a relative clause that begins with **who.** It also contains another kind of clause that begins with **because:**

> I know some people who hate the books I write, and because they hate my books they hate me.

▶ What is the relative clause that begins with **who?** What is the expanded noun phrase that contains it? What sentence might such an expanded noun phrase have come from?

This example results not only from the relative clause transformation, but from two other transformations which you will study later. One of these puts a sentence like "They hate my books" into a sentence like "They hate me," by putting the word **because** before "They hate my books." The other transformation joins these two sentences with the word **and:**

> I know some people who hate the books I write.
> Because they hate my books they hate me.

This sentence also contains the remains of still another relative clause: **I write.** The expanded noun phrase originally was "the books that I write," but the relative pronoun **that** has been dropped out. The expression **I write** is called the **residue** of a relative clause.

The relative clause transformation is usually used in combination with other transformations, as you have seen. The exercises that follow will concentrate on using the relative clause transformation by itself, however, on the principle of practicing things as you learn them.

■ Use the relative clause transformation to combine the following groups of shorter sentences into single longer sentences. Before you write the longer sentences, you will have to figure out which shorter sentences to transform into expanded noun phrases. They are not labeled **a** and **b,** or given in the same order as those in the exercises on page 131.

1. A baker worked for my uncle. A baker made my sister's wedding cake.

2. A bird had built its nest in the chimney. A bird caused the fire.

3. We sang a song. A song was too difficult for the girl. The girl had the solo part.

4. The carpenter built the garage. The carpenter made a mistake. A mistake delayed the project two weeks.

5. Some leaves clogged the drain. Some leaves flooded the terrace.

6. The road passes our house. The road leads to a valley. The valley is a famous landmark.

7. The cowboy sold the bronco. The bronco had kicked him. The cowboy bought a new horse.

8. The young actress spoke the opening lines. The young actress dropped the torch. The torch furnished the only light.

9. The audience lost sight of the scene. The scene depended on torchlight.

10. An electrician was on duty. An electrician turned on a spotlight. The spotlight revealed the young actress in tears.

A Poem

The greatest of all poets was an Englishman who lived about four hundred years ago, William Shakespeare. Here is a little song about winter from one of the plays he wrote.

Winter

When icicles hang by the wall,
And Dick the shepherd blows his nail,
And Tom bears logs into the hall,
And milk comes frozen home in pail,
When blood is nipp'd, and ways be foul,
Then nightly sings the staring owl,
      Tu-whit;
Tu-who, a merry note,
While greasy Joan doth keel the pot.

When all aloud the wind doth blow,
And coughing drowns the parson's saw,
And birds sit brooding in the snow,
And Marian's nose looks red and raw,
When roasted crabs hiss in the bowl,
Then nightly sings the staring owl,
      Tu-whit;
Tu-who, a merry note,
While greasy Joan doth keel the pot.

Winter

The first thing to remember is that this was written a long time ago, when one didn't pass the winter as comfortably as one does now. There was little heat in winter then and little protection from the snow and winds.

▶ The **nail** that Dick the shepherd blows is a fingernail. Why do you think he would blow on his fingernail in winter?

135

► What do you think the logs that Tom carries into the hall are used for? What word in the poem means **carries?**

► How does the milk arrive at the house? The **ways** mentioned in the fifth line are roadways. What does **foul** mean?

► What are the notes that the owl sings?

► **Greasy Joan** is the kitchen maid. She is greasy because cooking makes one greasy. To **keel** meant to cool a boiling liquid by stirring it or skimming it, so as to keep it from boiling over. What did greasy Joan keel? What do you think it might have contained?

► A **saw** is a wise saying. Whose saw is mentioned in the second stanza? Where would he utter his saw? What drowned it out? What does this have to do with the winter?

► Where do the birds sit? What does **brooding** mean?

► **Marian** is a girl in the family. What do you think made her nose look red and raw?

► **Crabs** are crabapples, which are ready to eat in the wintertime. What are the crabs doing?

► What lines in the second stanza repeat those of the first?

What Words Come From

Most of the very common words in our language — like **day, man, see, mother** — come down to us from a form of the language called Old English. Old English was the form of English spoken in England from about A.D. 450 to about 1100.

► Of course in Old English, words were spoken and written quite differently than they are now. **Day** was **dæg,** and **see** was **seon.** Old English had a pair of homonyms both written **sagu.** **Homonym** means "same name." One of these had the meaning "to cut." It was related to the Latin word **secare** which had the same meaning. We have part of this word in **bisect** and **intersect.** What has cutting to do with bisecting an angle? What has it to do with an intersection?

► The other **sagu** was related to the word **say.** It meant a wise saying. It was also related to the word **saga.**

The homonyms **sagu** both developed into the modern homonyms **saw.** What do these homonyms mean in modern English? What form of **see** is a third homonym?

► The following sentence contains a nonsense word used as a noun. What is it?

Jack noticed that the pistash had swallowed an acorn.

► Make up five other nonsense words and make them nouns by using them in that place in that sentence. Try to make English-sounding nonsense words and be ready to give a normal English spelling of them.

► What nonsense word is used as a verb in this sentence?

Nobody had grottled the wigwam.

Make up five other nonsense verbs and use them in the same place in the same sentence. Notice that you must use them in the participle form.

► In the following sentence, what nonsense word is used as an adjective?

The smaller bear seemed rather frabjous.

► Make up five other nonsense adjectives and use them in the same place in the same sentence. They don't have to end in **ous,** since not all adjectives do. The following are all adjectives: **helpful, comic, golden, funny, central.**

■ Make an adverb of manner of each of the nonsense adjectives you made, and use each one in a sentence.

■ The following sentence contains a nonsense noun, a nonsense verb, a nonsense adjective, and a nonsense adverb of manner. Rewrite the sentence, substituting a real word for each of these. Think of a combination that makes sense.

The vorpal blade spittered the lendox borgfully.

■ Do the opposite in the following sentence. Substitute nonsense words for the real noun, verb, adjective, and adverb of manner.

A wistful child was weeping pitifully.

► What words in the sentence above do not belong to one of the four large word classes?

► What words in the sentence above could **not** be replaced by nonsense words?

► Two verbs in the poem "Jabberwocky" were nonsense when Lewis Carroll wrote the poem, but aren't any more. These are **chortle** and **galumph.** They have become part of the language. What do they mean? See a dictionary.

Practice with Word Classes

▶ There are four large word classes. One is the class of nouns. What are the other three?

▶ There are a number of smaller word classes, whose members we mainly learn one by one. One such word class is the group of prepositions. Can you think of any others?

▶ Each sentence below contains two nouns. From each sentence make another sentence which is exactly like it but with two different nouns. For instance, if the sentence were "The man chased a bear," you might suggest "The boy chased a rabbit."

1. The lady read a poem.
2. The book was on the stove.
3. A cat has fur.
4. Our duck swims in the pond.
5. His brother is a doctor.
6. The youngster walked to the farm.

▶ The following sentences each contain two nonsense nouns. Repeat each sentence using actual English nouns instead.

7. This quiggle is a blatch.
8. The rast was behind the pladge.
9. His monch lived in a quork.
10. A nable has porge.

▶ Repeat each of the following sentences, but use a different verb. Do not change the tense. For instance, if the sentence were "John skated on the lake," you might say "John sailed on the lake." If it were "Mary was sewing," you might say "Mary was smiling."

11. Beth recited the poem.
12. We were polishing the silver.
13. Someone tapped on the door.
14. Pedro hates milk.
15. He had whipped the child.

▶ Repeat each of the following using a real verb in place of the nonsense one.

16. They gimbled in the lake.
17. He whimped through the wood.
18. The bears outgrabed the cobras.

▶ The following sentences each contain two adjectives, one in the predicate and one between a determiner and a noun. Say each sentence again, using different adjectives. For example, if the sentence were "The huge bear looked dangerous," you might say "The little bear looked frightened."

19. The tall man was angry.
20. His little brother seems sad.
21. A strong back is useful.
22. The hungry children were impatient.

▶ Repeat each of the following using a real adjective in place of the nonsense one.

23. It was very brillig.
24. The borogoves were mimsy.
25. He shunned the frumious Bandersnatch.
26. He took his vorpal sword in hand.
27. He stood in uffish thought.
28. It whiffled through the tulgey wood.
29. The day was rather frabjous.
30. Come to my arms, my beamish boy.

▶ Repeat each of the following sentences, replacing the adverb of manner with another one.

31. She played beautifully.
32. Lance walks slowly.
33. He turned angrily to Peter.
34. They walked happily into the wood.
35. Mark always does his work well.
36. Was it done carefully?
37. He scrubbed the rabbits hastily this morning.

▶ Repeat each of the following, using a real adverb of manner in place of the nonsense one.

38. The Bandersnatch retreated frumiously.
39. He was thinking uffishly.
40. The boy smiled beamishly at us.
41. The borogoves rose mimsily above them.
42. They answered everyone frabjously.
43. The raths had outgrabed momely.
44. Stan behaves stookily to everyone.
45. The children were looking indatically at the stoat.

▶ You have already had some practice in making a word of one class into a word of another class by adding a derivational morpheme. Thus we make the verb **teach** into a noun by adding the "one who does" morpheme. How do we spell this morpheme when we add it to **teach?** What are two other ways to spell it?

■ 1. Add the "one who does" morpheme to the following verbs, two of which are nonsense words. Then use each new word in a sentence.

       walk   plan   deceive   burkle   brutch

■ 2. We make verbs from adjectives and a few nouns by adding a morpheme we have called v-en. Add this morpheme to the following, and use each new verb in a sentence.

       sweet   ripe   red   length

■ 3. We make adjectives from nouns by adding a morpheme we have called adj-en. Add this morpheme to the following nouns, and use each new adjective in a sentence.

       oak   wood   gold   earth   pold

■ 4. We make adverbs of manner from adjectives by adding a morpheme which is spelled **ly.** Most adjectives can be made into adverbs of manner in this way, so there are nearly as many adverbs of manner as there are adjectives. Make the following adjectives into adverbs of manner and use each one in a sentence:

      careful   wooden   moral   manxome   slithy

■ 5. We make adjectives from nouns by adding a morpheme which is spelled **al.** This ending is added both to English nouns like **person** and to Latin nouns like **vita.** Add it to the following nouns and use each new adjective in a sentence.

      vita   tribe   manus   dorb

■ 6. We make abstract nouns from certain adjectives by adding **ity.** Add this ending to the following adjectives, and use each abstract noun in a sentence.

      moral   timid   humid   dorbal

▶ 7. When we add certain endings, we change the syllable that has first stress. How does **ity** added to the adjective **moral** change the stress? How does **ity** added to the adjective **humid** change the stress?

▶ Which of these relative pronouns may be used with human noun phrases: **who, that, which?** Which may be used with nonhuman noun phrases? Can any of them be used with both human and nonhuman noun phrases?

■ Review the relative clause transformation by studying the following examples of **a** and **b** sentences. Write the transforms — the **c** sentences.

1. a. Something awakened her. → NP + awakened her. ⎫
   b. Something sounded like thunder. → something ⎬ →
      that sounded like thunder ⎭

2. a. They found a boy.   They found + NP ⎫
   b. A boy could speak English. → a boy who could ⎬ →
      speak English. ⎭

■ In the following, the relative pronoun will sometimes be used with human noun phrases and sometimes not. Write the **c** sentences, using the relative pronoun **who** when the noun phrase refers to people, **that** when it doesn't.

3. a. They saw a colt.
   b. A colt seemed afraid of the snow.
4. a. People can get good jobs.
   b. People speak Spanish.
5. a. They rewarded the child.
   b. The child found the money.
6. a. This is the light.
   b. The light failed.
7. a. The door opened into the study.
   b. The door was locked.
8. a. The outfielder is Jim Daniels.
   b. The outfielder caught the fly.
9. a. He heard about it from a friend.
   b. A friend lives in Buffalo.
10. a. We bought a sofa.
    b. A sofa had seen better days.
11. a. Sam pulled out a nail.
    b. A nail had entered the tire.
12. a. The girl forgot the hiding place.
    b. The girl hid the book.

141

Study the expanded noun phrase that was made from the **b** sentence of Exercise 12 on page 141:

b. The girl hid the book. → the girl who hid the book

The relative clause **who hid the book** tells which girl it was. We say that this relative clause modifies the noun phrase subject of the **b** sentence: **the girl.**

► Tell what noun phrase the relative clause modifies in each of the following. Tell what the function of the modified noun phrase is in the **b** sentence.

  13. b. People speak Spanish. → people who speak Spanish

  14. b. The door was locked. → the door that was locked

All the relative clauses you have made so far have been like those in the examples above. They have modified the noun phrase that functioned as subject of the **b** sentence.

► 15. Relative pronouns may also modify noun phrases that function as objects in the **b** sentence. But this transformation is a little more complicated. Study the following:

  a. The house is on Elm Street. → NP + is on Elm Street.
  b. Mr. White built the house. → the house that Mr. White built } →

  c. The house that Mr. White built is on Elm Street.

► What is the function of the noun phrase **the house** in Sentence **b?** What is the relative clause that modifies this noun phrase in the expanded noun phrase made from the **b** sentence?

► 16. When a relative clause modifies a noun phrase that functions as object in a **b** sentence, the noun phrase object comes first, the relative pronoun follows, and then comes the subject of the **b** sentence followed by what remains of the **b** sentence. Here is another example:

  a. The dog chewed a bone. → The dog chewed + NP }
  b. John had found a bone. → a bone that John had found } →

What noun phrase does the relative clause after **b** modify? What was the function of this noun phrase in the **b** sentence? What noun phrase will the expanded noun phrase from **b** replace in Sentence **a?**

■ Write the **c** sentence.

■ Following the pattern of Number 16, write expanded noun phrases from the following:

  17. b. We sold the refrigerator.

  18. b. Mr. Wallace rents a garage.

■ Apply the relative clause transformation to the following. Write the **c** sentences, and tell what the function of the modified noun phrase was in the **b** sentence.

19. a. The bicycle is in the garage.
    b. Bob bought the bicycle.
20. a. The money is in the safe.
    b. Mr. Drum keeps the safe in his office.
21. a. The noise awakened Mrs. Springfield.
    b. They made the noise.
22. a. They played a game.
    b. Max had taught them a game.
23. a. We ate a cake.
    b. Mrs. Garrell had baked a cake.
24. a. The cat climbed a tree.
    b. The dog chased the cat.
25. a. He met a boy.
    b. A boy knew Jim Talby.
26. a. The marshall was tracking an outlaw.
    b. An outlaw had robbed a bank in Tombstone.

Recursive Relative Clauses

Relative clauses are recursive — that is, it is possible to use relative clause after relative clause after relative clause in the same sentence. You may know the rhyme that begins this way:

This is the house that Jack built.
This is the malt that lay in the house that Jack built.

And finally it builds up to this:

This is the farmer sowing his corn that kept the cock that crowed in the morn that waked the priest all shaven and shorn that married the man all tattered and torn that kissed the maiden all forlorn that milked the cow with the crumpled horn that tossed the dog that worried the cat that killed the rat that ate the malt that lay in the house that Jack built.

▶ This is a famous example of the relative clause transformation repeated beyond all reason. How many relative clauses are there? (Just count the relative pronouns.)

Now that you have studied relative clauses that expand noun phrase objects, you can use the transformation in your own writing with greater freedom.

Study the following sentence written by a former President of the United States, Woodrow Wilson:

> A man who works in order that he may be distinguished is sooner or later going to do some selfish thing that will disgrace him, because his object is himself and not the ideals which he serves.

This sentence contains three relative clauses. The first one is this: "who works in order that he may be distinguished." This relative clause comes from a sentence that already contains another clause "in order that he may be distinguished." But this is not a relative clause. The sentence from which the relative clause might be made goes something like this: "A man works in order that he may be distinguished."

▶ The second relative clause comes from a sentence like "Some selfish thing will disgrace him." What is the relative clause? What is the expanded noun phrase that contains this relative clause?

▶ The third relative clause comes from a sentence like "He serves the ideals." The expanded noun phrase including the relative clause is this: "the ideals which he serves." How do we get "the ideals which he serves" from "He serves the ideals"?

Now study the following sentence about style of writing, from an essay by John Ruskin:

> No man is worth reading to form your style who does not mean what he says; nor was any great style ever invented but by some man who meant what he said.

This sentence too contains more than one relative clause, as well as expressions which result from other transformations. One of these is the negative transformation, which you have already studied.

▶ What is the first relative clause? Can you figure out what the expanded noun phrase is?

The expanded noun phrase that functions as subject in the first part of the Ruskin sentence is this:

No man who does not mean what he says

To get this expanded noun phrase, we may begin by applying the negative transformation to an affirmative statement, and then we apply the relative clause transformation, like this:

A man means what he says.
A man does not mean what he says.
a man who does not mean what he says

We still have to change **a man** to **no man** in the first part of the finished sentence — the part before the semicolon.

▶ What is the second expanded noun phrase, the one which comes at the end of the Ruskin sentence? It contains the relative clause "who meant what he said." But there is a clause within a clause here: "what he said." This last clause is related to the **wh** question "What did he say?" You have not studied this type yet.

So you see that a single sentence by a skillful writer may result from several different transformations. This is not to say that writers consciously think "I will use Transformation A, then Transformation B, then Transformation C." The transformations we study are just a way to get a clear picture of the structures that lie beneath the surface of complex sentences. The point of studying them is to build familiarity with different ways of expressing ideas — the same kind of familiarity that many writers gain only through long experience.

■ Practice using the relative clause transformation by rewriting these groups of sentences as single sentences:

1. The player made the error. The error cost us the game last week. The player scored the run. The run won the game this week.
2. Any student doesn't attend the meeting. The meeting is scheduled for Friday. Any student will not be allowed to vote in the election. We expect to hold the election next week.
3. The mice ate the cheese. We were saving the cheese. The mice avoided a trap. We set the trap.

TESTS

1. Each of the following sentences contains one nonsense word. Copy it and tell its word class by writing after it **noun, verb, adjective,** or **adverb of manner.** If you make mistakes, study pages 118–21, 128–29.

   a. The spakes breathed deeply.
   b. He thrust the blade frumiously into the sack.
   c. Mark was feeling rather frobish.
   d. They were snoofing the children's toys.
   e. Who left the money in the spinge?
   f. Someone had whimped each desk.
   g. Was the cobra as nugful as the bear?
   h. Where were they going so wappishly?

2. Make words of a different word class from the groups of words below by adding an ending that represents a derivational morpheme. If you make mistakes, study page 140.

   a. Add the "one who does" morpheme to the following verbs to change them to nouns: **write, teach, speak.**
   b. Make verbs from the following adjectives by adding the morpheme which we call v-en: **dark, wide, deep.**
   c. Make adjectives from the following nouns by adding the morpheme which we call adj-en: **gold, wool, earth.**
   d. Make adverbs of manner from the following adjectives by adding a morpheme spelled ly: **thoughtful, merry, wide.**
   e. Make adjectives from the following by adding a morpheme which we spell al: **person, vita, tide.**
   f. Make abstract nouns from the following adjectives by adding a morpheme spelled ity: **rigid, moral, personal.**

3. Make expanded noun phrases containing relative clauses from the following sentences. Use **who** when the relative pronoun refers to a person and **that** when it does not. If you make mistakes, study pages 122–23, 130–31.

   a. The light burned out.
   b. An electrician came to see about it.
   c. The driver stopped his truck suddenly.
   d. The accident cost Mr. Hillyer his license.
   e. The owl built a nest behind the house.

4. In each of the following pairs, decide what noun phrase in **a** to replace with an expanded noun phrase made from **b**. Use **who** when the relative pronoun refers to a person, **that** when it doesn't. Apply the relative clause transformation and write the **c** sentences. If you make mistakes, study pages 122–23, 130–31.

(1) a. The dog was lost.
    b. I found the dog.
(2) a. A boy caught his coat on the fence.
    b. A boy tried to get into our yard.
(3) a. The plumber lost some tools.
    b. Some tools were worth a good deal of money.
(4) a. The plumber advertised in the paper.
    b. The plumber lost some tools.
(5) a. A freight engine hit a switch.
    b. A switch had been left open.

5. Apply the relative clause transformation to the following, using the object of the verb as the noun phrase to be modified, and writing the expanded noun phrase. If you make mistakes, study page 142.
    a. Bob broke the lawnmower.
    b. Miss Ellis assigned some homework.
    c. Mr. Johnson sold the car.
    d. Faith knitted a sweater for Bill.

6. Apply the relative clause transformation to the following pairs and write the **c** sentences. Use **who** for human noun phrases, **that** for nonhuman ones. If you make mistakes, study pages 122–23, 130–31, 141–42.

(1) a. The furnace is out of order.
    b. Mr. Robins bought the furnace.
(2) a. The driver left the motor running.
    b. The driver parked the bus.
(3) a. The door fell off its hinges.
    b. The bicycle hit the door.
(4) a. We saw a fisherman.
    b. A fisherman was sitting on the railroad bridge.
(5) a. Alice bought a dress.
    b. Her mother didn't like a dress.

147

PART

6

In this poem the author, Sir Arthur Quiller-Couch, has fun with English spelling.

The Harbor of Fowey

O the harbor of Fowey
   Is a beautiful spot,
And it's there I enjowey
   To sail in a yot;
Or to race in a yacht
   Round a mark or a buoy —
Such a beautiful spacht
   Is the harbor of Fuoy!

When her anchor is weighed
   And the water she ploughs,
Upon neat lemoneighed
   O it's then I caroughs;
And I take Watts's hymns
   And I sing them aloud
When it's homeward she skymns
   O'er the waters she ploud.

But the wave mountain-high,
   And the violent storm,
Do I risk them?　Not Igh!
   But prefer to sit worm
With a book on my knees
   By the library fire
While I list to the brees
   Rising hire and hire.

And so whether I weigh
   Up the anchor or not,
I am happy each deigh
   In my home or my yot;

Every care I resign
  Every comfort enjoy,
In this cottage of mign
  By the Harbor of Foy.

And my leisure's addressed
  To composing of verse
Which, if hardly the bessed,
  Might be easily werse.
And, the spelling I use
  Should the critics condemn,
Why, I have my own vuse
  And I don't think of themn.

Yes, I have my own views:
  But the teachers I follow
Are the lyrical Miews
  And the Delphic Apollow.
Unto them I am debtor
  For spelling and rhyme,
And I'm doing it bebtor
  And bebtor each thyme.

The Harbor of Fowey

► In this poem, one can figure out from the first stanza that the proper noun **Fowey** is a one-syllable word rhyming with **toy** or **boy.** What clues tell us this?

► How is the word **yacht** pronounced? What is the proper spelling of **spacht?** **Buoy,** since it is the first of two rhyming words, is spelled in the proper way. What is a buoy?

► What is to **weigh anchor?** **Neat lemonade** is a drink of lemonade without anything else in it. The spelling **caroughs** stands for the word **carouse.** What does it mean?

► What does the poet sing as the yacht "skymns" homeward? Actually there are two usual spellings for the word spelled here as **ploud.** One is **ploughed.** What is the other?

► What are the right spellings of **Igh, worm, brees,** and **hire** in the poem?

► **Address** in the fifth stanza means direct or use. What does the poet address and what does he address it to?

The Spelling of Morphemes

▶ One reason that English spelling is rather complicated is that we use letters for two distinct purposes: sometimes to spell sounds and sometimes to spell morphemes. For instance, we have a regular way of spelling words that end in the sound of the consonant cluster /st/ — simply **st,** as in **best** and **test.** Can you think of other words that rhyme with these and end in **st?**

▶ But we also have a regular way of spelling the past tense morpheme. In regular verbs we spell it with the letters **ed,** no matter how the last part of the word is pronounced. So when we make a past tense of **guess,** we spell it **guessed,** even though **guessed** is an exact rhyme for **best** and **test.** Can you give other examples of verbs in the past tense that rhyme with **guessed?**

▶ **Past** and **passed** are homophones. Which one contains the past-tense morpheme? Give other words that rhyme with **past** and are spelled in the same way. **Massed** and **gassed,** like **passed,** contain the past-tense morpheme.

▶ Here is another pair of homophones: **bold — bowled.** What two consonant sounds do they both end with? Which word is an adjective and which the past-tense form of a verb?

▶ Give a homophone for **made.** Which of the homophones has the past tense morpheme, spelled irregularly?

▶ Other morphemes that have regular spellings — no matter what the sound may be — are the plural of nouns, the **s** form of verbs, and the possessive of nouns. We spell the first of these usually with just **s: tables, pools.** After some sounds we spell it **es.** What sounds? In certain circumstances we spell it **ies.** What circumstances?

▶ We spell the **s** form of verbs by the same rules: **comes, reaches, tries.** Give another example of each.

But we spell the singular possessive with just the apostrophe and **s: John's, the fox's, Sally's.**

▶ However, words which do not have these morphemes do not follow these rules. **Muse** rhymes with **views.** Which word consists of two morphemes? **Praise** rhymes with **days.** Which word consists of two morphemes? Give two other words that rhyme with **days.**

▶ We have many signals in our language — position, accompanying words, endings — which tell what word class a word belongs to. So we can often use the same word in more than one word class. For instance, **watch** is used both as a verb and as a noun. Tell which it is in each of these sentences:

    a. My watch is slow.

    b. We will watch it closely.

▶ Can you tell how you knew that **watch** is a noun in Sentence **a?** What signals were there to tell you? What helped tell you that **watch** was a verb in Sentence **b?**

▶ Tell what word classes the word **bear** belongs to in each of the following. Try to tell how you know.

    1. The bear went over the mountain.

    2. Crockett found an enormous bear.

    3. I can't bear it.

    4. They bear their troubles bravely.

■ The words in heavy black type in the following sentences can all be used either as nouns or as verbs. Tell which each one is. Then make a sentence using it in the other word class. For instance, if the sentence were "John will **watch** it," you might say "His watch is slow."

    5. What did they **name** the baby?

    6. It's in the **sink.**

    7. We should **garage** the car.

    8. That ought to **floor** them.

    9. He had a handsome **face.**

    10. His **stay** was very short.

Of course not all nouns are easily used as verbs. **Boy** and **girl** and **car** are not. But a great many are.

▶ Some words used as nouns or verbs may also be used as adjectives. What different word classes does **sweet** belong to in the following sentences? Tell how you know.

    11. This is very sweet.

    12. Would you like a sweet?

▶ What is **dry** in each of the following?

    13. He should dry it.

    14. It isn't dry.

■ Make sentences using the following words first as verbs and then as adjectives:

       warm   smooth   quiet   brave   wet

Use the following in sentences first as adjectives and then as nouns. Use an indefinite article — **a, an, some,** or ∅ — with the word when you use it as a noun.

      emerald   calm   delinquent   regular   commercial

▶ Some words can occur without change of form as noun, verb, or adjective. Tell what **calm** is in each sentence:

    15. He is very calm.

    16. We were conscious of a great calm.

    17. We'll try to calm him.

■ Write three sentences for each of these words, using them first as nouns, next as verbs, next as adjectives:

      quiet   equal   total   light   initial

▶ The form **well** occurs in all four of the large word classes — noun, verb, adjective, adverb of manner. Tell which it is in each of the following sentences:

    18. Harry does his work well.

    19. I saw tears well up in her eyes.

    20. Julia was sick, but she is well now.

    21. They dug a well in the back yard.

There are not many such words, however. Usually we must make a change in the form of the word: "They are **neutrals**" (noun); "They are **neutral**" (adj.); "We'll **neutralize** them" (verb).

■ Most words have a special form which marks them as one class or another. This is usually an ending. Thus we can't just use the word **thick** as a verb. We don't say "I'll thick it." Instead, we say "I'll thicken it," adding the verb-making morpheme v-en. Make verbs of the following adjectives and use them in sentences:

      sweet   deep   rough   hard   soft

▶ Most adverbs of manner have the ending **ly** which distinguishes them from adjectives. What are the adverbs of manner corresponding to the following adjectives?

      rough   true   loose   angry   calm

▶ Of course, you know that a derivational morpheme that makes adjectives from nouns is spelled **al.** How do we spell a morpheme that makes abstract nouns from some adjectives?

The Relative Pronoun <u>Whom</u>

■ You have learned to expand **b** sentences into noun phrases in which a noun phrase object in the **b** sentence is modified by a relative clause. Review this transformation by writing **c** sentences for the following:

1. a. Bill dropped a ball. → Bill dropped + NP
   b. He was carrying a ball. → a ball that he was carrying } →

2. a. A cat climbed a tree. → NP + climbed a tree.
   b. The dog was chasing a cat. → a cat that the dog was chasing } →

3. a. The apricots looked good. → NP + looked good.
   b. He bought the apricots. → the apricots that he bought } →

Are any of the noun phrases modified by **that** clauses human — do any of them refer to people?

When a relative clause with **that** modifies the noun phrase object of a **b** sentence, we can omit the relative pronoun **that** and just let the position show that the structure which modifies the noun phrase is a relative clause:

   a. The apricots looked good. → NP + looked good.
   b. He bought the apricots. → the apricots he bought } →
   c. The apricots he bought looked good.

In **c** the relative clause is "(that) he bought," with the **that** left out. We can only do this when the relative clause modifies a noun phrase that functions as object in the **b** sentence.

■ Make **c** sentences of these, omitting the relative pronoun:

4. a. The house is on Cedar Street.
   b. Mr. Winkler bought the house.
5. a. The cat climbed a tree.
   b. The dog was chasing the cat.
6. a. We found some papers.
   b. Mildred had left some papers.
7. a. The radio works fine.
   b. Max fixed the radio.
8. a. We saw the movie.
   b. I liked the movie.
9. a. A noise frightened him.
   b. He heard a noise.

In the sentences we have worked with so far, none of the relative clauses have modified human noun phrases. We have seen that we may modify the nonhuman noun phrases with **that** clauses. When the modified phrase is an object, we may omit the relative pronoun **that**.

You know that **whom** is the object form of **who** because you have used **whom** in **wh** questions.

      a. John saw the man.   b. Whom did John see?

When the noun phrase functioning as object in a sentence is human, we can use the relative pronoun **whom:**

      a. The man was limping. → NP + was limping. ⎫
                                                               ⎬ →
      b. John saw the man. → the man whom John saw ⎭
      c. The man whom John saw was limping.

The form **whom** is not used in relative clauses as often as it is in questions, but still you should be familiar with it.

■ Make **c** sentences of the following, using the relative pronoun **whom** in the relative clauses.

10. a. The girl was crying.
    b. Edith saw the girl.
11. a. The people were Nigerians.
    b. We met the people.
12. a. The teachers were very grateful.
    b. The parents helped the teachers.
13. a. The driver threatened revenge.
    b. Mr. Wheeler had fired the driver.
14. a. Mr. Walker comforted the driver.
    b. Mr. Wheeler had fired the driver.
15. a. Nobody recognized the person.
    b. Marian described the person.
16. a. Harry knows a man.
    b. We can trust a man.
17. a. A librarian knew the answer.
    b. Helen asked a librarian.
18. a. Cousin Bob recommended the carpenter.
    b. Uncle Bill hired the carpenter.
19. a. The clerk gave us a receipt.
    b. We paid the clerk.
20. a. A detective arrested the fugitive.
    b. We had recognized the fugitive.

An Autobiography

This story is about the schooldays of a boy who became a very famous man, Winston Spencer Churchill. He was a great leader of the Second World War. He became also a great writer of English. But you will see as you read that school wasn't any easier for him that it is for most people.

Days at Harrow

I did not do well in examinations. This was especially true of my entrance examination to Harrow. The Headmaster, Mr. Welldon, however, took a broad-minded view of my Latin prose: he showed discernment in judging my general ability. This was the more remarkable, because I was found unable to answer a single question in the Latin paper. I wrote my name at the top of the page. I wrote down the number of the question "1." After much reflection I put a bracket round it thus "[1]." But thereafter I could not think of anything connected with it that was either relevant or true. Incidentally there arrived from nowhere in particular a blot and several smudges. I gazed for two whole hours at this sad spectacle, and then merciful ushers collected my piece of foolscap with all the others and carried it up to the Headmaster's table. It was from these slender indications of scholarship that Mr. Welldon drew the conclusion that I was worthy to pass into Harrow. It is very much to his credit. It showed that he was a man capable of looking beneath the surface of things: a man not dependent upon paper manifestations. I have always had the greatest regard for him.

In consequence of his decision, I was in due course placed in the third, or lowest, division of the Fourth, or bottom, Form. The names of the new boys were printed in the school list in alphabetical order; and as my correct name, Spencer-Churchill, began with an "S," I gained no more advantage from the alphabet than from the wider sphere of letters. I was in fact only two away from the bottom of the whole school; and these two, I regret to say, disappeared almost immediately through illness or some other cause.

The Harrow custom of calling the roll is different from that of Eton. At Eton the boys stand in a cluster and lift their hats when their names are called. At Harrow they file past a Master in the schoolyard and answer one by one. My position was therefore revealed in its somewhat invidious humility. It was the year 1887. Lord Randolph Churchill had only just resigned his position as Leader of the House of Commons and Chancellor of the Exchequer, and he still towered in the forefront of politics. In consequence a large number of visitors of both sexes used to wait on the school steps in order to see me march by; and I frequently heard the irreverent comment, "Why, he's last of all!"

I continued in this unpretentious situation for nearly a year. However, by being so long in the lowest form I gained an immense advantage over the cleverer boys. They all went on to learn Latin and Greek and splendid things like that. But I was taught English. We were considered such dunces that we could learn only English. Mr. Somervell — a most delightful man, to whom my debt is great — was charged with the duty of teaching the stupidest boys the most disregarding thing — namely to write mere English. He knew how to do it. He taught it as no one else has ever taught it. Not only did we learn English parsing thoroughly, but we also practiced continually English analysis. Mr. Somervell had a system of his own. He took a fairly long sentence and broke it up into its components by means of black, red, blue, and green inks. Subject, verb, object: Relative Clauses, Conditional Clauses, Conjunctive and Disjunctive Clauses! Each had its color and its

bracket. It was a kind of drill. We did it almost
daily. As I remained in the Third Fourth three times
as long as anyone else, I got three times as much of it.
I learned it thoroughly. Thus I got into my bones the
essential structure of the ordinary British sentence —
which is a noble thing. And when in after years my
schoolfellows who had won prizes and distinction for
writing such beautiful Latin poetry and pithy Greek
epigrams had to come down again to common English,
to earn their living or make their way, I did not feel
myself at any disadvantage. Naturally, I am biased
in favor of boys learning English. I would make them
all learn English; and then I would let the clever
ones learn Latin as an honor and Greek as a treat.
But the only thing I would whip them for is not knowing English. I would whip them hard for that.

Schools like Harrow and Eton are what we would call private schools, but the British call them public schools. Boys went to them — boys whose families could pay quite a lot of money for them to do so.

► The headmaster is what we would call the principal. What was the name of the headmaster at Harrow? Look up **discernment** in a dictionary. How did the headmaster show **discernment?** What does **relevant** mean?

► Even young boys were supposed to know Latin. Did Churchill? What did he put on his Latin paper?

► The **ushers** were people who supervised the examination. Look up the word **foolscap.** Why did Churchill have a great regard for Mr. Welldon? What are **paper manifestations?** Look up **manifestation** in a dictionary.

► The **form** was what we would call grade. What form was Churchill in? What division in the form was he in? Where did he come in the alphabetical list of that division of that form? **Invidious** means offensive, or creating ill will. What does **somewhat invidious humility** mean?

► Lord Randolph Churchill was Winston Churchill's father. **Leader of the House of Commons** is like our "Speaker of the House of Representatives." The British **Chancellor of the Exchequer** is like the American "Secretary of the Treasury." How did this make it hard on his son when roll was called? Look up **irreverent** in a dictionary.

► Look up **pretentious** in a dictionary. What does **unpretentious** mean? What did the cleverer boys go on to learn? What was Churchill taught? Who was his teacher? What do you think **the most disregarding thing** means?

► **Parsing** is telling about grammatical forms — whether a noun is countable or noncountable, whether a verb is present or past. You do quite a lot of parsing and analysis too. What was Mr. Somervell's system of teaching grammar?

► Why did Churchill learn three times as much as anyone else? How did what he learned help him later?

► **Pithy** means short and full of meaning. Find out what **epigram** means. What would Churchill let clever boys do as an honor? What as a treat?

The passage from Churchill's autobiography tells you a good deal about his character, but nothing at all about his appearance. If he had been writing a biography instead of an autobiography, he would probably have described the appearance of this young student.

Here is a brief description of the owner of a tavern, from "The Croxley Master," by A. Conan Doyle.

He was a coarse, clean-shaven man, whose fiery face made a singular contrast with his ivory-white bald head. He had shrewd, light-blue eyes with foxy lashes, and he also leaned forward in silence from his chair, a fat, red hand upon either knee, and stared critically at the young assistant.

▷ 1. The first sentence uses several adjectives to describe the tavern owner's appearance. Two of these adjectives are hyphenated. What are the adjectives? What color is his face? What color is his bald head? Is this why the author says his face and head made a singular contrast?

▷ 2. The second sentence begins by telling what his eyes looked like but then tells two things that he did. Could this sentence have ended after the word lashes? How are the two parts of the sentence that tell what he did connected? How are his hands described as the author tells what he did?

■ The following details are from a description in a *New Yorker* story, "Wallace" by Richard H. Rovere. The details are given, not as Rovere wrote them, but just as short statements. Rewrite these details, putting them into longer, better-written, more interesting sentences.

He was fourteen. He was somewhat shorter than he should have been. He was a good deal stouter than he should have been. His face was round. His face was owlish. His face was dirty. He had eyes. The eyes were big. The eyes were dark. He had hair. The hair was black. The hair hardly ever got cut. The hair was arranged on his head. The four winds wanted the hair arranged that way.

161

You have seen that many words can be used in various word classes without any change of form. Not all words can be used in this way, though — not even most words. Most of the words we use are marked in some way as belonging to one word class or another.

► The word **reject** in the sentences below does not change its form, even though it is used as a verb in one sentence and as a noun in another. It does change in a way that is not shown by its spelling, however. Can you tell what this change is?

   a. The inspectors **reject** one part in ten.

   b. Every **reject** is melted and used again.

► What word class does **reject** belong to in Sentence **a?** Which syllable has first stress when **reject** is used as a verb?

► What word class does **reject** belong to in Sentence **b?** Which syllable has first stress when **reject** is used as a noun?

■ A number of English words shift their stress in this way when they are used first in one word class and then in another. Copy the words in heavy black type in each sentence below, and put an accent mark over the vowel in the syllable with first stress. Write **n.** (for noun) or **v.** (for verb) after the word to show what its word class is in that sentence.

   1. He caught the ball on the **rebound.**
   2. Tennis balls **rebound** well on clay courts.
   3. Ship captains **record** facts about their voyages daily.
   4. Such a **record** is called a "log."
   5. The **subject** of his description was a cab driver.
   6. Professors **subject** graduate students to searching examination.
   7. Writers **contract** to complete a book by a given date.
   8. Mr. Watkins signed a **contract** with a publisher.
   9. Our country **exports** much machinery.
   10. Our **exports** include automobiles, tractors, and tools.

■ Write sentences using the following words either as nouns or as verbs, according to the stress marks that are given.

   11. a. óbject   b. objéct
   12. a. projéct   b. prój333

162

The Suffix able

You have seen that with some words the word class is indicated only by stress, with no help from the spelling. In other words there is a visible sign of the word class — **al** for adjective, **ity** for abstract noun, and so on. Another such visible sign is a very common suffix — the ending spelled **able.**

The derivational morpheme which **able** represents has about the same meaning as the modal **can,** and it is added to verbs to make adjectives:

a. That hill can be climbed.

b. That hill is climbable.

■ Make similar sentences with adjectives ending in **able** from these sentences with verbs.

1. That package can be mailed.
2. This fence can be jumped.
3. The soldiers can be counted.
4. The coat can be worn.
5. The story can be believed.

When we add **able,** we follow the same spelling rules that we do with other suffixes beginning with vowels. For instance we usually drop the final **e** in the verb. Make adjectives ending in **able** from the following verbs:

love　　deceive　　observe　　adore　　excite

However, when the verb ends in the sound /s/ spelled **ce,** or the sound /j/ spelled **ge,** there would be a problem if the final **e** is dropped.

What sound does **c** represent when the letter after it is not **i** or **e?** Then what would be the regular pronunciation of **trace + able → tracable,** or **manage + able → managable,** if we dropped the **e** in **trace** and **manage?**

To show that the **c** stands for /s/, not /k/, and the **g** for /j/, not /g/, we keep the **e** at the end of words like these:

traceable　　manageable

▶ What happens when the verb ends in a consonant followed by **y,** as in **rely?**

■ Write adjectives ending in **able** from the following:

justify　　pay　　fortify　　deny　　replace

change　　erase　　enforce　　charge　　pity

163

You know that when a relative clause modifies a noun phrase object that is nonhuman, we may use the relative pronoun **that** (or **which**) or we may omit the relative pronoun. When the noun phrase is human, we may use the relative pronoun **whom.** But **whom** is not used much in relative clauses because people feel that it is a little awkward. We have two perfectly respectable alternatives. We can use the relative pronoun **that** with both human and nonhuman noun phrases. So this gives us one choice:

a. The man was limping. → NP + was limping. ⎫
b. John saw the man. → the man that John saw ⎬ →
c. The man that John saw was limping.

▶ What word in **c** has been used instead of **whom?**

The other alternative is the one you learned about with **that** clauses modifying nonhuman noun phrase objects. This is to omit the relative pronoun altogether.

a. The man was limping. → NP + was limping. ⎫
b. John saw the man. → the man (whom) John saw ⎬ →
c. The man John saw was limping.

■ Write **c** sentences from each of the following. First, use **whom** as the relative pronoun. The second time use **that.** The third time omit the relative pronoun entirely.

1. a. The child was crying.
   b. They found the child.
2. a. The dentist is very good.
   b. Mr. Baxter recommended the dentist.
3. a. Maria liked the dentist.
   b. Mr. Baxter recommended the dentist.
4. a. Everyone listened to the astronaut.
   b. The principal introduced the astronaut.
5. a. Dorothy is a girl.
   b. Everyone likes a girl.
6. a. Mack has a teacher.
   b. He admires a teacher very much.
7. a. He was a fighter.
   b. Everybody feared a fighter.
8. a. The policeman had saved some children.
   b. Everyone honored the policeman.

Delete means take out. You have made deletions from relative clauses by taking out, or omitting, the relative pronouns **that** (or **which**) and **whom.**

▶ 1. When a relative clause contains a relative pronoun and a form of **be,** there is another deletion we can make. Study the following string of morphemes for a **b** sentence and for the expanded noun phrase made from this sentence:

b. the + lady + pres. + be + downstairs →
   the + lady + who + pres. + be + downstairs

What is the relative clause? What relative pronoun does the clause contain? What is the tense morpheme? To what morpheme does the tense apply?

▶ 2. Let's apply the relative clause transformation, using an **a** sentence, but using a morpheme string for the expanded noun phrase:

a. The lady wants to see you. → NP + wants to see you ⎤
b. The lady is downstairs. → the + lady + who + pres. + ⎬ →
   be + downstairs ⎦
c. the + lady + who + pres. + be + downstairs +
   wants to see you

In relative clauses that contain **be** as the tense-carrying morpheme, we can delete the relative pronoun, tense, and **be.** What three morphemes in **c** can be deleted?

When the relative pronoun, tense, and **be** are deleted, we have the following:

c. the + lady + downstairs + wants to see you

What is the actual **c** sentence?

▶ 3. Here is another example with a morpheme string representing the expanded noun phrase. We delete the relative pronoun, tense, and **be** just as we did in the first example.

a. NP + looks like your brother
b. The boy is standing on the porch. → the + boy + who +
   pres. + be + ing + stand + on + the + porch

What are the actual words of the expanded noun phrase made from the **b** sentence? What is left of the expanded noun phrase when we delete who, pres., and be? To what does ing apply? What is the actual **c** sentence?

▶ 4. Here is one more example, but this time we will use the actual words of the expanded noun phrase instead of a morpheme string:

    a. Jerry spoke to the gentleman. → Jerry spoke to + NP ⎫
    b. The gentleman was leading a horse. → the gentleman ⎬ →
       that was leading a horse ⎭

What is the relative clause in the expanded noun phrase after Sentence **b?** What is the relative pronoun which you will delete? What is the form of **be** in the relative clause? What tense does this word show? Then you can delete both tense and **be** by deleting one word in the relative clause. What word?

▶ What is the actual **c** sentence after you have deleted **that** and **was** and completed the transformation?

■ Deleting the relative pronoun, tense, and **be** is called the **relative clause deletion transformation.** Apply the regular relative clause transformation and then the relative clause deletion transformation to each of the following pairs of sentences. Write just the final **c** sentences.

   5. a. I know the lady. → I know + NP
     b. The lady is in the blue dress. → the lady who is in the blue dress

   6. a. A man wants to see you. → NP + wants to see you.
     b. A man is painting the garage. → a man who is painting the garage

   7. a. I saw the key. → I saw + NP
     b. The key was in the lock. → the key that was in the lock

   8. a. The water has smoothed the stones. → The water has smoothed + NP
     b. The stones were in the brook. → the stones that were in the brook

   9. a. The boys laugh too much. → NP + laugh too much
     b. The boys are studying upstairs. → the boys who are studying upstairs

 10. a. The clerk spilled the sugar. → NP + spilled the sugar
     b. The clerk was waiting on Nancy. → the clerk who was waiting on Nancy

We often delete the relative pronoun or the relative pronoun, tense, and **be** when we use the relative clause transformation to combine two or more shorter sentences into a single longer one. Such deletions usually speed up the sentence and make it sound freer and less formal.

■ Use the relative clause transformation to combine each group of sentences below into a single longer sentence. You will have to figure out which sentences to convert to expanded noun phrases. Write the complete sentence first, without deletions. Then, delete the relative pronoun if the relative clause modifies a nonhuman phrase object. Delete the relative pronoun, tense, and **be** when you can do so.

1. The lady has a parrot. The lady is visiting us. The parrot speaks with an accent. The accent sounds French.
2. The piano tuner wants to borrow the crowbar. The piano tuner is in the parlor. The crowbar is in the woodshed.
3. We'll eat the cheese on the crackers. Mabel bought the cheese. The crackers are on the shelf. The shelf is in the cupboard.
4. I introduced a boy to the girl. I know the boy. The girl runs the contest. He wants to enter the contest.
5. Bill borrowed the knife. I got the knife as a prize in the game. I won the game.
6. The girl wants to bring the friend. You invited the girl. The friend is staying at her house.
7. The fish won first prize in the fishing contest. Tom caught the fish. The sporting club puts on the contest.
8. The man hired the contractor. The man is building that house. We recommended the man.
9. The lifeguard supervises the pool. The lifeguard is on duty. The pool is reserved for adults.
10. The silver belongs to the lady. The silver is in the shoebox. Mother knows the lady.
11. The man delivered the dishwasher. The man is in the kitchen. My parents ordered the dishwasher last week.
12. The child has lost the skates. I met the child. I found the skates.

A Poem

You may have read last year "The Quiet Season" — a poem by the same poet about the fall of the year.

The Coming of the Cold

The small brook dies within its bed;
The stem that holds the bee is prone;
Old hedgerows keep the leaves; the phlox,
That late autumnal bloom, is dead.
All summer green is now undone:
The hills are grey, the trees are bare,
The mould upon the branch is dry.
The fields are harsh and bare, the rocks
Gleam sharply on the narrow sight.
The land is desolate, the sun
No longer gilds the scene at noon;
Winds gather in the north and blow
Bleak clouds across the heavy sky.
And frost is marrow-cold, and soon
Winds bring a fine and bitter snow.

THEODORE ROETHKE

The Coming of the Cold

▶ How might cold weather make a small brook "die" within its bed?

▶ **Prone** means lying flat. What kind of stem would hold a **bee?** Why would the flowers be lying flat?

▶ Do you think that the leaves **old hedgerows keep** are green leaves growing on the hedges? Why would the poet say that hedgerows keep the leaves? What kind of leaves?

▶ The poem tells what **phlox** is. What is it?

▶ The adjective **undone** may mean not tied or fastened. It may also mean ruined. Which meaning did the poet intend in saying "All summer green is now undone"?

169

► **Mould** is another spelling of **mold.** Look up **mold** and find a meaning that explains what Roethke meant by the word.

► "The Coming of the Cold" contains many adjectives, some of them used in unusual ways. The most usual meaning of **narrow,** for example, is the one Emily Dickinson used when she called a snake "a narrow fellow in the grass." But narrow is sometimes used to mean detailed, close, or painstaking. Find the expression in the poem that means something like this:

To the person who looks closely, the rocks gleam sharply.

► What does **desolate** mean? Guess if you do not know, and then check your guess by using a dictionary.

► What does **gild** mean in the expression "the sun no longer gilds the scene . . ."?

► What does the word **bleak** mean? What kind of word is it?

► Is the sky actually **heavy?** What does the poet mean by describing it this way?

► You have heard the expression "chilled to the bone." What do you think **marrow-cold** means?

► The adjective **fine** may mean good or excellent. It may also mean powdery or composed of small particles. Which meaning is intended in the last line?

► Look up the adjective **bitter** in a dictionary and copy the definition that you think best fits the use of this word in the last line of the poem. Be prepared to defend your choice.

Appealing to the Senses

► 1. In "The Coming of the Cold," Roethke makes use of words that appeal to the senses of sight and touch, or feeling. Give some examples from the poem of words or expressions that appeal to each of these senses.

■ 2. Think of a scene that you have observed carefully — a frosty lawn; brick walls on a day so clear and sunny that each brick stood out; streets half hidden by the spray of heavy, wind-blown rain; surf breaking on a rocky shore. Choose a scene that you can make vivid by using words that appeal to the senses — sight, touch, taste, hearing, smell. Then write a paragraph or two in prose, describing the scene you have chosen.

Writing Conversation

The following quotation comes from the novel *Tom Sawyer,* by Mark Twain. Tom and his friend, Becky, have been lost for days in a cave. While they were in the cave, Tom discovered that a murderer named Injun Joe was using it as a hiding place. Now, two weeks after his rescue, Tom is talking to Becky's father, Judge Thatcher, and has stated that he wouldn't mind going to the cave again.

> The judge said, "Well, there are others just like you, Tom, I've not the least doubt. But we have taken care of that. Nobody will get lost in that cave any more."
>
> "Why?"

▶ Study the conversation. When the quotation — the actual words of the speaker — follows an introductory expression like **The Judge said,** what punctuation mark may be used to separate this expression from the quotation? Does this punctuation mark come before or after the quotation mark?

▶ Notice that the second quotation, "Why?" does not have an expression like **asked Tom** after it. How can you tell from what the Judge said that Tom asked the question?

■ The following exercises will give you a chance to write some conversation. Each exercise is in the form called indirect discourse. It tells what was said, but does not give the actual words of the speaker. Rewrite each bit of indirect discourse as a direct quotation, using quotation marks. The parts in parentheses are not discourse, but are part of the story.

1. The Judge said this was because he had its big door sheathed with boiler iron two weeks before, and triple-locked — and he had the keys.
   (Tom turned white as a sheet.)
2. The Judge asked the boy what the matter was. He told somebody to run and to fetch a glass of water.
   (The water was brought and thrown into Tom's face.)
3. The Judge told Tom that he was all right now. He asked Tom what had been the matter with him.
4. Tom exclaimed to the Judge that Injun Joe was in the cave.

The Suffix ible

The derivational morpheme that means **can** and is added to verbs to make adjectives has two spellings: **able** and **ible**. This creates a spelling problem, especially because the **a** of **able** and the **i** of **ible** are both pronounced with the vowel sound /ə/, and therefore the pronunciation gives us no clue to the spelling.

▶ The spelling **ible** for the most part is added to words that are verbs in Latin. An example is **legible.** This is an adjective made by adding **ible** to the Latin verb **legere,** which means **read.** We don't use this verb in English. If we want to make an adjective of the English verb **read,** we would use **able.** What would this adjective be?

■ Here are some more words like **legible,** made by adding **ible** to forms of Latin verbs. Study them. Look up any that you don't know. Then write them in sentences.

edible   plausible   possible   visible   flexible

▶ There are some recognizable sets among the **ible** words. One is made by adding **ible** to English verbs that end in **duce.** Make adjectives of these words. What letter will you drop?

produce   deduce   reduce

▶ Look up any of these three words that you don't know.

Another set that takes **ible** consists of English verbs which end in **st.** Make adjectives of the following:

digest   combust   resist

■ A number of verbs ending in **nd** change the **d** to **s** and then add **ible.** Make adjectives of the following:

defend   respond   comprehend

▶ Look up any of the words whose meaning you don't know.

The following verbs that end in **mit** change the **t** to **ss** and then add **ible.** Make adjectives of the following:

admit   permit   omit

The following verbs take **ible.** Make adjectives of them.

force   reverse   convert

Study the following miscellaneous **ible** words:

sensible   divisible   susceptible   feasible

■ Write all of the **ible** words on this page from dictation.

One might well ask why we have two forms of the morpheme that means **can** and makes adjectives from verbs. We have seen the same thing, of course, in the three spellings of the "one who does" morpheme: **worker, actor, beggar.**

▶ The answer lies, as often, in Latin. Most Latin verbs had the ending **are,** like **stare,** which meant **to stand.** These verbs formed adjectives with **abilis: stabilis.** What English adjective do you think we have from **stabilis?**

▶ Other Latin verbs had endings other than **are,** and they all made their adjectives with the ending **ibilis.** For instance, the Latin verb **credere,** which meant believe, added **ibilis** to form **credibilis.** What English adjective do we have from **credibilis?**

This explains why we have the two forms, but it isn't much help to most of us in spelling the suffix. However, there are some things we can bear in mind that will help.

▶ The first is to know which form is the more likely. The form **able** is. There are over seven hundred words that end in **able** and only about two hundred and fifty that end in **ible.** So if you had to guess — if there were no clue at all — which spelling would you choose, **able** or **ible?**

▶ Another thing to know is that **able** is a living suffix and **ible** is not. That is, if we add this morpheme to a new word, which never had it before, we always add the form **able.** Make an adjective by finishing **b** below:

   a. Bertram grouped the daisies.

   b. The daisies were group_____.

We can even add this form to phrases: "The marbles were pick-uppable." In these new creations, we always add **able.**

Then we reduce the guesswork by knowing as many as we can of the smaller group. That is why some of the **ible** words are listed on page 171. We learn them and then, if we have to guess, we guess **able** for others.

▶ It is a good idea to pay attention to relationships in the smaller groups. If you know **admissible,** how would you expect to spell **permiss–ble?** If you know **eligible,** how would you expect to spell **inelig–ble?**

► 1. You have learned that the relative pronoun, tense, and **be** can be deleted from a relative clause that contains a form of **be** as the tense-carrying word. Does the relative clause in this expanded noun phrase contain a relative pronoun, tense, and **be?**

> the lady that was on the platform

We can delete two words from the relative clause and leave it without a relative pronoun, tense, or **be.** What two words are these? What will the expanded noun phrase be after you have applied the relative clause deletion transformation?

► 2. You know that one structure which can follow a form of **be** as complement is an adjective. So a relative clause that contains a relative pronoun, tense, and **be** could also contain an adjective. Here is a morpheme string for such a **b** sentence and for the expanded noun phrase:

b. the + child + past + be + hungry →
   the + child + that + past + be + hungry

Now, suppose we apply the relative clause deletion transformation to the string for the relative clause in the expanded noun phrase. What three morphemes do we remove?

The expanded noun phrase is now reduced to this:

> the + child + hungry

We would not be likely to say "the child hungry." What would we say?

When a relative clause modifying a noun phrase is reduced by deletion to one word, and that word is an adjective, the adjective is moved to a position before the noun:

> **the hungry child**

This is called the **noun modifier transformation.**

► 3. Here is another example of a **b** sentence and expanded noun phrase in the form of morpheme strings:

b. the + teacher + pres. + be + patient →
   the + teacher + who + pres. + be + patient

What three morphemes can we delete?

When you deleted the relative pronoun, tense, and **be,** the following morphemes were left:

> the + teacher + patient

What does the + teacher + patient become when the noun modifier transformation is applied?

■ First, apply the relative clause transformation to each of the following. Then change the **c** sentence by deleting the relative pronoun, tense, and **be,** and applying the noun modifier transformation. You can perform the deletion and apply the noun modifier transformation in a single step. An example is provided for you:

Example:

   a. We admired the lady. → We admired + NP
   b. The lady was beautiful. → the lady that was beautiful

       →

   c. We admired the lady that was beautiful.
     We admired the beautiful lady.

4. a. The dog barked fiercely. → NP + barked fiercely.
   b. The dog was huge. → the dog that was huge
5. a. The boy cried for his mother. → NP + cried for his mother.
   b. The boy was little. → the boy who was little
6. a. The fire gave off an odor. → The fire gave off + NP
   b. An odor was peculiar. → an odor that was peculiar
7. a. The policeman arrested the driver. → NP + arrested the driver.
   b. The policeman was angry. → the policeman who was angry
8. a. The moon glowed with a light. → The moon glowed with + NP.
   b. A light was mellow. → a light that was mellow
9. a. A mother was looking for her child. → NP + was looking for her child.
   b. A mother was anxious. → a mother who was anxious
10. a. Mr. Wilson lives in this house. → Mr. Wilson lives in + NP.
   b. This house is old. → this house that is old
11. a. The kitten purred loudly. → NP + purred loudly.
   b. The kitten was happy. → the kitten that was happy
12. a. We heard a noise. → We heard + NP.
   b. A noise was ghastly. → a noise that was ghastly

You now know a good deal about relative clauses that should be useful to you in expressing a number of ideas in a single sentence. You know how to rewrite a sentence as an expanded noun phrase that you can embed in another sentence. You also know when the relative pronoun can be deleted, when the relative pronoun, tense, and **be** can be deleted, and what to do when all that is left after the deletion is an adjective.

■ Use this information to combine each group of sentences that follows into a single longer sentence. If you can do so, write the longer sentence at once, deletions, adjectives, and all.

1. The man sold the farm to the contractor. The man was elderly. The man loved the farm. The contractor made the bid. The bid was the highest.
2. Some children have a dog. The children are noisy. The children live next door. The dog is large. The dog barks all night.
3. The boat was caught in the current. The boat was small. The boat was approaching the falls. The current was powerful.
4. The musician comes from a country. The musician is remarkable. The musician composed the music. We heard the music on television last night. A country never appreciated him.
5. We glimpsed a light. A light was distant. A light blinked out a code. None of us could understand a code.
6. A stranger poured a spoonful of shot into the frog. The stranger was dishonest. The shot was lead. The frog had been the jumper.
7. Alice was the girl. The girl made the sandwiches. The sandwiches were delicious. We ate the sandwiches for lunch.
8. A wind blew the leaves off the trees. The wind was strong. The wind sprang up suddenly. The leaves were dead. The trees shelter the farmhouse.
9. The movie showed scenes. We saw the movie. The scenes were taken in cities. Cities were famous. Cities were European.

10. Mrs. Sanchez told us stories. Stories were true. Stories happened in Puerto Rico.
11. The snow covered the roads in drifts. The snow was fine. The roads are hilly. Drifts were impassable.
12. We had a dinner at the restaurant. A dinner was wonderful. The restaurant was inexpensive. Mr. Waterhouse recommended the restaurant.
13. We fed the cat. The cat was hungry. Eddie found the cat.
14. Mr. Nichols knows a man. A man is old. A man can make whistles from trees. Trees grow by the river.
15. The houses were bleached by the sun. The houses were gaunt. The houses were still standing in the ghost town.
16. The horseman rode a mare. The horseman was solitary. The horseman appeared in the street. The street was empty. A mare had a limp. A limp was bad.
17. Rocks marked the camping grounds of the tribe. Rocks were black. Rocks were stained by the soot of fires. Fires were many. The camping grounds were ancient.
18. The rabbits are really hares. The rabbits are big. The rabbits live in the North. The North is snowy. Hares turn white in the winter.
19. The boys had hung pails on pegs in the maple trees. The boys lived in the house. The house was little. The maple trees were old. The maple trees grew beside the road.
20. The Spanish moss waved gently in the breeze. The Spanish moss covered the trees. The trees were great. The trees were gray. The breeze blew from the sea.
21. The strangers were carrying packs on their backs. The strangers were weary. We met the strangers at the bridge. The bridge was over the river. The packs were heavy.
22. The ants entered a crack in the wall. The ants were black. We saw the ants. The ants were carrying grains of sand. The crack was small.
23. The horseman was leading a string of pack animals. The horseman was lone. The horseman was riding towards us. A string of pack animals was long. A string of pack animals carried loads. Loads were heavy.

T E S T S

1. The word in **heavy black type** in each sentence below is used as a noun. Make another sentence using it as a verb. If you make mistakes, study pages 152–53.

    a. I'll make a **mark** on it.

    b. He has an **interest** in it.

    c. The **march** was a long one.

    d. The **object** was an animal tooth.

2. The word in heavy black type in each sentence below is used as an adjective. Make another sentence using it as a verb. If you make mistakes, study pages 152–53.

    a. The clothes aren't **dry.**

    b. The children are **thin.**

    c. The room is very **warm.**

    d. The children are **quiet.**

3. For each word below write two sentences. In the first use it as a noun, in the second as a verb. Each time make a mark over the syllable that has the heavier stress. If you make mistakes, study page 162.

        record   object   rebound

4. Make adjectives ending in **able** from the following verbs. If you make mistakes, study page 163.

        pay   rely   trace   manage   desire

5. Copy the words in each set, completing the spelling in each set with either **a** or **i.** If you make mistakes, study pages 163, 172.

Set a: deduc–ble   vis–ble   respons–ble   admiss–ble

Set b: enjoy–ble   lov–ble   change–ble   loan–ble

Set c: sens–ble   ed–ble   digest–ble   forc–ble

Make **c** sentences of the following, omitting the relative pronoun if the relative pronoun modifies a noun phrase object. If you make mistakes, study page 154.

  6. a. I have the apples.

     b. Tom picked the apples.

  7. a. The key is under the mat.

     b. I hid the key.

  8. a. Mary ate the candy.

     b. The candy belonged to Sally.

Make **c** sentences of the following, using **who** if the relative clause modifies a human noun phrase subject, **whom** if it modifies an object. Then rewrite the **c** sentences with **whom,** deleting the relative pronoun. If you make mistakes, study pages 155, 164.

9. a. The stranger was walking.
   b. We met the stranger.
10. a. We knew the boy.
    b. Tom beat the boy at tennis.
11. a. Jerry helped the woman.
    b. The woman had dropped her groceries.

Make **c** sentences from the following, and apply the relative clause deletion transformation. If you make mistakes, study pages 165–66.

12. a. We heard the birds.
    b. The birds were in the trees.
13. a. A boy is at the door.
    b. A boy is whistling a tune.
14. a. The boat has no oars.
    b. The boat is on the pond.

Make **c** sentences from the following, and apply the noun modifier transformation. If you make mistakes, study pages 174–75.

15. a. Your sister is a girl.
    b. A girl is pretty.
16. a. The dogs want their dinner.
    b. The dogs are hungry.

Make **c** sentences from the following, making all permissible deletions. Use the noun modifier transformation if it applies. If you make mistakes, study pages 155, 164–66, 174–75.

17. a. The boat hit a rock in the rapids.
    b. The rapids are swift.
18. a. Tom knows the lady.
    b. The lady is playing the piano.
19. a. A policeman gave him directions.
    b. Mr. Hanson asked a policeman.
20. a. The eggs splattered the wallpaper.
    b. Mary dropped the eggs.

A Poem

People who *like* to study don't always fit into the modern scheme of things.   Read this poem by J. E. Faulks.

Problem Child

How *shall* I deal with Roger,
　　　　　　Mrs. Prodger?
I've never yet been able
To sit him at a table
And make him paint a label
For the salmon in the kindergarten shop.
　But he's full of animation
　When I mention a dictation,
　And he never wants a spelling test to stop.
I've encouraged self-expression
And intentional digression
But I think I'll have to let the system drop.
　For the normal child, like Roger,
　Is a *do*-er, not a dodger,
And your methods, Mrs. Prodger, are a flop.

How *shall* I deal with Roger,
　　　　　　Mrs. Prodger?
I've had projects on the fairies,
On markets, shops, and dairies;
I've had projects on the *prairies,*
But the little fellow doesn't want to play:
　Instead he has a yearning
　For unreasonable learning,
　And wants to do Arithmetic all day.
He shows a strong proclivity
For purposeless activity,
And doesn't want experience in clay.
　So I rather think that Roger
　Is a *do*-er, not a dodger,
And how *would* you deal with Roger, can you say?

181

► The person who is supposed to be speaking in the poem is a teacher in one of the early grades in school. She is talking to the principal, Mrs. Prodger. What does she say in the first few lines that she has been unable to get Roger to do?

► What does **animation** mean? Do you think Roger liked to have a dictation exercise or not? What did he feel about spelling tests?

► How might one "encourage self-expression" among kindergarten children or first graders? **Digression** means turning away from the main subject and doing something else instead. What does **intentional** mean? The teacher says that Roger, however, wants to *do* the subjects, not dodge them. What in the last part of the first stanza suggests that she thinks most little children are like Roger?

► What projects has the teacher tried in an effort to interest Roger? How did Roger respond to these? What did he have a yearning for? What did he want to do?

► **Proclivity** means a liking for something or a tendency to do something. What does Roger show a strong proclivity for? What are these activities that Roger likes to engage in? Do you think the teacher really thinks that they are purposeless? What kind of experience does Roger *not* want?

Morphemes, Spellings, and Word History

A morpheme that makes adjectives and sometimes nouns from verbs is spelled **ent** in many words, but it is spelled **ant** in others.

Some of the verbs to which we add this morpheme in the spelling **ent** are ordinary English verbs:

differ + ent → **different**

■ Write similar adjectives ending in **ent** from the following verbs. Look up any of the adjectives you make whose meaning you don't know.

indulge   urge   insist   persist   consist

There are also nouns ending in **ent,** such as **student, agent, rodent.**

► You remember that adding **ity** to an adjective like **moral** shifts the stress from one syllable to another. Which syllable in **moral** has first stress? Which syllable in **morality** has first stress? How can this help you to remember the spelling of **moral?**

► Add the morpheme <u>ent</u> to the following verbs, and then say both the verb and the adjective:

provide   reside   confide   excel

► Does adding **ent** shift the stress in these words? What syllable in each verb has first stress? What syllable has first stress in each of the adjectives you made? How might pronouncing **confide** help you to spell **confident?**

► The adjective **provident** is made from the English verb **provide,** which goes back to the Latin verb which means to foresee, **providere.** But most adjectives ending in **ent** go back directly to the Latin and have no underlying English verbs. The adjective **prudent,** for example, goes back to **prudentis,** a form of the Latin verb, **providere.** We don't have an English verb **prude.** What connection in meaning is there between **prudent** and **foreseeing?**

■ Study the following Latin verbs and verb forms and their meanings. These verbs and their forms are the origins of the English adjectives given at the right. Copy sentences **a** to **f** and replace the blanks with the adjectives.

Underlying Latin Verb	Meaning	Adjective
decere (decens, decentis)	to be proper	decent
silere (silens, silentis)	to be silent	silent
evident (evidens, evidentis)	out + to see	evident
currere (currens, currentis)	to run	current
ardere (ardens, ardentis)	to burn	ardent
efficere (efficiens, efficientis)	to bring about	efficient

a. A _____ engine is one that makes no noise.
b. A fact that is _____ is clear or plain.
c. The _____ thing to do is the proper thing to do.
d. An _____ debate is a fiery or hot argument.
e. Events happening at this time are _____ events.
f. A procedure that gets things done is an _____ procedure.

Telling someone else how to make a pie, construct a bird-house, or play a game is difficult. The problem is to remember all of the details that must be followed and to give these details in the proper order. It does little good to say "Bake the pie for 20 minutes in a 350° oven" and then add "Be sure to use very cold water in mixing the crust."

Study the following directions for a game that is fun to play at parties:

Shoe-Box Basketball

Collect five shoe boxes, and have on hand a box of checkers. Before the game begins, write the following values on the bottoms of the five boxes: 0, 5, 10, 15, 20. Use a marking pen or black crayon. Then conceal the numbers which tell the value of the box by taking off the cover and slipping it over the bottom of the box, leaving the box open.

When the players are ready to begin, choose sides, dividing the red checkers among the players of one team and the black among those on the other side.

Put shoe boxes in a group ten feet from a line. The players stand behind the line and try to pitch their checkers into the boxes without, of course, knowing what values are written on the bottom.

When all the checkers have been pitched, the scores are counted, one box at a time. Suppose the first box to be scored contains 1 black checker and 3 red ones. When the lid is removed from the bottom, it is found that this box is marked 15 and the black team scores 15 and the red team 45. Each box is emptied in turn, and the score for each team is totaled. Then the lids are replaced on the bottoms of the boxes, the boxes are shuffled so that no one knows the value of any box, and the game continues until one team or the other reaches a winning score of 300.

▶ 1. What materials are needed to play this game?

► 2. Tell what the steps are in concealing the numbers which tell the values of the boxes.

► 3. Tell what the players do when the game of "Shoe-Box Basketball" begins.

► 4. Tell what the steps are in continuing the game after all of the checkers have been pitched.

■ Use the information given in the short sentences below to write directions for the game called "Baker's Dozen." Illustrate your directions with a chart like this one, but use a different number and show a different score. You will need to improve the organization of the directions and rewrite them, paragraphing them and using longer sentences.

Baker's Dozen

A player is first. The player is **A**. **A** chooses a number from 1 to 13. Here is a game. Two can play the game. The game requires a pencil. The game requires paper. The game requires only these things. Suppose that **A** chooses 10. The second player is **B**. **B** does not know **A**'s number. **B** marks a chart. The chart is simple. **B** marks it as shown below. He makes an X beside one figure after another on the chart. He tries to avoid something as long as possible. That is marking the number. **A** has the number. **B** has a turn. The turn is over as soon as he marks the space. This space contains **A**'s number. The numbers are marked during **A**'s turn. **B**'s score is the total of all these numbers. These numbers include his opponent's chosen number. **B** scores 5 + 8 + 13 + 10, or 36, in the example. The example is shown here. **B** chooses a number now. **A** marks the chart. **A** uses the right-hand side. The right-hand side contains no X's. A chart is used twice. A new chart is made then. The winning score may be set at 300. The winning score may be set at 500.

X	13
	12
	11
X	10
	9
X	8
	7
	6
X	5
	4
	3
	2
	1

185

► 1. Study the noun phrase in heavy black type in each of the following sentences and decide what its function is:

a. Her weakness was **her selfishness.**
b. **Her selfishness** was well known.
c. Everybody regretted **her selfishness.**

What is the function of **her selfishness** in Sentence **a?** In Sentence **b?** In Sentence **c?**

► 2. Now study the words in heavy black type in the following sentences:

a. Her weakness was **that she was selfish.**
b. **That she was selfish** was well known.
c. Everybody regretted **that she was selfish.**

In which sentence does **that she was selfish** function as subject? In which does it function as object of a verb? In which does it function as complement after a form of **be?**

■ 3. As you can see, the expression **that she was selfish** functions in these sentences in just the same way that the noun phrase **her selfishness** does.

Suppose we remove the word **that** from **that she was selfish.** The words **she was selfish** are left. Does this group of words contain a noun phrase subject? Does it contain a predicate? Then is **she was selfish** a sentence? Write it as a sentence.

► 4. The expression **that she was selfish** was made simply by putting the word **that** in front of the sentence "She was selfish." We call a group of words like **that she was selfish** a **clause.** It is called a clause, rather than a phrase, when it contains a subject and a predicate, just as a sentence does, yet it is part of a longer sentence. It is called a **noun clause** when it functions the way a noun phrase does either as subject, object of a verb, or as complement after **be.**

■ Find the noun clauses in the following sentences and tell what the function of each noun clause is:

5. That John is sick may delay the performance.
6. I regret that we broke the window.
7. The problem was that we lost the key.
8. That Mary is a genius was clear to everyone.
9. That Mr. Elkins lost his job seems tragic.

10. He said that she had left.
11. That he hates dogs is a fact.
12. The difficulty was that the engine wouldn't start.
13. The engineers reported that the dam was weakened.
14. Our fear is that nobody can come.
15. That the movie was dull is undeniable.

▶ Now study the clauses in the following sentences and try to decide which is a noun clause and which is a relative clause.

    a. Everybody knew the story **that I told.**
    b. Everybody knew **that I told the story.**

▶ What would be left of the clause in Sentence **a** if the word **that** were omitted? **I told** has a subject and a verb, but the verb phrase is not complete: the verb **tell** must be followed by an object. If what is left when we remove the word **that** is not a complete sentence, we have removed the relative pronoun from a relative clause. What expanded noun phrase functions as object of the verb in Sentence **a?** What does the relative clause **that I told** modify in Sentence **a?**

▶ What would be left of the clause in Sentence **b** if the word **that** were omitted? Is **I told the story** a sentence? If what is left when we remove the word **that** is a complete sentence, we have removed it from a noun clause. In a noun clause like **that I told the story,** the word **that** is called a **subordinator** and the clause is called a **subordinate clause.**

▶ Each of the following sentences contains either a relative clause or a subordinate clause. Point out each clause which begins with **that** and tell which kind it is.

16. We believe that she is telling the truth.
17. We believe the story that she tells.
18. The box that we opened surprised Mr. Bouton.
19. That we opened the box surprised Mr. Bouton.
20. The idea is that Tom will dream up something.
21. The idea is a notion that Tom dreamed up.
22. The part that she played enchanted the audience.
23. That she played the part enchanted the audience.
24. Roger guessed that we had opened the box.
25. Roger found that the box had been opened.
26. The trouble that worried us was imaginary.
27. The trouble was that we worried about nothing.

A Famous Speech

When a President of the United States takes office, there is a ceremony known as the inauguration. On this occasion, the President always makes a speech, which is called the **inaugural address.** He usually talks about the problems the nation has and how he thinks they might be solved.

In 1865, after President Abraham Lincoln had been elected for the second time, he made a very famous speech, his Second Inaugural Address. At that time, Americans were fighting each other in the Civil War. Lincoln made a plea that when the war was ended all Americans might live together in good will and charity. The major part of this speech follows. Read it thoughtfully.

Lincoln's Second Inaugural

On the occasion corresponding to this four years ago, all thoughts were anxiously directed to an impending civil war. All dreaded it. All sought to avoid it. While the Inaugural Address was being delivered from this place, devoted altogether to saving the Union without war, the insurgent agents were in the city seeking to destroy it without war — seeking to dissolve the Union, and divide the effects by negotiating. Both parties deprecated war, but one of them would make war rather than let it perish, and war came. One eighth of the population were colored slaves, not distributed generally over the Union, but located in the southern part. These slaves contributed a peculiar and powerful interest. All knew the interest would somehow cause war. To strengthen, perpetuate, and extend this interest was the object for which the insurgents would rend the Union by war, while the government claimed no right to do more than restrict the territorial enlargement of it. Neither party expected the magnitude or duration which it has already attained; neither anticipated that

189

the cause of the conflict might cease even before the conflict itself should cease. Each looked for an easier triumph and a result less fundamental and astonishing. Both read the same Bible and pray to the same God. Each invokes His aid against the other. It may seem strange that any man should dare to ask a just God's assistance in wringing bread from the sweat of other men's faces; but let us judge not, that we be not judged. The prayer of both should not be answered; that of neither has been answered fully, for the Almighty has His own purposes. "Woe unto the world because of offenses, for it must needs be that offense come; but woe unto that man by whom the offense cometh." If we shall suppose American slavery one of those offenses which, in the providence of God, must needs come, but which, having continued through His appointed time, He now wills to remove, and that He gives to both North and South this terrible war, as was due to those by whom the offense came, shall we discern that there is any departure from those divine attributes which believers in the living God always ascribe to Him? Fondly do we hope, fervently do we pray, that this mighty scourge of war may speedily pass away; yet if it be God's will that it continue until the wealth piled by bondsmen by two hundred and fifty years' unrequited toil shall be sunk, and until every drop of blood drawn with the lash shall be paid by another drawn with the sword, as was said three thousand years ago, so still it must be said that the judgments of the Lord are true and righteous altogether.

With malice toward none, with charity for all, with firmness in the right, as God gives us to see the right, let us strive on to finish the work we are in, to bind up the nation's wounds, to care for him who shall have borne the battle, and for his widow and orphans; to do all which may achieve and cherish a just and lasting peace among ourselves and with all nations.

▶ When Lincoln spoke these words, more than a hundred years ago, the long and cruel war was drawing near an end. It had started just after the First Inaugural. What was "the occasion corresponding to this"? How long before had that been?

▶ What is a **civil war**? What does **impending** mean? Does he say that people wanted war four years before? What does he say? What does **insurgent** mean? What are insurgent **agents**? What were they trying to do to the Union? Look up **deprecate** in a dictionary. One party was willing to make war rather than let **it** perish. What does **it** refer to? Which party wanted to preserve the Union?

▶ What proportion of the nation were slaves before the war? How were they distributed in the United States? The remark that they "contributed a peculiar and powerful interest" means that they were valuable property. What did everyone know that this interest would cause? What does Lincoln say the insurgents wanted to do? The phrase "restrict the territorial enlargement" means keep slaves from being taken into the new territories opening in the West.

▶ What did neither party expect? What do **magnitude** and **duration** mean? The cause of the conflict ceased before the conflict did because Lincoln freed the slaves. The Emancipation Proclamation in which he did this took effect in conquered territory in 1863.

▶ Did Lincoln think one of the parties more religious than the other? What did each ask of God? Why does Lincoln think that they should not judge — that is, say that the others are quite wrong?

▶ In reading the rest of the paragraph, use a dictionary to make sure that you know the meaning of the following words: **providence, appointed, discern, attribute, ascribe, scourge, bondsmen, unrequited, lash.**

▶ With what three things, in the famous last lines, does he propose to finish the work? What does he want to bind up? Whom does he want to care for? What does he want to be achieved and cherished?

▶ It often helps, in understanding long and complex sentences like those in Lincoln's Second Inaugural, to sort out the ideas and express them in shorter, less complex sentences. The following groups of shorter sentences express the ideas that single, longer sentences express in the selection on pages 189–190. Study each group of sentences below. Then turn back to pages 189–190 and find the related sentences.

1. The insurgent agents were in the city. The agents were seeking to destroy the city without war. They were seeking to destroy the Union. They were seeking to divide the effects (what was left). They were seeking to do this by negotiation. This was while the Inaugural Address was being delivered from this place. The Inaugural Address was devoted altogether to saving the Union without war.

2. The insurgents would rend the Union by war for an object. The object was to strengthen, perpetuate, and extend this interest (slavery). The government claimed the right to restrict the territorial enlargement of it (to keep slavery out of places that did not already allow it). The government did not claim the right to do more than this.

3. Woe (will come) unto the world because of offenses. It must needs be (it is inevitable) that offense come. Woe unto that man by whom the offense cometh.

4. We shall suppose American slavery (to be) one of those offenses. Those offenses must needs come. This is required by the providence of God. This offense has continued through His appointed time. He now wills to remove this offense. He gives this terrible war to both North and South. This was due to those by whom (through whose acts) the offense came. Shall we discern (detect) that there is any departure from those divine attributes (qualities)? Believers in the living God always ascribe (consider as belonging) those divine attributes to Him.

5. The prayers of both (parties) should not be answered. The prayers of neither (party) has been answered fully. (For the reason that) the Almighty has His own purposes.

You have studied words with the morpheme <u>ent</u>, spelled **ent.** Some of these were made from English verbs, but most of them were made from Latin verbs and we have simply adapted the adjective from Latin. Here are some familiar adjectives with <u>ent</u>:

        decent   excellent   current   confident   efficient

► Although most of the **ent** words in English are adjectives, not all are. A number of them were adjectives in Latin, but are used as nouns in English. Here are some examples. Use each in a sentence as a noun.

        student   talent   agent   rodent   client

Just as the morpheme <u>able</u> appears in many words in the form **ible,** so <u>ent</u> appears in many in the form **ant.** Indeed the problem of whether to spell a word with **ent** or with **ant** is even more puzzling than the **able/ible** problem. For though there are only about a third as many **ible** words as **able** words, there are very nearly as many **ant** words as **ent** ones.

However, as always, there are a few points we can note before turning to memory or the dictionary.

► Words that have the sound / k / with the spelling **c,** before the morpheme <u>ent</u> are all spelled **ant** at the end. Can you figure out a reason why? How would we pronounce **vacant** according to the regular / k / rule if the word were spelled **vacent?** Two other words with this sound and spelling are **applicant** and **significant.**

► You may remember that the letter **g** before the vowel letters **i** or **e** may represent either the / g / sound, as in **get** and **give,** or the / j / sound as in **gem** and **giant.** But in American English, the letter **g** has the sound / g / when the next letter is **a.** Can you see a reason why words that have the sound / g / before the morpheme <u>ent</u>, like **elegant** and **extravagant,** are spelled **ant?**

► Can you see a reason why <u>ent</u> is usually spelled **ent** after the sound / j /?

► Can you see why there is an **e** after the **g** in **pageant** and **sergeant?** How might we try to pronounce these words if they were spelled **pagant** and **sergant?**

In a number of words we have the ending **ient** in place of **ent.** In some of these, the **i** makes a preceding **c** stand for the sound / sh / instead of / s /. Say each of the following words, listen to the sound / sh /, and use the word as an adjective in a sentence:

sufficient   efficient   ancient

▶ What sound do the letters **ti** stand for in **patient** and **quotient?** This is the usual pronunciation for **ti** in such words. Does the / sh / sound come in the same syllable as the **ent?** Check by using a dictionary.

▶ In some words with **ient,** the letter **i** stands for the consonant sound / y /. Does the / y / come in the same syllable as the / ent /? Check by looking up **convenient** and **resilient** in a dictionary.

▶ In some words, such as **obedient** and **lenient,** the **i** stands for the vowel sound / ē /. Does the / ē / fall in the same syllable as the / ent /?

▶ Whether we spell a word **ent** or **ant** usually depends on what Latin word the English one comes from. For example, the Latin origin of **quotient** is **quotiens,** meaning how many times. But the Latin origin of **radiant** is the verb **radiare** meaning to emit rays, which has the forms **radians** and **radiantis.**

■ Study the Latin verbs and their forms given below. Then write the complete spelling of the English word that contains the morpheme <u>ent</u> and use it in one of the sentences with the letters **a** to **e.**

Latin Verb and Forms	Meaning of Verb	English Word
abundare (abundans, abundantis)	to overflow	abund–nt
fervere (fervens, ferventis)	to boil	ferv–nt
rodere (rodens, rodentis)	to gnaw	rod–nt
fragrare (fragraus, fragrantis)	to smell sweet	fragr–nt
distare (distans, distantis)	to stand apart	dist–nt

    a. A _____ is a creature with teeth suited for gnawing.
    b. When acorns are _____, the squirrels grow fat.
    c. Far away we saw the flash of _____ lightning.
    d. The garden was _____ with the scent of roses.
    e. The speaker made a _____, emotional plea for his cause.

1. You know that we can convert a sentence into an expanded noun phrase by using one of the relative pronouns:

    a. The man stole the money. → the man who stole the money

    b. The police caught the man. → the man whom the police caught

    c. The police returned the money. → the money that the police returned

▶ What relative pronoun is used to expand a human noun phrase in Sentence **a?** What other relative pronoun could have been used?

▶ Did the noun phrase that is modified by a relative clause in **b** function as subject or as object in Sentence **b?** Is this noun phrase human or nonhuman? What relative pronoun is used? What other relative pronoun could have been used?

▶ Is the noun phrase that is modified by a relative clause in **c** human or nonhuman? What relative pronoun is used? What other relative pronoun could have been used?

2. In the relative clause transformation, one sentence is converted into an expanded noun phrase, and the expanded noun phrase is used to replace a noun phrase in another sentence.

    a. The man stole the money. → NP + stole the money. $\Big\} \to$

    b. The police caught the man.

    c. The man whom the police caught stole the money.

We could, in this case, make an expanded noun phrase of either sentence and insert it in the other. However, an order must be agreed upon, and in the exercises of this book we expect the **b** sentence to be inserted into the **a** sentence in the form of an expanded noun phrase. To change the **c** sentence above, we would arrange the **a** and **b** sentences in this order:

    a. The police caught the man. → The police caught + $\Big\} \to$ NP.

    b. The man stole the money.

▶ What would the **c** sentence be now?

▶ Tell what can be deleted from the following sentences:

    3. A policeman who was on duty arrested a burglar.

    4. The man whom the police caught stole the money.

    5. The money that the man stole belonged to Don.

▶ 1. You have seen that we can make any statement into a noun clause by putting the word **that** in front of it:

Clarissa spoiled the party by losing her temper. →

that Clarissa spoiled the party by losing her temper

The word **that,** when it is used in this way to make a noun clause, is not a relative pronoun. It belongs to a small word class called **subordinators.** What kind of clause do we call a noun clause that begins with a subordinator like **that?**

▶ 2. What is left when you remove the subordinator from a noun clause like **that Clarissa spoiled the party by losing her temper?**

▶ 3. The fact that we have a sentence left when we remove the subordinator from a subordinate clause is a test for subordinate clauses. Is the following clause a subordinate clause by this test?

that Bill chose the smaller package

▶ 4. Is the clause in the following sentence a subordinate clause or a relative clause?   Use the test for subordinate clauses.

The package that Bill chose was the smaller one.

Then is the word **that** in the sentence above a subordinator or a relative pronoun?

In the relative clause transformation, we replace an NP in the **a** sentence with an expanded noun phrase that contains a relative clause:

a. The package was the smaller one. → NP + was the smaller one

b. Bill chose the package. → The package that Bill chose

$\left.\begin{array}{l}\\ \\ \end{array}\right\}$ →

▶ 5. The transformation that is shown below is similar to the relative clause transformation in many ways. But we use the symbol "S" for Sentence in this transformation because the subordinate clause we use to replace the S is a sentence with a subordinator before it, rather than an expanded noun phrase:

a. Mr. Woods regretted + S.

b. He was away last week. → that he was away last week

$\left.\begin{array}{l}\\ \\ \end{array}\right\}$ →

c. Mr. Woods regretted that he was away last week.

What replaces the S in Sentence **a** to make Sentence **c?**

► 6. This transformation is called the **subordinate clause transformation.** Here is another example of it:

a. S + made very little difference.
b. They were late. → that they were late
c. That they were late made very little difference.

What noun clause was made by putting **that** in front of Sentence **b?** What takes the place of S in Sentence **a?** What is the more complex sentence that results from replacing S with the noun clause? What is the function of the subordinate noun clause in Sentence **c?**

■ Apply the subordinate clause transformation to the following pairs of sentences. Make a subordinate clause by putting **that** in front of the **b** sentence. Then use the subordinate clause to replace the symbol **S** in the **a** sentence and write the **c** sentence.

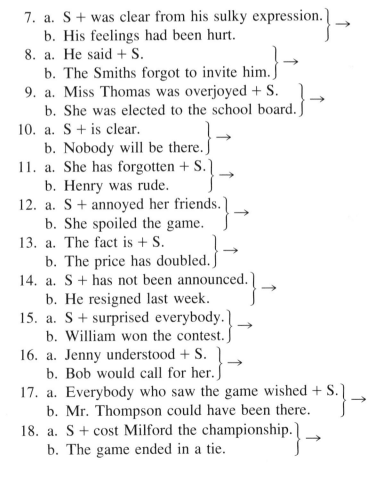

7. a. S + was clear from his sulky expression.⎱→
   b. His feelings had been hurt.

8. a. He said + S.⎱→
   b. The Smiths forgot to invite him.

9. a. Miss Thomas was overjoyed + S.⎱→
   b. She was elected to the school board.

10. a. S + is clear.⎱→
    b. Nobody will be there.

11. a. She has forgotten + S.⎱→
    b. Henry was rude.

12. a. S + annoyed her friends.⎱→
    b. She spoiled the game.

13. a. The fact is + S.⎱→
    b. The price has doubled.

14. a. S + has not been announced.⎱→
    b. He resigned last week.

15. a. S + surprised everybody.⎱→
    b. William won the contest.

16. a. Jenny understood + S.⎱→
    b. Bob would call for her.

17. a. Everybody who saw the game wished + S.⎱→
    b. Mr. Thompson could have been there.

18. a. S + cost Milford the championship.⎱→
    b. The game ended in a tie.

197

Read this poem by Rosemary and Stephen Vincent Benét.

Wilbur Wright and Orville Wright

Said Orville Wright to Wilbur Wright,
"These birds are very trying.
I'm sick of hearing them cheep-cheep
About the fun of flying.
A bird has feathers, it is true,
That much I freely grant.
But, must that stop us, W?"
Said Wilbur Wright, "It shan't."

And so they built a glider first,
And then they built another.
— There never were two brothers more
Devoted to each other.
They ran a dusty little shop
For bicycle repairing.
And bought each other soda pop
And praised each other's daring.

They glided here, they glided there,
They sometimes skinned their noses,
— For learning how to rule the air
Was not a bed of roses —
But each would murmur afterward,
While patching up his bro,
"Are we discouraged, W?"
"Of course we are not, O!"

And finally at Kitty Hawk
In Nineteen-Three (let's cheer it!),
The first real airplane really flew
With Orville there to steer it!
— And kingdoms may forget their kings
And dogs forget their bites,
But, not till Man forgets his wings,
Will men forget the Wrights.

199

► Sometimes we use the word **trying** in the sense of annoying or disturbing. What did Orville Wright say were very trying? Why were they?

► What has the fact that a bird has feathers to do with what he is talking about?

► Did these poets find a rhyme for **W?**

► We said that **shan't** is a rather rare contraction, but it is sometimes used, as in the first stanza of this poem. What is it a contraction of?

► How many morphemes are there in the word **glider?** What does the word mean? What kind of shop did the Wright brothers run?

► We sometimes say of something difficult or unpleasant that it is **no bed of roses.** What did the Wright brothers find was no bed of roses? In the third stanza, the poets playfully use the abbreviation **bro.** What is it an abbreviation of? How should it be pronounced here? Why?

► Orville Wright flew the first heavier-than-air machine at Kitty Hawk, North Carolina, in December, 1903. This is when the age of the airplane began. What is meant by **wings** in the second line from the end?

► Does the word **Man,** in the last stanza, mean just a man — not a woman, a boy, or a girl? What does it mean?

■ Writing a Report

Prepare a report on the development of aviation. You may do it in two or three stages, according to the decision you and your teacher make on how far to carry the assignment.

The first stage is to study the first part of such a report, which is given on page 201. This part of the report is a summary of early developments in man's attempts to fly. Read it carefully and notice the way in which several ideas are given in a single sentence.

The second stage is to organize and write in your own words the facts which are given on page 202 about the first successful fliers — the Wright brothers.

The final and optional stage is to carry out your own investigation and report on the development of air travel and airplanes from the Wright brothers to Lindbergh's solo flight across the Atlantic to Paris in 1927. Some of you may want to include the Apollo moon flights, but then you will have to include rockets.

The Airplane From Daedalus to the Wright Brothers

The ancient story of Daedalus and Icarus, who flew with wings of feathers and wax, is a myth, but it reflects an ambition that may be as ancient as the human race. Aesop, that wisest of all slaves, tells of a tortoise four thousand years ago who wanted to fly and fell to his death, thus demonstrating the folly of creatures who try to do what they're not equipped for. But equipped or not, men have never heeded Aesop's moral. Throughout recorded history, they have tried to fly.

Men tried it and failed in the 11th and 12th centuries. Roger Bacon, that resourceful Englishman of the 13th century, suggested a plan for an airplane with wings that a flier could flap to propel himself, birdlike, through the air. The famous Italian painter, sculptor, inventor, and engineer, Leonardo da Vinci, drew up some pretty convincing plans for an ornithopter — an aircraft driven by wings like Bacon's. But there is no record that anyone flew anything successfully until the first balloon carried a man aloft about the time our Revolutionary War ended.

In the nineteenth century there was a great deal of progress in heavier-than-air flight, especially in Europe. French experimenters studied the principles of flight and actually flew power-driven aircraft, which were not, however, capable of carrying a pilot. Experiments with gliders, too, were successful, and in the 1890's a German named Otto Lilienthal made glider flights up to 1000 feet. Man at last was about to realize one of his oldest dreams — flight through the air.

■ In the three paragraphs of the report on page 201, find and copy a single sentence that says about what the following group of sentences says:

Roger Bacon suggested a plan for an airplane. Roger Bacon was an Englishman. He was resourceful. He lived in the 13th century. The airplane had wings. A flier could flap the wings. This would propel him through the air like a bird.

■ Now rewrite the statements about the Wright brothers that are given below. You may wish to reorganize the facts, leave some out, put some additional facts in, and write this part of the report in more than one paragraph.

The Wright Brothers

The Wright brothers ran a bicycle factory. It was in Dayton, Ohio. They also repaired bicycles. They were mechanics. They were skillful. They read about Otto Lilienthal. They studied his books. They made gliders. They flew the gliders often in 1900. They tested the gliders at Kitty Hawk, North Carolina. They invented skids for gliders. The gliders landed on these skids. These skids are still used on gliders today. They decided something. They would put an engine on their glider. Orville Wright designed the engine. Orville made the first flight on December 17, 1903. The flight was successful. The flight lasted 12 seconds. Wilbur Wright flew for 59 seconds on the same day. His flight covered 852 feet. The airplane was a success.

■ Now, if you and your teacher agree that you should do so, try writing the rest of this report yourself. Get the facts on the development of the airplane and air travel from 1903 to 1927 by consulting encyclopedias, books on aviation, biographies of aviation figures from the Wrights to Lindbergh, or any sources you can find. Make notes of the facts you discover. Then organize your notes around topics for paragraphs and write this stage of the report in your own words.

You remember that a morpheme that makes abstract nouns from adjectives has the spelling **ity:**

<u>severe</u> + <u>ity</u> → **severity**   <u>moral</u> + <u>ity</u> → **morality**

There is a similar morpheme that makes abstract nouns from adjectives and nouns that end in **ent** or **ant.** We will call this morpheme <u>ence</u>, just as we called the morpheme that makes adjectives from verbs the morpheme <u>ent</u>. When the adjective or noun ends in **ent** we spell the morpheme <u>ence</u> with an **e: ence.** But when we add <u>ence</u> to an **ant** word, we spell the morpheme **ance:**

<u>excellent</u> + <u>ence</u> → **excellence**   <u>assistant</u> + <u>ance</u> → **assistance**

■ Write abstract nouns by adding the morpheme <u>ence</u> to the following **ent** and **ant** words. Remember that the way you spell the morpheme <u>ence</u> depends on how the morpheme <u>ent</u> is spelled in the word you add <u>ence</u> to.

innocent	obedient	present
silent	violent	evident
fragrant	distant	brilliant
radiant	defiant	abundant

If you know how to spell words ending in **ence** or **ance,** you can spell the corresponding words ending in **ent** or **ant.** Can you explain the rule?

■ Make **ent** words from the following:

impudence   intelligence   patience
convenience   residence

Make words that end in **ant** from the following:

importance   abundance   ignorance
elegance   tolerance

■ Study the Latin verbs and verb forms. Read the meanings. Complete the word that has the morpheme <u>ent</u> on the right, spelling it with **e** or **a.** Then write the abstract noun with **ence.**

Latin Verb and Forms	Meaning	English Word
haesitare (haesitans, haesitantis)	to stick	hesit–nt
differre (differens, differentis)	apart + to carry	differ–nt

203

In the following sentences, find the clauses which begin with the word **that.** In each sentence, tell whether this clause is a subordinate clause or a relative clause. What test can you use for this?

1. We were surprised that a man was selling peanuts.
2. The man that was selling peanuts has disappeared.
3. That he is your uncle was news to me.
4. The rumor is that he is your uncle.
5. We bought some peanuts that the man sold.
6. The news that we heard cheered us up.

► Apply the subordinate clause to the following. Tell what the function of the subordinate clause is in each **c** sentence.

7. a. Mr. Walter said + S.
   b. He has accepted a new position.
8. a. The ladies' excuse was + S.
   b. The men were ready to go home.
9. a. S + is certain.
   b. We will enter the contest.

The **c** sentence for 9 above is this:

That we will enter the contest is certain.

This is a perfectly good sentence, except that we usually say it another way. We start the sentence with **it,** put the verb phrase **is certain** next, and end the sentence with the subordinate clause:

It is certain that we will enter the contest.

Here is another example. The subordinate clause transformation is applied first. Then the **it** transformation is applied to the **c** sentence:

a. S + was a shame.
b. Walter lost the race. } → (by **subordinate clause transformation**)

c. That Walter lost the race was a shame. (by **it transformation**) → It was a shame that Walter lost the race.

► When the **it** transformation was applied to Sentence **c,** where did the **it** come? What structure in the **c** sentence followed the **it?** What structure comes last?

► Which sentence sounds more natural to you: "That Walter lost the race was a shame" or "It was a shame that Walter lost the race"?

204

■ Apply the **it transformation** to the following **c** sentences, and write the sentences that result.

10. That dogs dug up our garden made us angry.

11. That we will be there goes without saying.

12. That Janet refused the prize seemed odd.

13. That dinner was late was my fault.

14. That Ann forgot her lines must have surprised the audience.

■ Apply the subordinate clause transformation to each of the following. First write the **c** sentence. Then apply the **it transformation** to the **c** sentence and write the sentence that results.

15. a. S + pleased Roberta.
    b. Maude took her picture.

16. a. S + irritated Mr. Whiteside.
    b. His wife criticized his manners.

17. a. S + never entered her head.
    b. She had failed.

18. a. S + is unfortunate.
    b. He forgot the address.

19. a. S + surprised the coach.
    b. We won.

20. a. S + bothered my teacher.
    b. I misspelled the word grammar.

21. a. S + made Tom happy.
    b. We praised his report.

22. a. S + is a wonder.
    b. We found our way.

23. a. S + disappointed his father.
    b. Walter failed the test.

24. a. S + disturbed the audience.
    b. The lights kept going out.

25. a. S + made everybody uneasy.
    b. The river kept rising.

26. a. S + was hard luck.
    b. He broke his arm.

27. a. S + was a coincidence.
    b. We both arrived at the same time.

28. a. S + seemed strange.
    b. Roberta refused the invitation.

Two Kinds of Noun Clauses with <u>That</u>

▶ Study the following sentences that contain subordinate noun clauses.   Tell what the noun clauses are.

1. It is sad that Alice missed the party.
2. That Bill made the team surprised his father.
3. That the Browns had bought a yacht was the chief topic of conversation at the party.
4. The judge was aware that this was the prisoner's first offense.

▶ In Sentence 1, is it assumed as a fact that Alice did miss the party?   In Sentence 2, did Bill really make the team?   In Sentence 3, is it considered a fact that the Browns had bought a yacht?   In Sentence 4, does the noun clause state a fact?

All of the subordinate noun clauses you have worked with so far are assumed to give actual facts.   But the **a** sentences were of two kinds.

▶ Study the following **a** sentences for 1–2 above:

1. It is sad + S.
2. S + surprised his father.

In these two cases, does the **a** sentence express some feeling or emotion about the facts stated by the subordinate noun clauses? What feelings?

▶ Now study the following **a** sentences for 3–4 above:

3. S + was the chief topic of conversation at the party.
4. The judge was aware + S.

In these two cases, does the **a** sentence express some feeling toward the fact stated by the subordinate clause?   If not, does the **a** sentence give a judgment or conclusion about the fact?

▶ Tell whether the **a** sentence in each of the following is like 1 and 2, or like 3 and 4.

5. The banker bore in mind that Jack's credit was excellent.
6. It was regrettable that you lost your opportunity.
7. That Janet has a part in the play is fascinating.
8. John has forgotten that he borrowed your book.
9. The speaker made clear that he supports the President.
10. That we have no fire escape is alarming.

▶ All of the subordinate clauses so far have been considered to be true, whether the rest of the transform expressed fact or feeling. But not all noun clauses with **that** give actual facts. Often, they suggest what might happen, but hasn't. Study the following transforms and find the noun clauses:

11. It is possible that Harry arrived last night.
12. That Bill bought a new car is unlikely.
13. I am afraid that the gamble will lose.
14. We regret that Sally might move to Chicago.

▶ In Sentence 11, is it assumed that Harry actually did arrive last night? In 12, is it assumed to be true that Bill bought a new car? In 13, is it assumed that the gamble actually has lost? In 14, has Sally actually moved to Chicago?

▶ Which two sentences in 11–14 express feelings or emotions about the possibilities suggested by the noun clauses?

■ Apply the subordinate clause transformation to the following and write the **c** sentence. Write **yes** or **no** after each transform to tell whether the subordinate noun clause does or does not give an actual fact.

15. a. The factory foresees + S
    b. Next year could be very prosperous.
16. a. S + seems tragic.
    b. The victim of the accident may be crippled.
17. a. S + was clear to his lawyer.
    b. Mr. Mellon was telling the truth.
18. a. S + is nonsense.
    b. Jack stole the money.
19. a. The actors took into account + S
    b. The theater was poorly lighted.
20. a. Mr. Williamson regrets + S
    b. His intentions were misunderstood.
21. a. S + is probable.
    b. Helen took the morning train.
22. a. The musicians fear + S
    b. Their instruments are lost.
23. a. Alice reported + S
    b. The fire had damaged her room.
24. a. S + is not impossible.
    b. The clerk had lost the money.
25. a. Mr. Oates suspects + S
    b. The business is losing money.

1. Make adjectives of the following verbs by adding to each one the morpheme ent. If you make mistakes, study pages 182–83.

reside   confide   provide

2. Write the headings **Noun** and **Adjective** on your paper. Write each of the following words under the proper heading on your paper, according to whether it is generally used as a noun or as an adjective. If you make mistakes, study pages 182–83, 193–94.

prudent	talent	agent	decent
student	silent	recent	rodent

3. Complete the words in each of the following sets, using **a** or **e** to complete it. If you make mistakes, study pages 182–83, 193–94.

Set a: vac_nt   eleg_nt   page_nt   serge_nt
Set b: confid_nt   provid_nt   resid_nt   urg_nt
Set c: fragr_nt   abund_nt   applic_nt   radi_nt
Set d: ferv_nt   rec_nt   effici_nt   pati_nt

4. Make abstract nouns by adding the morpheme ence to the following. If you make mistakes, study page 203.

present	different	obedient
radiant	distant	brilliant

5. Copy the clause which begins with **that** in each of the following sentences. After each clause write **subordinate** or **relative** to tell what kind of clause it is. If you make mistakes, study pages 186–87, 195.

  a. Our problem was that the bell rang too soon.
  b. Our problem was the mistake that caused the bell to ring.
  c. The mistake that caused the bell to ring cost us the game.
  d. That the bell rang too soon was Harry's mistake.
  e. We claimed that the bell rang too soon.
  f. Our hope was that the bus would be on time.
  g. The bus that was on time was not ours.
  h. The play that we saw was exciting.
  i. That we saw the play was an adventure.
  j. The wheel that squeaked got the grease.

Apply the subordinate clause transformation to the following. If you make mistakes, study pages 196–97.

6. a. We hope + S.
   b. You will be able to go to the movies.
7. a. S + appeared obvious to everyone.
   b. The game was lost.
8. a. The difficulty that arose was + S.
   b. The bus began to lose power.
9. a. Mr. Whiteside said + S.
   b. The drive for funds had fallen short of its goal.
10. a. The story is + S.
    b. The principal is in the hospital.
11. a. The driver acknowledged + S.
    b. He was in the wrong.

Apply the **it** transformation to the following **c** sentences. If you make mistakes, study pages 204–05.

12. That we can do it seems perfectly clear.
13. That they will elect Arthur was Harry's prediction.
14. That somebody missed the signal irritated the coach.
15. That Mollie can sew surprised her friends.
16. That Miss Kibbey is gentle was clear from her actions.

Apply the subordinate clause transformation to the following and write the **c** sentences. Then apply the **it** transformation to the **c** sentences and write the sentences that result. If you make mistakes, study pages 196–97, 204–05.

17. a. S + pleased the committee.
    b. Bob told the truth.
18. a. S + seemed impossible.
    b. Mabel had refused to help us.
19. a. S + angered the spectators.
    b. The referee penalized the home team.
20. a. S + discouraged me.
    b. You turned down my request.
21. a. S + hurt our case.
    b. We had avoided the question.
22. a. S + astonished the crowd.
    b. The quarterback did not see the open receiver.
23. a. S + offended Mr. Mendez.
    b. We did not ask his opinion.

A Famous Story

Several thousand years ago the poet Homer wrote two books, the *Iliad* and the *Odyssey*. The *Iliad* told the story of the Trojan war. The *Odyssey* is the story of Odysseus' long voyage home. The tale below of how the Greeks finally captured Troy is from the *Iliad*.

The Trojan Horse

Paris, the son of the King of Troy, carried off Helen, the wife of the Greek chieftain Menelaus. To regain his wife and take revenge, Menelaus raised a mighty army among the Greeks and sailed for Troy, which he besieged.

For ten years the Trojans and the Greeks fought on the windy plain before Troy without bringing the war to an end. The Trojans were unable to make the Greeks lift the siege, and the Greeks could not fight their way into the city.

Among the Greek chiefs, the cleverest man was Odysseus. When it became clear that Troy could not be taken by force of arms, Odysseus devised a stratagem to conquer the city by trickery. He engaged carpenters and instructed them to build an enormous wooden horse, a horse as tall as the walls of Troy themselves. He had them make the inside hollow, and the horse was so large that many men could be contained within it.

When the horse was completed, Odysseus and the bravest of the Greek warriors entered the horse and were concealed in it. The rest of the army broke camp. They gathered their tents and the rest of their equipment and boarded their ships. The ships set sail and disappeared from the sight of Troy, but they went only behind the nearest island, where they could not be seen by the watchers on the walls.

The next morning, the people of Troy awoke to find

211

the plain before them empty, for the first time in ten years, of the Greek army. In its place stood a huge wooden horse. They rushed from the walls into the plain, joyful at being free to leave the city.

In the place where the Greek camp had been, they found only one human being, a Greek, Sinon by name, who had been stationed there by Odysseus and carefully instructed in the tale he was to tell. He said that the Greeks had marked him as a human sacrifice to appease the wrath of the goddess Athena, whom they had displeased. But he, Sinon said, learning of this, had run away and hidden himself until the army had sailed away. He said that because they no longer had Athena's favor they knew they could never capture Troy, and had returned to their homes.

He told them that the horse was an offering to Athena. It had been made so large, he said, to discourage the Trojans from bringing it inside the walls. He said that the Greeks hoped that the Trojans would destroy it and thus bring the anger of Athena on themselves. For if they brought it into the town, her favor would shift from the Greeks to the Trojans.

While Sinon was talking, Odysseus and his men were huddled inside the horse, listening.

So it was that the horse was brought into the city. When night came, the Trojans went to their houses happy in the belief that the siege was lifted and that they had won the favor of the goddess Athena. But then at midnight, when all were asleep, Odysseus and the other warriors emerged from the horse. First they threw open the gates and admitted the rest of the Greek army. Then they set fire to the city.

The Trojans, awakened from sleep, and without their armor, fought valiantly, but they had been taken too completely by surprise. The fight raged all night, but by morning Troy was in ruins and most of the Trojans dead. Of all the Trojan leaders, only Aeneas escaped. He fled through the fire and found the kingdom of Rome.

▶ Who was Paris? Whom did he carry off?

▶ Find and read one sentence that expresses the following ideas:

Menelaus raised an army among the Greeks. The army was mighty. He did this to regain his wife. He did this to take revenge. He sailed for Troy. He besieged Troy.

▶ How long did the Greeks and Trojans fight before the walls of Troy? What is a **siege?** What does "lift the siege" mean? What were the Greeks unable to do?

▶ To **devise** means to **think up.** What is a **stratagem?**

▶ When the Greek ships sailed, where did they go? Which Greeks stayed behind? Where did they hide?

▶ What did the people of Troy see the morning after the Greeks sailed? Why were they joyful?

▶ Whom did they find in the Greek camp? Who had told him to stay there?

▶ Find the sentence that contains the following sentence in the form of a subordinate clause: "The Greeks had marked him as a human sacrifice." What does "marked as a human sacrifice" mean?

▶ What is meant by **wrath** and **appease?** Use a dictionary if you don't know.

▶ Find the sentence that contains the following sentences as subordinate clauses. One subordinate clause begins with the subordinator **that** and this clause contains the other subordinate clause which begins with the subordinator **because.**

"They knew they could never capture Troy."

"They no longer had Athena's favor."

▶ How did Sinon explain the great horse? What did he say would happen if the Trojans brought it inside the walls?

▶ What did the Trojans believe as they went to bed that night? When did Odysseus and the others emerge from the horse? What did they do first? Then what did they do?

▶ Why were the Trojans at a disadvantage? What had happened by morning?

▶ Who was the only Trojan leader to escape? What did he do afterward?

The story of "The Trojan Horse" really begins with a beauty contest between three goddesses. The story is told below in short, simple statements. Rewrite it, using longer, more interesting sentences. Make use of the transformations you have studied. You may also use ways of combining sentences that you have observed but have not actually studied yet. The superlative transformation (T-sup.) and the negative transformation (T-neg.) are specifically called for. Try to use the relative and subordinate clause transformations also.

The Golden Apple

A king invited all the gods and goddesses of Olympus to his wedding. The king was legendary. He invited the goddess of discord (T-neg.). She was troublesome. The goddess was angry. She was invited (T-neg.). She tossed an apple among the guests. The apple was golden. The apple was inscribed "To the most beautiful." Three of the goddesses claimed the apple. Hera claimed it. She was wife of Zeus. Athena claimed it. She was goddess of wisdom. Aphrodite claimed it. She was goddess of love. Three of the goddesses asked Zeus to judge a beauty contest among them. Zeus was king of the gods.

Zeus declined the honor. A man accepted the position. A man was young. A man was named Paris. Zeus had declined the position wisely. A man awarded the apple to Aphrodite. His decision made Aphrodite his friend. His decision made enemies of the other two goddesses.

Something is said often. "I can handle my enemies. Save me from my friends." Aphrodite was his friend. Aphrodite persuaded Paris. Paris ran away with Helen to Troy. Helen was wife of King Menelaus. Helen was beautiful (T-sup.). The women in the world are beautiful. The Greeks pursued Paris. The Greeks were under King Menelaus. The siege of Troy began.

About fifteen hundred English words have the ending **ate.** Most of these words are borrowed from the Latin.

■ 1. Study the Latin verbs and verb forms below, read what they mean, study the spelling of the English verb, and then use the English verbs in Sentences **a** to **f.** Some of the Latin verbs contain prefixes or are made up of two words.

Latin Verbs and Verb Forms	Meaning	English Verbs
excavare (excavatus)	*ex* out + *cavus* hollow	excavate
abbreviare (abbreviatus)	*ad* to + *breviare* shorten	abbreviate
operari (operatus)	to work	operate
punctuare (punctuatus)	*punctus* point	punctuate
nominare (nominatus)	to name	nominate
navigare (navigatus)	*navis* boat + *agere* to direct	navigate

a. When we name a person to run for office, we _____ him.
b. People who make machinery work _____ it.
c. We dig out the earth to _____ for a foundation.
d. Captains of ships _____ by compass.
e. When we shorten an expression, we _____ it.
f. We _____ writing when we use either a period or a question mark.

▶ What consonant sound in **punctuate** is spelled with the first letter **t** in the word?

▶ 2. Though most **ate** words are verbs, many are nouns or adjectives. Find the **ate** words in the sentences below, and tell of each whether it is a noun, a verb, or an adjective.
a. They appreciate it.
b. He is Mr. Abel's associate.
c. This clock is accurate.

▶ 3. Say these sentences aloud:
a. We will **separate** them.
b. Then they will be **separate.**
In which sentence is **separate** an adjective? The **ate** in the verb has middle stress. What stress does this syllable have in the adjective?

▶ 4. Use **duplicate** as an adjective, then as a verb. Does the stress shift in **duplicate** as it does in **separate?**

215

Softening Statements

We often want to soften a statement, either to avoid hurting someone's feelings or to show that we don't think we know all the answers. Here are two statements that we might want to soften:

a. You're wrong.

b. He misunderstood the question.

▶ 1. One way to modify such statements is to use modals. What is the tense of Sentence **a?** Does the verb phrase contain a verb or a form of **be?** One thing we could do is to insert the modal **may,** keeping the tense the same:

You may be wrong.

We could also change the tense. Try using **past** and the modal **may.** What sentence do you get? Try using **past** and the modal **can.** What is the sentence?

▶ 2. Does the verb phrase of Sentence **b** contain a verb or a form of **be?** What is the tense? One thing we could do to soften Statement **b** is to use a modal and <u>have</u> + <u>part.</u>, using the present tense:

He may have misunderstood the question.

Try using the past tense of **may** and <u>have</u> + <u>part.</u> Try using the past tense of **can** and <u>have</u> + <u>part.</u>

Another way to soften such statements is to use words like **maybe, perhaps, possibly:**

Maybe you're wrong.

Possibly he misunderstood the question.

▶ 3. Try **perhaps** and **possibly** with the "You're wrong" statement.

▶ 4. Try **maybe** and **perhaps** with the "He misunderstood the question" statement.

■ Rewrite each of the following statements, softening it in the ways suggested above that are appropriate.

5. You made a mistake.

6. She is being stubborn.

7. He didn't do his best.

8. His facts were not accurate.

9. You didn't speak clearly enough.

Commands

▶ 1. You have been working with two kinds, or types, of sentences: **statements** and **questions.** Which of these sentence types says that something is or is not so?

Another type of sentence is called a **command.** A command tells someone to do something or not to do something. The subject of a command is the pronoun **you,** but the subject is left out of a simple command:

(you)　Study the lesson.　　(you)　Act justly.

(you)　Be reasonable.　　　(you)　Watch what happens.

▶ 2. We use the base form of verbs in commands. What form of **be** do we use?

The commands above are affirmative, but like a statement and a question, a command may be negative. Study the following affirmative and negative commands:

Affirmative	**Negative**
Be silly.	Don't be silly.
Use that exit.	Do not use that exit.

▶ 3. What words or contraction do we use at the beginning of a negative command?

■ Write the numeral for each of the following sentences. After it, write **statement, question,** or **command** to tell what type of sentence it is. Then write **aff.** if the sentence is affirmative, **neg.** if it is negative.

4. Do not feed the animals.

5. Can't they finish the work?

6. You are walking on the flowers.

7. The police won't search the room.

8. Should he take the train?

9. Work harder.

10. Doesn't somebody have an eraser?

11. Steve mustn't leave before noon.

12. Did Jenny see Peter?

13. Don't open that drawer.

14. Close the door.

15. He was behind the screen.

16. Use the dictionary.

A Poem

What happened in the place called Lyonesse to put magic in the poet's eyes? Did he fall in love?

Lyonesse

When I set out for Lyonesse,
    A hundred miles away,
    The rime was on the spray,
And starlight lit my lonesomeness
When I set out for Lyonesse
    A hundred miles away.

What would bechance at Lyonesse
    While I should sojourn there
    No prophet durst declare,
Nor did the wisest wizard guess
What would bechance at Lyonesse
    While I should sojourn there.

When I came back from Lyonesse
    With magic in my eyes,
    All marked with mute surmise
My radiance rare and fathomless,
When I came back from Lyonesse
    With magic in my eyes.

THOMAS HARDY

Lyonesse

▶ Lyonesse is not the real name of a town. It is a kind of magic name of a place where magical things might happen. What does **set out** mean?

▶ The word **rime** is not just another spelling for **rhyme.** Here it is a different word. Look up **rime** in a dictionary and see what it means. Does this help you understand the meaning of **spray?** Guess what **spray** means here. Check your guess by using a dictionary.

219

► At what time of day did the poet set out for Lyonesse? How can you tell? What abstract noun in the first stanza tells you how he was feeling?

► Can you tell from the way it is used what **bechance** means? What is another verb that means about the same thing as **bechance?**

► What does **sojourn** mean? Use a dictionary.

► What is a **prophet? Durst** is an old modal, the past tense form of **dare.** How would we now say **durst declare?**

► What is a **wizard?** What was the wisest wizard unable to do?

► **All** means everybody — the people in his home town. To **mark** means to notice or pay attention to, and **surmise** means guess. What is a **mute surmise?**

► What did all the people mark with mute surmise? What does the abstract noun **radiance** mean? Guess. Then check your guess in a dictionary. What adjective ending in **ant** could you make from it?

Fathomless means too deep to be measured or understood.

► The poem treats the journey to Lyonesse as though it was a real journey. Is it possible, do you think, that Lyonesse could be an experience and not a journey at all?

Stress and Sound

► 1. Study the stresses in the first three lines of "Lyonesse" as they are shown below:

> When Í set oút for Lýonésse,
> A húndred míles awáy,
> The ríme was ón the spráy,

How many syllables are there in each foot? How many feet does the first line have? How many do the second and third lines have?

■ 2. Copy the last three lines of the first stanza and use stress marks in the same way to show the stressed syllables.

► 3. How many feet does the fourth line have? The fifth? How many does the last line of the first stanza have?

► 4. In stanzas two and three does the number of feet per line also go this way: 4, 3, 3, 4, 4, 3?

220

► 5. You remember that we can show the rhyme scheme of a stanza by using letters. Here are the rhyming words of Stanza 1 of "Lyonesse" with letters to show the rhyming pattern:

Lyonesse	a
away	b
spray	b
lonesomeness	a
Lyonesse	a
away	b

Which "a" rhyming word occurs twice in the first stanza? Which "b" rhyming word is repeated?

■ 6. Make a similar listing of rhyming words with letters to show the rhyme scheme for the second and third stanzas.

► 7. Poets make use of pleasing repetitions of sounds in many ways in poems. Rhyme is only one of these ways. Say the following line from "Lyonesse" and listen for repeated sounds:

And starlight lit my lonesomeness

What consonant sound in **starlight** is repeated twice at the beginning of words in the same line?

► 8. The repetition of sounds, as the /l/ sound in "starlight lit my lonesomeness," is called **alliteration.** What example of alliteration can you find in the following line: "Nor did the wisest wizard"? What consonant sound within **wisest** is repeated in **wizard?**

► 9. Find another example of alliteration in the poem.

Organizing a Story in Three Parts

Look again at the poem "Lyonesse" on page 219 and note its structure. In the first stanza, the poet tells how he felt when he set out for Lyonesse; in the second, he tells of something important that happened there; in the third, he tells how it was when he came back.

■ Write a story with a similar structure, in three paragraphs. In the second, tell of something important that happened to you, or to a character you make up. In the first, tell how things were before, and in the third tell how they were afterward.

Now that you know about verbs that end in **ate,** you can notice something that will help you to spell certain words **ant** rather than **ent.** A number of the **ate** verbs form nouns or adjectives in this fashion:

> radiate → radiant   emigrate → emigrant

▶ What letters take the place of the **te** of the verb?

■ Make a noun or adjective of the verb printed in heavy black type before each sentence below.   Copy the sentence and use the noun or adjective to complete it.   Write **n.** or **adj.** after the sentence to tell whether you made a noun or an adjective. Some **ant** words can be used both as nouns and as adjectives.

1. **migrate**   A _____ worker is one who travels from job to job.

2. **migrate**   The man who asked for work is a _____.

3. **hesitate**   Jane spoke in a shy, _____ way.

4. **participate** Each _____ in the conference will wear a badge.

5. **tolerate**   My father is a kindly, _____ man.

6. **immigrate**   The greatest _____ years were in the nineteenth century.

7. **immigrate**   Now an _____ must be able to support himself.

8. **stimulate**   Coffee is a _____ that keeps some people from sleeping.

You are familiar with a morpheme that makes abstract nouns and is spelled **ity:** moral + ity → **morality.**

Another morpheme that makes abstract nouns is often spelled **ion.** This morpheme is added mostly to verbs, although it is also added to words of other classes.   There are over two thousand English words that contain this morpheme, which we will call the morpheme ion.

This ending has the same effect on the stress of verbs to which it is added that **ity** does.   Pronounce the following:

> educate → education   prosecute → prosecution

▶ Which syllable has first stress in **educate?**   Which in **education?**   Which in **prosecution?**

▶ You remember that adding **ity** puts the first stress on the first syllable before the ending.   Is this also true of **ion?**

222

About half of the <u>ion</u> words are made from verbs that end in **ate.** In fact, nearly all of the **ate** verbs can become **ation** nouns. Naturally, we drop the **e** of **ate** in adding <u>ion</u>:

<u>migrate</u> + <u>ion</u> → migration   <u>hesitate</u> + <u>ion</u> → hesitation

▶ In the **ation** words above, what sound do the letters **ti** stand for? What vowel sound does the last syllable have?

■ Make an abstract noun of the verb printed in heavy black type before each sentence below by adding the morpheme <u>ion</u>, spelled **ion.** Copy the sentence and use the abstract noun.

9. **liberate**   Lincoln proclaimed the _____ of slaves.
10. **operate**   The _____ of a helicopter is difficult.
11. **elevate**   A high _____ may cause dizziness.
12. **calculate**   Much _____ is done by computer.

The morpheme <u>ion</u> is spelled **ation** when it is added to a number of verbs which do not end in **ate:**

<u>vary</u> + <u>ion</u> → **variation**   <u>provoke</u> + <u>ion</u> → **provocation**

▶ What change was made in **vary** when **ation** was added? What letter was dropped and what letter changed in forming **provocation?** Why was the **k** changed to **c** in this word?

■ Make abstract nouns of the verbs in heavy black below by adding <u>ion</u> spelled **ation.** Use the abstract nouns in the sentences. Use a dictionary when you need help in spelling.

13. **recommend**   A _____ is often requested in application forms.
14. **imagine**   Ghosts exist in the _____ of some people.
15. **condemn**   The President's _____ of the action had an effect.
16. **resign**   Tom's _____ was announced.
17. **recite**   Jenny's _____ of "Lyonesse" was excellent.
18. **examine**   _____ revealed a flaw in the engine.
19. **starve**   War causes the _____ of innocent people.
20. **confirm**   The seller wants a _____ of the order.

▶ How might the pronunciation of **resignation** and **condemnation** help you remember how to spell **resign** and **condemn?**

▶ Tell what verbs underlie these abstract nouns:

explanation   occupation   application

What changes in sound or spelling have been made in each?

■ Add the morpheme <u>ion</u>, spelled **ation,** to the verb **multiply** and use the abstract noun that results in a sentence.

1. A command is more likely to give offense than any other type of sentence. No one likes to take orders. To avoid offending people, we often add the word **please** to a command without changing it in any other way:

a. Be careful.   Please be careful.

b. Don't tease the cat.   Please don't tease the cat.

The word **please,** with a comma before it, is often used at the end of a command, as well as at the beginning. Rewrite the commands above, putting **please** at the end.

► 2. Since a command may sometimes seem too abrupt, we often express our wishes in the form of a suggestion instead of a command. Compare the commands below with the suggestions:

Commands	Suggestions
a. Leave.	You may leave.
b. Stop.	You should stop.
c. Wash the dishes.	You might wash the dishes.
d. Work harder.	You ought to work harder.

What word that appears in every one of these suggestions is not used in any of the commands? What other words are used in the suggestions, but not in the commands?

■ Rewrite the suggestions above, using **can** and **could.**

► 3. Study the following:

You must leave.   You have to leave.

Are these sentences stronger or weaker than "You may leave"?

■ When we want to make a suggestion that has about as much force as a command, we use the modal **must** or the expression **have to.** Rewrite suggestions **b, c,** and **d** above, using **must** and **have to.**

■ 4. The following sentences are commands. Put each command in the form of a suggestion. Write each suggestion in as many of the ways suggested above as you think are appropriate.

a. Shut the door.   b. Be ready at six.

c. Open your books.

5. We can express negative commands in the form of suggestions, too. Instead of "Don't leave," we can say "You shouldn't leave," or "You mustn't leave."

224

■ Write each of the following negative commands in the form of a suggestion. Use as many modals and modal-like expressions as you think are appropriate.

a. Don't look out the window.

b. Do not stare.

c. Don't mimic your brother.

▶ 6. Another way to avoid the abruptness of a command and still make our wishes known is to make a **request.** A request is expressed as a question:

Commands	Requests
a. Please be still.	Will you please be still?
b. Give me that knife.	Would you give me that knife?
c. Pass the butter.	Could you pass the butter?
d. Give me some help.	Can you give me some help?

What word that appears in every one of these requests is not used in any of the commands? What other words are used in the requests, but not in the commands?

■ 7. Write each of the following commands in the form of a request. Express each request in as many different ways as you think are appropriate, using modals.

a. Get out.

b. Pay attention.

c. Be a good sport.

d. Take the dog for a walk, please.

8. Another way to express the idea of a command is to use a negative request.

Command: Speak more distinctly, please.

Negative Request: Won't you please speak more distinctly?

■ Write each of the following commands in the form of a negative request, using contractions of modals and **not.** Express each negative in as many ways as you think appropriate.

a. Stop wriggling, please.

b. Stay awhile.

c. Work harder.

9. We can't express negative commands as negative requests without the danger of confusion. "Don't mumble" can't be expressed as "Won't you mumble?" What does "Won't you mumble?" mean? Could "Will you not mumble?" have two meanings?

As you know, conversation is **direct discourse** — the exact words spoken by one or more persons:

> Ralph was feeding his dog a chicken carcass as Bill looked on. "They tell me chicken bones are bad for dogs," said Bill. "The bones splinter into sharp pieces."
>
> Ralph was irritated. "Don't tell me how to feed my dog," he snapped.

► 1. What were the exact words spoken by Bill? What punctuation mark comes at the end of Bill's first sentence, before the words **said Bill?** Is this punctuation mark inside the quotation marks, or outside?

► 2. What did Ralph actually say? To whom was he speaking? What kind of sentence did Ralph use?

The same scene could have been reported without using conversation. You have learned that a report of conversation without the actual words of the speakers is called **indirect discourse:**

> Ralph was feeding his dog a chicken carcass as Bill looked on. Bill said that chicken bones were bad for dogs because they splinter into sharp pieces.
>
> Ralph was irritated and ordered Bill not to tell him how to feed his dog.

► 3. What kind of sentences were used in the indirect discourse? Are they affirmative or negative?

► 4. Direct discourse allows you to use questions and commands, as well as statements. The sentences may be either affirmative or negative. Which kind of discourse do you think is more lifelike, direct or indirect?

■ Each of the incidents that follows is reported in indirect discourse. Rewrite each incident, using the actual words that you think the persons might have said. Be careful to enclose in quotation marks the actual words the people used.

5. Alice was tying her little sister's shoes. She commanded the child to be still and asked if she couldn't stop wriggling even for a minute.

Alice's father spoke to her and told her that it is necessary to be patient with little children. He ordered her not to scold the baby.

6. George pointed to the top of a tree and told his friend Jack to look at the nest there. He said it was huge, and he asked what would build a nest of sticks like that.

Jack said that anybody ought to know that. He said it was a crow's nest.

Just then a squirrel poked its head over the edge of the nest and looked down at them. George laughed and told Jack to look at that. He said that Jack's crow had turned gray and lost its wings.

7. Helen asked her brother Bob to lend her a quarter, promising to pay him back the next Saturday.

Bob asked her what she wanted it for.

Helen was a little annoyed with her brother and said to him that she would not tell him, that it was a secret.

He commanded her to tell him what she wanted it for, and he asked if she could not trust him with a secret.

Helen insisted that she could not tell him, that it would spoil everything.

He replied in a mean voice that he would not lend her the quarter and turned to walk away.

Helen wearily told him to suit himself, that she needed a quarter more to buy his birthday present.

In a voice now hearty with friendly generosity, Bob asked why she hadn't said so and demanded that she take the quarter. He asked if she did not want to borrow more than that.

8. Jane called to Ellen and told her to wait a minute. She asked Ellen if she had heard the news.

Ellen ordered Jane not to tell her. She commanded Jane to let her guess. She guessed that there was a new boy in the neighborhood.

Jane replied that she had not said it was good news; it was bad news.

Ellen anxiously ordered Jane not to tell her that a boy was moving out of the neighborhood.

A Poem

From 1854 to 1856 the British, the French, and the Turks fought a war against the Russians in the Crimea, an area between Turkey and Russia. Through a mistake, a single British brigade, armed mainly with a kind of sword, was sent against the Russian cannons and infantry. The poet Alfred, Lord Tennyson wrote a famous poem about what happened.

The Charge of the Light Brigade

Half a league, half a league,
Half a league onward,
All in the valley of Death
　　Rode the six hundred.
"Forward, the Light Brigade!
Charge for the guns!" he said.
Into the valley of Death
　　Rode the six hundred.

"Forward, the Light Brigade!"
Was there a man dismay'd?
Not, tho' the soldier knew
　　Someone had blundered.
Theirs not to make reply,
Theirs not to reason why,
Theirs but to do and die.
Into the valley of Death
　　Rode the six hundred.

Cannon to right of them,
Cannon to left of them,
Cannon in front of them
　　Volley'd and thunder'd;
Storm'd at with shot and shell,
Boldly they rode and well,
Into the jaws of Death,
Into the mouth of hell
　　Rode the six hundred.

229

Flash'd all their sabres bare,
Flash'd as they turn'd in air
Sabring the gunners there,
Charging an army, while
  All the world wonder'd.
Plunged in the battery smoke
Right thro' the line they broke;
Cossack and Russian
Reel'd from the sabre stroke
Shatter'd and sunder'd.
Then they rode back, but not,
  Not the six hundred.

Cannon to right of them,
Cannon to left of them,
Cannon behind them
   Volley'd and thunder'd;
Stormed at with shot and shell,
While horse and hero fell,
They that had fought so well
Came thro' the jaws of Death,
Back from the mouth of hell,
All that was left of them,
   Left of six hundred.

When can their glory fade?
O the wild charge they made!
   All the world wonder'd.
Honor the charge they made!
Honor the Light Brigade,
   Noble six hundred!

ALFRED, LORD TENNYSON

The Charge of the Light Brigade

▶ On a map or a globe, find the Crimea, where this battle was fought. What is a **brigade?** Is it larger or smaller than a regiment? Use a dictionary. A **light** brigade was one that was not heavily armed, so that it could move fast. What did these soldiers ride?

▶ Use a dictionary to find out how long a **league** is. Who do you think the **he** might be in the fifth line of the first stanza?

▶ In older poetry, an apostrophe is often used to show that the **ed** spelling of past tenses and participles is not to be pronounced as a separate syllable: **dismay'd, thunder'd.** Of course, it wouldn't be anyway in modern English. What does **dismay'd** mean? Note the apostrophe in **tho'.** How is this word usually spelled? What is meant by "Theirs not to make reply"?

▶ What do the first three lines of the third stanza tell about the nature of the charge? Where were the enemy positions?

► Are **shot** and **shell** in the third stanza nouns, verbs, or adjectives? Look these words up in a dictionary.

► Look up **sabre** in a dictionary. How is it spelled nowadays? The words in the first line of stanza four are put in a very poetic order. What would their normal order be? In what word is **sabre** made into a verb? How many syllables does the verb have? How many syllables does the modern form **sabering** have?

► A **battery** is a group of guns. What would **battery smoke** be? A **cossack** was a kind of Russian soldier. Find out what kind by using a dictionary. What do **reel'd** and **sunder'd** mean? What is told to us about the cost of the charge by the last two lines of this stanza?

► What do the first three lines of the next stanza tell about the new situation on the battlefield? What does **volley'd** mean? What is the usual spelling of the word here spelled **thro'**?

Tennyson used a punctuation mark after the following sentence to show strong feeling, but it is not an exclamation.

> Honor the charge they made.

► What is the subject of this sentence? What kind of sentence is it?

What Words Come From

It may seem from our study of morphemes and spelling that all of our borrowed words come from Latin. Most of them do, but not all.

The word **brigade** comes from the Italian word **brigata.** **Brigata** is made from the Italian verb **brigare** meaning to fight.

The word **cossack** comes from a Russian word, **kazak,** which the Russians, in turn, borrowed from a Turkish word that meant a kind of outlaw, or freebooter.

The word **sabre,** which is more commonly spelled **saber,** is a French word which they borrowed from the Germans, who in turn took it from a Hungarian word meaning to cut.

League has been in the English language longer than the words above that are borrowed from Italian, Russian, or French. It comes from the Celtic, the language spoken in Britain thousands of years ago.

232

■ Make a noun of the verb printed in heavy black type before each sentence below by adding the morpheme <u>ion</u>. Copy the sentence and use the noun to complete it. You may need to use the plural form.

1. **regulate**   The Navy has strict _____.
2. **create**   New fashions are often referred to as _____.
3. **relate**   Our _____ with Great Britain are cordial.
4. **illustrate**   He told a story as an _____ of his point.
5. **cultivate**   Most _____ of crops is performed by machines.
6. **irritate**   He showed his _____ by his frown.
7. **populate**   India's _____ is growing faster than the food supply.
8. **irrigate**   Deserts are reclaimed through _____.
9. **punctuate**   Many writers are _____ rather sparingly.
10. **navigate**   The North Star is still an aid to _____.

▶ 11. When the verb does not end with **ate,** the morpheme <u>ion</u> is often added in the spelling **ation,** frequently with other spelling changes as you have seen:

apply + ion → **application**   invoke + ion → **invocation**

In application, the **y** was changed to **i.** What letter was added before **ation?** An **invocation** is an appeal for help, as in a prayer. The **e** of **invoke** is dropped. What letter is substituted for **k?** What general spelling rule would be violated if the **k** were retained before **ation?**

Make nouns of the verbs in heavy black type below by adding the morpheme <u>ion</u>, spelled **ation.** Use the nouns in the sentences. You may need to use the plural form.

12. **imply**   An _____ is an indirect suggestion.
13. **accuse**   The prisoner denied the _____.
14. **expect**   Our _____ is that Sally will visit us.
15. **alter**   Mother's new dress needed some _____.
16. **present**   The _____ of prizes followed his speech.
17. **exhale**   Inhalation, or breathing in, is the opposite of _____.
18. **invite**   The guests will be admitted only by _____.
19. **occupy**   Mr. Jonathon's _____ is deep-sea diving.

► 20. Study the noun formed by adding ion to pronounce:

pronounce + ion → **pronunciation**

What is the difference in spelling between the second syllable of the verb **pronounce** and the second syllable of the noun **pronunciation?** The **ou** in **pronounce** stands for the sound /au/, as in **down** or **bounce.** The **u** in **pronunciation** stands for the sound /u/, as in **bun** or **ton.**

► 21. Many verbs ending in the sound /d/ spelled **de** change the spelling to **s** when adding the morpheme ion:

evade + ion → **evasion**   decide + ion → **decision**

How does the vowel sound in the second syllable of **decide** change when the verb is made into a noun?

► 22. Verbs that end in the sound /d/ spelled **d** or the sound /t/ spelled **t** may also change **d** or **t** to **s** in adding ion:

extend + ion → **extension**   divert + ion → **diversion**

What letter in **extension** stands for the sound /sh/? What letter in **diversion** stands for the sound /zh/?

► 23. When the morpheme ion is added to verbs that end in the sound /z/, we drop the **e** if /z/ is spelled **se.** If the final sound is /s/ spelled **ss,** we just add the ending **ion.**

revise + ion → **revision**   confess + ion → **confession**

The letters **se** in **revise** stand for the sound /z/. What letter in the noun **revision** stands for /zh/? The letters **ss** in **confess** stand for the sound /s/. What two letters in the noun **confession** stand for the sound /sh/?

■ Write nouns by adding the morpheme ion to the verbs in heavy black type below, as shown in 21 to 23 above. Use the nouns in the sentences.

24. **oppress**   The refugees complained of _____.
25. **convert**   The _____ of water power to electricity is done by generators.
26. **provide**   There is a strange _____ in the contract.
27. **divide**   We reverse multiplication by _____.
28. **repulse**   The opposite of attraction is _____.
29. **suspend**   The parents protested Bob's _____.
30. **possess**   It is said that _____ is nine points of the law.
31. **persuade**   What force can't do, _____ often can.
32. **seclude**   A hermit is a man who lives in _____.

► 1. We make affirmative statements negative by putting **not** into the affirmative statement. Where do we put **not** when the verb phrase begins with a modal, a form of **have,** or a form of **be?** What do we add besides the word **not** when the verb phrase begins with a verb? To what word does the tense morpheme, <u>pres.</u> or <u>past</u>, apply when the verb phrase begins with a verb?

► 2. Make the following affirmative strings negative. Then write the finished negative statements:

   a. <u>the</u> + <u>cake</u> + <u>past</u> + <u>be</u> + <u>ready</u> + <u>by</u> + <u>dinnertime</u>
   b. <u>Alice</u> + <u>past</u> + <u>eat</u> + <u>his</u> + <u>candy</u>
   c. <u>he</u> + <u>pres.</u> + <u>study</u> + <u>history</u>
   d. <u>Jim</u> + <u>pres.</u> + <u>have</u> + <u>part.</u> + <u>go</u>
   e. <u>they</u> + <u>past</u> + <u>may</u> + <u>be</u> + <u>ing</u> + <u>try</u>

► 3. When a string of morphemes for an affirmative statement contains a verb as the first word in the verb phrase, with what morpheme do we begin the matching "yes/no" question string? What morpheme do we add to carry the tense? What two morphemes come first when the verb phrase of the statement begins with a modal, a form of **have,** or a form of **be?**

■ 4. Write the matching "yes/no" question strings for the following. Then write the finished "yes/no" questions.

   a. <u>she</u> + <u>pres.</u> + <u>ride</u> + <u>a</u> + <u>horse</u>
   b. <u>they</u> + <u>past</u> + <u>have</u> + <u>part.</u> + <u>buy</u> + <u>a</u> + <u>house</u>
   c. <u>I</u> + <u>pres.</u> + <u>be</u> + <u>ing</u> + <u>miss</u> + <u>the</u> + <u>point</u>
   d. <u>Walter</u> + <u>past</u> + <u>write</u> + <u>a</u> + <u>preface</u>
   e. <u>Susan</u> + <u>past</u> + <u>may</u> + <u>have</u> + <u>part.</u> + <u>misunderstand</u>

► 5. What do we add after tense-**have,** tense-**be,** or tense-**do** to make an affirmative question negative?

■ 6. Write negative questions for the following, using contractions:

   a. Should she resign?
   b. Will you sit down?
   c. Is the window clean?
   d. Have the boys left?
   e. Did Wally buy the boat?
   f. Could we stay until eleven?
   g. Do the stores close at five?

► 1. What type of sentence tells someone to do something or not to do something? What is the subject of a command? Is this word actually used in a command?

■ 2. Write the letter for each of the following sentences. After it, write **statement, question,** or **command** to tell what type of sentence it is. Then write **aff.** if the sentence is affirmative, **neg.** if it is negative.

    a. You deserve a prize.

    b. Do not give up yet.

    c. Doesn't my dog know you?

    d. Be moderate in all things.

    e. He doesn't mow the lawn.

    f. Don't spill your milk.

    g. Is she in our class?

    h. Aim high.

► 3. We can use modals to soften statements. What are some other words that can be used for this purpose?

■ 4. Rewrite each of the following statements twice, softening it in two different ways:

    a. It is her fault.

    b. You are to blame.

    c. He was lazy.

■ 5. When you express the idea of a command in the form of a suggestion, what word do you use as subject? What are some words or expressions that you add to the verb phrase?

■ 6. Express each of the following commands in the form of a suggestion. Express each suggestion in three different ways.

    a. Be on time.

    b. Keep your temper.

    c. Don't argue.

► 7. When you express a command in the form of a request, does the request contain the word **you?** What are some other words that may appear in a request, but not in a command?

■ 8. Express the following commands in the form of requests. Write two requests for each — one affirmative, one negative.

    a. Get to work.

    b. Stop scratching.

    c. Be cheerful.

■ Each of the following statements will answer a question that begins with **where, when,** or **how.** Write the three matching "wh" questions.

1. My coat is in the closet.
2. They will leave at noon.
3. The boys behaved badly.

You have seen that a command can be expressed in the form of a question. In that form, what do we call it? This suggests that questions may be thought of as commands in another form. Study the following commands:

a. Please tell me the location of my coat.
b. Please tell me the time of their departure.
c. Please tell me the way in which the boys behaved.

▶ 4. Which statement matches Command **a?** Which of the questions you wrote puts Command **a** in question form?

▶ 5. Which statement matches Command **b?** Which of the questions you wrote puts Command **b** in question form?

▶ 6. Which statement matches Command **c?** Which of the questions you wrote puts Command **c** in question form?

■ Rewrite each command below in the form of a "wh" question.

7. Please tell me the way in which Mabel spoke.
8. Please tell me the location of the bus station.
9. Please tell me the way in which our team played.
10. Please tell me the time of his arrival.
11. Please tell me the location of the library.
12. Please tell me the time at which the meeting begins.
13. Please tell me the time at which the fire started.
14. Please tell me the location of their house.
15. Please tell me the way in which Harry sang.

■ The following commands can be expressed in the form of "yes/no" questions. Write the "yes/no" questions.

16. Please tell me whether or not we won the game.
17. Please tell me whether or not they were angry.
18. Please tell me whether or not she is Bob's sister.
19. Please tell me whether or not the boys are outside.
20. Please tell me whether or not I am right.

The <u>wh</u> Words

A great many English words come from the language called Old English that was spoken very long ago in England. In dictionaries, Old English is abbreviated OE.

You have used **wh** words to begin "wh" questions and to form relative clauses. These **wh** words are related in meaning because they all come from the interrogative forms in Old English. As you probably know, **interrogative sentence** is another name for question. The interrogative forms in Old English began with **hw.**

► The Old English word for **who** was **hwa,** and **hwa** was an interrogative form in Old English. **Who** is the basic interrogative word of the **wh** group. See if you can find anything that suggests this interrogative form in the Old English spelling of the following **wh** words:

what   hwaet   when   hwanne   where   hwaer

Do you see any evidence that **what, when,** and **where** are related to **who?**

► Although **what, when,** and **where** are now spelled **wh,** we pronounce the consonant cluster at the beginning as though it were still spelled the Old English way: / hw /. Do we pronounce **who** as though it began with the sounds / hw /? What sound do we use at the beginning of **who?**

► Another **wh** word that comes from the interrogative form **hwa** means "for what reason." Can you name this word?

► The word **which** is also related to **who.** **Which** at the beginning of a question asks the listener to tell what one thing in a set of things answers the question. When do we use **which** in a relative clause?

► Study the Old English spelling of the **wh** word **whether:**

whether   hwaeder

Do you see any evidence that **whether** is related to **who?** Actually, **which** is related to **what, what** is a form of **who,** and **whether** asks which of two: "He asked whether I would go or stay."

► The word that is used in asking "in what way" is closely related to **who,** even though it does not begin with the letters **wh,** but just with **h.** What word is it?

► The **wh** word **whence** is no longer commonly used in English. Once, we might have said, **"Whence** did he come?" But now we would say "Where did he come from?" What two words do we now use instead of **whence?**

► Another **wh** word that, like **whence,** has disappeared from ordinary English, is **whither.** **Whither** means "to what place?" Once we might have said, "Whither she went, we do not know." What would we say instead today?

There is a group of words from Old English which begin with the letters **th,** and which are related to the definite article **the.**

► We use two of these words in answering questions such as "What man did you see?" If the answer is "the more distant of the men," we would use **that:** "I saw **that** man." What **th** word would we use if the answer is "the nearer of the men"?

► Which of the two **th** words, **this** or **that,** do we use as a relative pronoun?

► There are two **th** words which are the plural forms of **this** and **that.** What **th** word is the plural of **this?** What **th** word is the plural of **that?** Use the plural form in sentences to illustrate the **more distant** and the **nearer** meanings.

► There is another **th** word which is closely related to the words **the** and **that** and which is used in answering questions that begin with **when:** "When did the bus leave?" The **th** word means "at that time." What is the word?

► The word that we use after **er** or after **more** (or less) to express the morpheme of comparison was originally the same word as **then.** What is this **th** word?

■ Another word that begins with **th** and is related to **that** is a word which means "in this way": **thus.** Write a sentence using the word **thus.**

► The common **th** word that means "in that place" is closely related to **the** and **that** also. It answers questions with **where:** "Where is my hat?" What word is it? What word means "in this place"?

► The old words **hither** and **thither** are also related to **the** and **that.** One means "to or towards that place." The other means "to or towards this place." Match the words with their meanings.

1. In each sentence below, find the word that ends in **ate.** Copy it and write **v., n.,** or **adj.** after it to tell whether it is used as a verb, noun, or adjective in that sentence. If you make mistakes, study page 215.

    a. Mr. Wallace is a graduate of Yale.

    b. This year's class will graduate in May.

    c. Mrs. Evans is a fortunate woman.

2. Make nouns from the verbs in heavy black type by adding the morpheme <u>ion</u>, spelled **ion.** Copy the sentences and put in the nouns. If you make mistakes, study pages 222–23.

    a. **immigrate**   There is a yearly _____ of people from other lands.

    b. **hesitate**   Ned's _____ was due to embarrassment.

    c. **educate**   A good _____ is priceless.

3. Make nouns from the verbs in heavy black type by adding the morpheme <u>ion</u>, spelled **ation.** Copy the sentences and put in the nouns. If you make mistakes, study pages 223, 233.

    a. **starve**   The refugees were threatened with _____.

    b. **invoke**   The priest gave the _____.

    c. **condemn**   The act drew vigorous _____.

    d. **accuse**   Tom said that the _____ was false.

    e. **vary**   He repeated the story without _____.

4. Make nouns of the verbs in heavy black type by adding the morpheme <u>ion</u>, making spelling changes in the verb when necessary. Copy the sentences and use the nouns to complete them. If you make mistakes, study page 234.

    a. **pronounce**   Betty's _____ has a Southern accent.

    b. **decide**   The judge's _____ was announced on TV.

    c. **divert**   The court permitted some _____ of water from the river.

    d. **revise**   The book was undergoing _____.

    e. **confess**   The prisoner's _____ was published.

5. Rewrite each of the following statements, softening it in one of the ways you have studied. Soften each statement in a different way. If you make mistakes, study page 216.

    a. You are mistaken.

    b. They missed the point.

    c. He was nervous.

6. Write the numeral for each of the following sentences. After it, write **statement, question,** or **command** to tell what type of sentence it is. If you make mistakes, study page 217.

a. When did the train leave?
b. The horse bucked violently.
c. Give me a drink of milk.

7. Put each of the following commands in the form of a suggestion. Use **must** or **have to** in one of the suggestions. If you make mistakes, study pages 224–25.

a. Go home.
b. Do your homework.
c. Get to bed.
d. Don't argue.

8. Put each of the following commands in the form of an affirmative request. If you make mistakes, study page 225.

a. Help me with my spelling.
b. Please bring the logs for the fireplace.
c. Speak more softly.

9. Put each of the following commands in the form of a negative request.

a. Come to see us.
b. Try a little harder.
c. Forgive my error.

10. Make the following affirmative strings negative. Then write the finished negative statements. If you make mistakes, study page 235.

a. she + pres. + have + part. + arrive
b. he + past + can + fix + the + toy
c. Mack + pres. + work + hard
d. they + past + be + at + the + party

11. Write affirmative "yes/no" question strings for the statements in **10 a, b, c,** and **d** above. If you make mistakes, study page 235.

12. Write negative questions for the following, using contractions. If you make mistakes, study page 235.

a. Did you finish your report?
b. Could I borrow the flashlight?
c. Have they bought the house?

A Poem

This is a tale of an Assyrian king, Sennacherib, who led his army against the Jewish peoples and besieged Jerusalem nearly three thousand years ago.

The Destruction of Sennacherib

The Assyrian came down like the wolf on the fold,
And his cohorts were gleaming in purple and gold;
And the sheen of their spears was like stars on the sea,
When the blue wave rolls nightly on deep Galilee.

Like the leaves of the forest when Summer is green,
That host with their banners at sunset was seen:
Like the leaves of the forest when Autumn hath blown,
That host on the morrow lay withered and strown.

For the angel of Death spread his wings on the blast,
And breathed in the face of the foe as he passed;
And the eyes of the sleepers waxed deadly and chill,
And their hearts but once heaved — and forever grew still!

And there lay the steed with his nostril all wide,
But through it there rolled not the breath of his pride;
And the foam of his gasping lay white on the turf,
And cold as the spray of the rock-beating surf.

And there lay the rider distorted and pale,
With the dew on his brow, and the rust on his mail:
And the tents were all silent — the banners alone —
The lances unlifted — the trumpet unblown.

And the widows of Ashur are loud in their wail,
And the idols are broke in the temple of Baal;
And the might of the Gentile, unsmote by the sword,
Hath melted like snow in the glance of the Lord!

GEORGE GORDON, LORD BYRON

This story is told in the Bible in the Second Book of Kings, Chapters 18 and 19. It is that the Assyrian King Sennacherib besieged Jerusalem with a mighty army, but in the night an angel of the Lord came and killed 185,000 of his men. Sennacherib escaped, but was killed on his return to his kingdom.

Sennacherib is pronounced with first stress on the second syllable. The **ch** stands for the sound / k /.

► Look up the word **fold.** What kind of fold would be in danger from wolves? A **cohort** was a group of warriors, something like a brigade. What colors did they wear? What does **sheen** mean? How does the poet tell that there were a great many soldiers?

The **Sea of Galilee** is a fresh-water lake in the northern part of Israel.

► What is the army compared to in the first two lines of the second stanza? Look up **host** if you need to. What is it compared to in the second two lines? What time passes between the first two lines and the second? **Strown** is an old participle form of the verb **strew.** What does strew mean? What has happened to the host?

► The third stanza tells what caused it to happen. **Blast** means a strong wind. What does "spread his wings on the blast" mean? Who did this? Explain the last two lines of this stanza.

► How does the poet say in the fourth stanza that the steeds, or horses, lay dead? What does **rock-beating surf** mean?

► How did the riders of the steeds lie? What does **distorted** mean in the fifth stanza? Look up **mail** and find the meaning that it must have in this stanza. How else in the fifth stanza does the poet describe the death and desolation in the camp? What is a **lance?**

► **Ashur** was the Assyrian god of war. The widows of Ashur are the women left widowed by the death of their soldier husbands. **Baal** was another Assyrian god. Find what **idol** means. A **gentile** is a person who is not Jewish. How do the last two lines tell again what happened to the Assyrians?

You have now studied a number of transformations that are very useful in writing, including the relative clause, the subordinate clause, and the **it** transformations.

■ Use transformations as you are directed to combine each group of sentences that follows into a single sentence. Your instructions are given in parentheses. Here is a key to the abbreviations used in these instructions:

T-rel: relative clause transformation

T-rel, deletion: relative clause deletion transformation

T-noun modifier: noun modifier transformation

T-sub: subordinate clause transformation

T-it: **it** transformation

T-comp and **T-sup:** comparative and superlative transformations

T-poss: possessive transformation

T-neg: negative transformation

The first exercise is done for you.

1. S + pleased the boy. **(T-sub):** Sally came to the party. **(T-rel):** The boy invited her. (Now apply **T-it**)

    S + pleased the boy. (T-sub): that Sally came to the party. (T-rel): the boy who invited her. S + pleased the boy: "That Sally came to the party pleased the boy who invited her." (Now, apply T-it): "It pleased the boy who invited her that Sally came to the party."

2. The girl said + S **(T-rel, deletion** and **T-noun modifier):** The girl was pretty. **(T-rel, deletion):** The girl was watching the game. **(T-sub):** She knew the umpire.

3. S + seemed likely. **(T-sub):** The storm would spoil the picnic. **(T-rel):** The storm was brewing. (Now apply **T-it.**)

4. The stranger told us + S **(T-rel):** The stranger asked us for directions. **(T-sub):** He is going to Illinois.

5. **(T-neg):** S + is surprising. **(T-sub):** The train arrived late. (Now apply **T-it.**)

6. The problem was + S **(T-sub** and **T-neg):** The gentleman would move over. **(T-rel, deletion** and **T-noun modifier):** The gentleman was stout. **(T-rel, deletion):** The gentleman was in the back seat.

7. The storekeeper had a wife. **(T-poss)**: The wife was helpful + S **(T-comp)**: The clerk was helpful. **(T-rel)**: He had hired the clerk. (Now delete any relative pronoun that you can.)

8. S + delighted my mother. **(T-sub)**: The pianist will play at the benefit. **(T-rel, deletion** and **T-noun modifier)**: The pianist is famous. **(T-rel)**: The pianist lives next door. **(T-rel, deletion)**: The benefit is for children. **(T-rel, deletion** and **T-noun modifier)**: The children are deaf. (Now apply **T-it**.)

9. The policeman thought + S **(T-rel, deletion)**: The policeman was on the beat. **(T-sub)**: The strangers were characters. **(T-rel, deletion)**: The strangers were in the car. **(T-rel, deletion** and **T-noun modifier)**: The characters were suspicious.

10. S + is a fact. **(T-sub)**: Alice is the pretty girl in school. **(T-sup)**: The girls in school are pretty. (Now apply **T-it**.)

11. **(T-neg)**: S + occurred to me. **(T-sub)**: The daughter might know + S **(T-poss)**: Mr. Brown has a daughter. **(T-sub)**: We were away. (Now apply **T-it**.)

12. Somebody must have planted the row of hollyhocks. **(T-rel)**: Somebody loves flowers. **(T-rel, deletion** and **T-noun modifier)**: The row of hollyhocks is lovely. **(T-rel)**: The row of hollyhocks grows along the stone wall. **(T-rel, deletion** and **T-noun modifier)**: The stone wall is old.

13. S + is surprising. **(T-sub)**: People will spend hours every day on a train so + S **(T-rel)**: People work in the city. **(T-rel, deletion** and **T-noun modifier)**: A train is uncomfortable. **(T-sub)**: They can live in the country. (Now apply **T-it**.)

14. The people promised + S **(T-rel)**: The people sold us the radio. **(T-rel, deletion** and **T-noun modifier)**: The radio is portable. **(T-sub)**: The batteries would last a year.

15. S + is the fault. **(T-poss)**: George has the fault. **(T-sub** and **T-neg)**: The groceries have been delivered. **(T-rel)**: You bought the groceries this morning. (Now apply **T-it** and delete any relative pronouns you can.)

When the noun-forming morpheme ion is added to some verbs, there are internal spelling changes as well as different spellings of the morpheme. Often, these internal changes go back to the Latin verb and its participle form.

The ion noun that matches our verb **pronounce,** as you know, is written with **u** instead of **ou: pronunciation.** Another example is the ion noun for our verb **explain,** which is spelled with **a** instead of **ai** in the second syllable.

▶ 1. Study the Latin verbs and the forms of the Latin verbs that are given, and see if you find anything that helps account for the spelling of the English noun.

Latin Verb and Verb Form	English Verb	English Noun
pronuntiare (pronuntiatus)	pronounce	**pronunciation**
explanare (explanationis)	explain	**explanation**

As you see, the nouns **pronunciation** and **explanation** go back to the Latin spelling instead of the English.

▶ 2. Now study the following Latin verbs and verb forms and the spelling of the related English verbs and **ion** nouns.

Latin Verb and Verb Form	English Verb	English Noun
decidere (decisionis)	decide	**decision**
applicare (applicationis)	apply	**application**
convertere (conversionis)	convert	**conversion**
suspendere (suspensionis)	suspend	**suspension**
omittere (omissionis)	omit	**omission**

Does the spelling of the English nouns resemble the spelling of the Latin verb forms that are given in parentheses? Does it seem that there may be a historical reason for English spellings that otherwise seem very inconsistent?

▶ 3. When the consonant sound / sh / comes between a vowel letter and the ending **ion,** the / sh / sound is usually spelled with **ss,** not a single **s.** Find one example of this in the five English nouns in 2, above.

▶ 4. The sound that comes between a vowel and **ion** in **decision** is spelled with only one **s.** Is the consonant sound / sh / or / zh /?

247

■ The **ion** nouns for the following verbs in heavy black type all have the sound / sh / between a vowel and ion, as **omission** does. Add the morpheme ion and use the nouns you make to complete the sentences.

5. **concede**   A _____ is something that is granted.
6. **permit**   You ask _____ of your parents.
7. **commit**   A _____ is an appointed group.
8. **admit**   We buy tickets for _____ to the movies.

Many verbs end in sounds spelled **ct**. The morpheme ion is added to these verbs just by adding the letters **ion**.

    subtract → subtraction   restrict → restriction

► What sounds do the letters **ct** stand for in **subtract?** What sounds do they stand for in **subtraction?**

■ Add the morpheme ion to each verb in heavy black type below, and use the noun to complete the sentence.

9. **act**   There was plenty of _____ at the game.
10. **subtract**   Addition can be reversed by _____ .
11. **affect**   Another word for _____ is love.
12. **elect**   Our _____ takes place in November.
13. **select**   The _____ of representatives is a right of the people.
14. **collect**   Do you have a _____ of stamps?
15. **connect**   A telephone _____ links two telephones.
16. **direct**   The _____ opposite from east is west.
17. **correct**   Proofreading is done for the _____ of errors.
18. **protect**   The _____ of our country rests with the armed forces.
19. **predict**   A weather _____ may prophesy rain.
20. **convict**   A _____ is a sincere belief.
21. **intersect** He was struck at a blind _____ .

■ Verbs that end in the sounds spelled **pt** also add just ion to form ion nouns. Add the morpheme ion to each verb in italics below, and use the noun to complete the sentence.

22. **adopt**   The _____ of a child was the Smiths' hope.
23. **erupt**   The _____ of a volcano causes lava flows.
24. **except**   The spelling of the plural **geese** is an _____ .
25. **corrupt**   Taking bribes is one form of _____ .
26. **interrupt** The _____ was caused by a fire drill.
27. **conscript** The draft for the armed forces is _____ .

► 1. You may remember that when we studied the comparison transformation on pages 26 and 27, it was pointed out that making a comparison is only one way of telling how strong or how beautiful or how sad someone is. Another way is to use words like those before the adjectives in the following sentences:

a. It is **very** hot.
b. It is **extremely** hot.
c. It is **so** hot.

Words like **very, extremely,** and **so** belong to a small class of words called **intensifiers.** They show, in this case, that there is a high degree of heat. Can you think of another intensifier that could be used with the adjective **hot?**

■ Rewrite the following sentences, using an intensifier before each adjective in the predicate position. Use as many different intensifiers as you can. Here are some others: **quite, terribly, awfully, remarkably, amazingly, astonishingly, unbelievably, surprisingly.**

2. The day is stormy.
3. The sea is rough.
4. It is cold.
5. The snow is deep.
6. Her voice is pleasant.

■ The question that naturally follows when someone says "The room is hot" is this: "How hot is the room?" Write the **how** questions that you could ask about these statements:

7. The pillows are soft.
8. The bed is comfortable.
9. His smile is happy.
10. The lady is beautiful.

11. To reply to the question "How hot is the room?" we could use the word **how** in somewhat the same way that we used the word **that** in the subordinate clause transformation, making a noun clause: **how hot the room is.** We could then use the clause in a noun phrase question:

a. **How hot the room is** is unbelievable.
b. **How hot the room is** is simply terrible.

249

► 12. Notice that the **how** noun clause **"how hot the room is,"** like the subordinate noun clause "that the room is hot," contains a noun phrase subject, **the room,** and a verb phrase predicate, **is hot.** In which noun clause does the adjective **hot** come before the noun phrase subject? What is the function of the noun clause **how hot the room is** in Sentences 11a and b on page 249?

■ Make **how** noun clauses from the following "how" questions and use them as subjects of sentences like "How hot the room is is unbelievable":

13. How soft are the pillows?
14. How comfortable is the bed?
15. How happy is his smile?
16. How beautiful is the lady?
17. How deep is the snow?
18. Now study the following sentence:

He plays very skillfully.

The word **skillfully** is not an adjective. What kind of word is it?

We use **how** clauses with adverbs as well as with adjectives. For the statement "He plays skillfully," we could, of course, ask the following "how" question:

How skillfully does he play?

■ Write "how" questions for the following statements that contain adverbs of manner:

19. She works carefully.
20. He sings well.
21. They swim fast.
22. The men walk slowly.
23. The rain fell hard.

■ Make **how** noun clauses from the following "how" questions and use them as subjects of sentences like "How skillfully he plays is unbelievable":

24. How thoroughly did she learn the lesson?
25. How quickly did the fire engine arrive?
26. How loudly did the boys talk?
27. How badly was the town flooded?
28. How rapidly did the ship sink?
29. How carefully does he drive?

A Story from the *Odyssey*

The following is an account of one of the dangers that Odysseus met on his long voyage home from Troy.

Odysseus and Polyphemus

After sailing for many days, Odysseus and his men came to the island of Sicily. They did not know it, but that island was inhabited by a race of one-eyed giants, all fierce and dangerous to men.

Odysseus' ship was beached on the shore, and he and his crew went on land to see if they could find food. Before long they came to a very large cave. There was no one there, but it was apparent that it belonged to a person of some wealth. For there were wines and cheeses, chickens and ducks, lambs and kids, and other foods of all sorts. Odysseus and the others went into the cave and, since they were very hungry, ate and drank ravenously of the good things they found there. When they had had their fill, they fell asleep.

They were awakened by a loud noise, and, opening

their eyes, they were terrified by what they saw. A flock of sheep were entering the cave, and driving them was a giant so large that he nearly filled the enormous door. He was a ferocious-looking creature, and he had but one eye, in the middle of his head. No sooner had he entered the cave and seen his visitors, than he rolled an immense stone to the mouth of the cave and blocked it.

"Now," he said, "since you have been so bold as to eat my food, I will eat you." With that, he seized a member of the crew and ate him up, bones and all. His appetite satisfied, he stretched out on the floor of the cave and fell asleep.

Odysseus and his men were terrified and grief-stricken for their dead comrade, but there seemed to be nothing that they could do. Not all of them together had strength enough to roll the great stone from the mouth of the cave.

When morning came, the giant, who was named Polyphemus, rose and immediately seized another member of the crew and breakfasted on him. Then he moved the stone from the entrance and drove the sheep out of the cave. He followed them and put the stone back, keeping the men imprisoned. But Odysseus was not called the Wise One for nothing. He formed a plan. Finding a huge beam in the cave, he showed his men how to shape the end to a point and harden it in the fire. Then he had them hide it away.

That night Polyphemus returned with his sheep and again made a horrible dinner. But when he had finished, Odysseus brought him wine to drink and kept replenishing his cup whenever it was empty. Soon Polyphemus sank into a drunken sleep. Then the men brought out the beam and heated it in the fire. Running, they thrust it into his eye and blinded him. Polyphemus, in a fury, roared about the cave trying to clutch the men who had injured him, but Odysseus and his companions kept out of his way.

When morning came, Polyphemus rolled aside the stone and placed himself in the doorway ready to seize his escaping enemies. But Odysseus had foreseen this, and he had another plan. He had his men tie three sheep together and told each man to lie under a set of three sheep, holding onto the fleece. Polyphemus let the sheep out to pasture. He felt over the back of each one to be sure that no man was riding on it, but he didn't think to feel underneath. Thus Odysseus and his men escaped from the cave.

When they had reached their boat and were putting out to sea, Odysseus could not resist shouting in mockery to Polyphemus. The wounded giant instantly seized a huge boulder and flung it in the direction of the voice. It missed the ship but set up a great wave which pushed the boat again toward the shore. However, the men bent instantly to their oars and finally pulled free of the land of the one-eyed giants.

► This story takes place after Odysseus and his men in the wooden horse brought about the capture of Troy. The island of Sicily is in the Mediterranean Sea. Find it on a map or globe. What modern European country is Sicily a part of? Who inhabited this island in the days of Odysseus, according to this story?

► What does **beached** mean in the second paragraph? What were Odysseus and his men looking for? What did they find? What made them think that the cave belonged to a person of some wealth? Does **some wealth** mean great wealth or moderate wealth? What did they do when they entered the cave?

► What awakened them? Who came in through the door of the cave? What was he driving? What subordinate clause with **that** tells how large the giant was? Describe the giant. What did he do first when he saw the visitors? What did he do next?

► What did Odysseus and his men not have strength enough to do?

► Polyphemus has the first stress on the second syllable from the end. That syllable has the vowel sound /ē/. What consonant sound do the letters **ph** stand for? Pronounce the name.

► What did Polyphemus do when he awakened? What do you think Polyphemus's occupation was? When he went out, how did he make sure that his captives could not escape? What is a **beam?** What did the men do with the beam they found?

► How did Odysseus make Polyphemus go to sleep? What does **replenish** mean? How did the men blind the sleeping giant? What did Polyphemus try to do then? Did he catch any more of them?

► Where did Polyphemus place himself in the morning, when he rolled the stone from the door? Why? Describe the place that Odysseus thought of to allow him and his companions to escape from the cave.

► What could Odysseus not resist doing as they put out to sea? What was the giant's response?

■ Use transformations as you are directed to combine each group of sentences that follows into a single longer sentence. Use contractions when you can. You will find a list of the transformations and their abbreviations on page 245 if you forget what the abbreviations mean. **T-comp, as,** which is not listed there, means the comparative transformation with **as.**

The first example is done for you. Notice that the relative pronoun **which** is used to avoid having the word **that** used three times in the same sentence.

1. S + is amazing. **(T-sub** and **T-neg):** The salmon have disappeared entirely. **(T-rel, deletion** and **T-noun modifier):** The salmon are wonderful. **(T-rel):** The salmon spawn in our rivers. (Now apply **T-it.)**

S + is amazing. (T-sub): that the salmon have disappeared entirely. (T-neg): that the salmon have not disappeared entirely. (T-rel, deletion): the salmon ~~that are~~ wonderful. (T-noun modifier): the wonderful salmon. (T-rel): the salmon which spawn in our rivers. S + is amazing. That the wonderful salmon which spawn in our rivers have not disappeared entirely is amazing. (By T-it): It is amazing that the wonderful salmon which spawn in our rivers have not disappeared entirely.

2. The difficulty was + S **(T-sub):** The ice cream had melted. **(T-rel):** We had brought the ice cream. (Now delete any relative pronoun you can.)

3. S + was a calamity. **(T-sub** and **T-neg):** The engineers foresaw + S **(T-rel):** The engineers built the dam. **(T-sub):** Mud slides might weaken the structure. (Now apply **T-it.)**

4. Everybody feared + S **(T-sub):** The governor would choose a staff. **(T-rel, deletion** and **T-noun modifier):** The governor was new. **(T-rel, deletion** and **T-noun modifier):** The staff was incompetent.

5. S + is astonishing. **(T-sub** and **T-neg):** The people have kept up the property. **(T-rel):** The people belong to the club. (Now apply **T-it.)**

6. The men say + S **(T-rel):** The men have been there. **(T-sub):** The side of the moon is colorless + S **(T-rel. deletion** and **T-noun modifier):** The side is bright. **(T-comp, as):**

The side is colorless. **(T-rel, deletion** and **T-noun modifier):** The side is dark.

7. **(T-neg):** S + was understood. **(T-sub** and **T-neg):** The winner of the contest could be an employee. **(T-rel):** The company put on the contest. (Now apply **T-it** and delete any relative pronoun you can.)

8. The lady said + S **(T-rel, deletion):** The lady was sitting behind us. **(T-sub** and **T-neg):** We should whisper.

9. **(T-neg):** S + is likely. **(T-sub):** Anyone will be at the party. **(T-rel):** Anyone knows the name. **(T-poss):** The newcomer has the name. (Now apply **T-it.**)

10. S + is possible. **(T-sub):** The plane will bring the luggage. **(T-rel):** The plane arrives at seven. **(T-rel):** We left the luggage behind. (Now apply **T-it** and delete any relative pronoun which can be deleted.)

11. We understand + S **(T-sub):** The teachers were the ones. **(T-rel):** The children helped the teachers. **(T-rel):** The ones gave the party. (Now remove any relative pronoun you can.)

12. The man told me + S **(T-rel):** The man awarded the prizes. **(T-sub):** The essay was interesting. **(T-poss):** Jane had an essay. **(T-comp):** The essay was interesting. **(T-poss):** Bill had an essay.

13. S + was lucky for the Greeks. **(T-rel):** He had captured the Greeks. **(T-sub):** The giant had only one eye. **(T-rel):** The giant lived in the cave. (Now apply **T-it** and delete any relative pronoun you can.)

14. S + was obvious. **(T-sub):** The fire would spread to the planes. **(T-rel):** The fire had started below decks. **(T-rel, deletion):** The planes were on the flight deck. (Now apply **T-it.**)

15. The official had witnessed the act. **(T-rel):** The official said + S **(T-sub):** The fireman deserved a medal. **(T-rel, deletion** and **T-noun modifier):** The act was heroic. **(T-rel):** The act saved a life. **(T-poss):** A child had life.

16. **(T-neg):** S + is always true. **(T-sub):** A word is good. **(T-poss):** A man has a word. **(T-comp, as):** Gold is good. (Now apply **T-it.**)

17. George said + S **(T-sub):** The friend had bought a bike. **(T-poss):** Bill has a friend. **(T-rel):** You know the friend.

You remember that when we add the noun-forming morpheme ion to verbs that end in **pt**, we simply add ion:

except + ion → **exception**   adopt + ion → **adoption**

► 1. The noun form of verbs that end in **ceive** and **scribe** may also have the letters **pt** before the **ion.** Study the following Latin verbs and verb forms. Then see if you can tell why the English verb is spelled differently from the verb.

Latin Verb and Verb Form	English Verb	English Noun
decipere (deceptionis)	deceive	**deception**
subscribere (subscriptionis)	subscribe	**subscription**

► 2. How does the vowel sound of the second part of **deceive** change in the making of the noun? How is this shown in the spelling? How does the second vowel sound **subscribe** change?

■ The spelling of the verbs in heavy black type below changes as the spelling of **deceive** and **subscribe** does when we add the morpheme ion to make nouns. Add the morpheme ion and use the nouns you make to complete the sentences.

   3. **receive**   The new principal held a ———.
   4. **describe**   I recognized the house from your ———.
   5. **perceive**   She is a woman of unusual ———.
   6. **prescribe**   The doctor's ——— cured my cough.

► 7. Like **deceive** and **subscribe,** the following words have **pt** before the ion in the noun form.

assume + ion → **assumption**   absorb + ion → **absorption**

What letter does **pt** replace in **absorb?** What letter is dropped in adding ion to the other three verbs?

■ A number of verbs that end in **t** with another consonant letter before it simply add ion to form the noun:

exert + ion → **exertion**   invent + ion → **invention**

Make nouns by adding ion and use them in the sentences:

   8. **resume**   The ——— of train service was announced.
   9. **suggest**   The mayor's ——— was adopted.
 10. **prevent**   The ——— of accident is our goal.
 11. **congest**   The new bridge will relieve traffic ———.
 12. **consume**   The ——— of milk keeps going up.

Exclamations with <u>How</u>

■ What are words like **very, extremely,** and **so** called? Re-write each of the following sentences, using an intensifier before each adjective or adverb in a predicate position.
1. The chair is uncomfortable.
2. The quarterback played skillfully.
3. Mr. Garcia runs his business wisely.
4. The children romped noisily.

▶ 5. A question that naturally follows a sentence like "The chair was uncomfortable," or "The quarterback played skill-fully," is a **how** question:
a. How uncomfortable was the chair?
b. How skillfully did the quarterback play?

To reply to the question "How uncomfortable was the chair?" we could use **how** as the first word in the subordinate clause **how uncomfortable the chair was.** We could then use the **how** clause as the subject of a sentence like:
How uncomfortable the chair was was incredible!

▶ You could make the **how** clause **how skillfully the quarter-back played** from Sentence **5b,** above. What is the subject in this clause? What is the verb phrase predicate? Make up a sentence in which you tell how skillfully the quarterback ran the team, using the **how** clause as subject.

▶ 6. You remember that when a subordinate clause with **that** is used as the subject of a sentence, we usually apply the **it** transformation. "That Maude took her picture pleased Roberta" would be transformed to "It pleased Roberta that Maude took her picture." What would the following sentences become if you applied the **it** transformation?
a. That Henry broke the dish embarrassed his mother.
b. That Alice made a high mark surprised Willa.

7. We would also apply the **it** transformation to sentences with a **how** clause functioning as subject:
a. How hot it is is unbelievable. →
   It is unbelievable how hot it is.
b. How skillfully the quarterback played is amazing. →
   It is amazing how skillfully the quarterback played.

258

■ Apply the **it** transformation to the following sentences:

8. How hot it is is simply terrible.
9. How gracefully she dances is remarkable.
10. How poorly they cook is astonishing.
11. How cheap it was is ridiculous.
12. How carelessly he drives is surprising.
13. How easy it was is unbelievable.
14. How conceited they are is absurd.
15. How badly he fails is incredible.

16. You remember that a command is a sentence like "Come here," which has no noun phrase in it to function as subject. We understand that the subject is **you.** We capitalize the first word of **come here** and put a period after it as we do with any sentence, even though the subject is not stated.

Another kind of sentence that is not completely stated is called an **exclamation.** To write an exclamation, we use just the **how** clause of a sentence that expresses strong feeling as surprise, like "it is amazing how hot it is." We drop the "amazing" part, and put an exclamation mark after the **how** clause:

It is amazing how hot it is. →
How hot it is!

We begin an exclamation with a capital letter. The exclamation mark means that the exclamation shows surprise or astonishment, even though it does not actually contain words like **it is astonishing.**

■ Make exclamations from the following **it** transforms:

17. It is surprising how pretty she is.
18. It is amazing how skillfully they ski.
19. It is ridiculous how easy it was.
20. It is incredible how silly I was.
21. It is astonishing how awkwardly they played.
22. It is terrible how poor they are.
23. It is unbelievable how quickly James learns.
24. It is absurd how lazy she is.
25. It is remarkable how cleverly he writes.
26. It is awful how hard it snowed.
27. It is shocking how old she looks.
28. It is incomprehensible how cruel they are.

SECTION 3

A Poem

You know that poets often write differently from other people. Some even leave out punctuation and capital letters, which we must use in our normal writing. Here is a poem by a poet who so disliked capitals and periods that he sometimes wrote his name e e cummings.

In Just-

in Just-
spring   when the world is mud-
luscious the little
lame balloonman

whistles   far   and wee

and eddieandbill come
running from marbles and
piracies and it's
spring

when the world is puddle-wonderful

the queer
old balloonman whistles
far   and   wee
and bettyandisbel come dancing

from hop-scotch and jump-rope and

it's
spring
and

      the

          goat-footed

balloonMan   whistles
far
and
wee

261

In Just-

▶ The poem is about spring, of course. Study the following definitions of **just** and decide which meaning of the word the poet had in mind in the title "In Just-."

> **just** (just) *adj.* **1.** Fair in judging. **2.** Honest. **3.** Deserved; well-earned: a *just* reward. — *adv.* **1.** Precisely: *just* right. **2.** A moment ago; very recently: He *just* arrived.

▶ Look up **luscious** in a dictionary. What does the poet mean by describing the world as **mud-luscious?**

▶ What is a balloon man? What are you told about the appearance of this one? How does he whistle? What do you think this means?

▶ Who come running? What two games had they been playing?

▶ What is said to be wonderful about the world? What does **puddle-wonderful** have to do with **mud-luscious?** Who might think the world to be mud-luscious and puddle-wonderful?

▶ Who come dancing to see the balloon man? What games had they been playing?

▶ What do you think **goat-footed** means? Remember what you have been told of the balloon man in the first stanza.

▶ There are only two words capitalized in the whole poem. Find them. Why do you think the poet might have decided to capitalize these two words?

A Paper to Write

■ Write a three-paragraph paper about early spring in the locality where you live.

In the first paragraph tell about how the weather and the appearance of things change when spring comes. Tell when it comes.

In the second paragraph tell about some of the different things you do in spring — the games you play and the work you do.

In the third paragraph tell what you feel about spring and why you feel that way.

When we replace the symbol **S** or the symbol **NP** with a clause or phrase made from another sentence, we say that we **embed** the second sentence in the first sentence.

▶ 1. What sentence results when we change Sentence **b,** below, to an expanded noun phrase by **T-rel** and embed it in Sentence **a?**

    a. The dog ran to the man. → The dog ran to + NP

    b. The man called him.

▶ 2. What sentence results when we change Sentence **b,** below, to a subordinate clause by **T-sub** and embed it in Sentence **a?**

    a. The man was pleased + S

    b. The dog was friendly.

■ 3. As you know, we can change sentences like "She is happy" to **how** clauses:

                She is happy. → how happy she is

Write this clause as an exclamation.

■ 4. We can embed a **how** clause in another sentence, just as we can embed a **that** clause. Embed Sentence **b** below in Sentence **a,** first using **that** and then using **how** to make the sentence into a subordinate clause. Write the two sentences that result from the two applications of **T-sub.**

    a. We know + S

    b. She is happy.

In which sentence you wrote does the adjective **happy** come before the subject of the subordinate clause?

■ Embed Sentence **b** in Sentence **a** in each pair below by applying **T-sub,** first using **that** and then **how.** If the subordinate clause functions as subject, rewrite the two sentences that result, applying **T-it.**

    5. a. S + did not occur to us.

       b. He would be disappointed.

    6. a. Mr. Smith understood + S

       b. The boy was trying hard.

    7. a. S + was surprising.

       b. Mr. Thomas could get angry.

    8. a. S + was remarkable.

       b. He worked carefully.

▶ You have used both **that** and **how** as the first word in a subordinate clause:

that a. S + disappointed us.
   b. Miss Jones wasn't there.
   c. That Miss Jones wasn't there disappointed us.

how a. S + was amazing.
   b. The train was uncomfortable.
   c. How uncomfortable the train was was amazing.

■ Make single sentences from the groups of sentences below. The abbreviations listed on page 245 are used here, except that when **T-sub** is called for, the word to be used in applying it is given: **(T-sub, that), (T-sub, how)**.

1. The driver thought + S **(T-rel)**: The driver called for us. **(T-sub, that)**: The roads would be icy.

2. S + was astonishing. **(T-sub, how)**: The trapeze artist could fly through the air gracefully. (Now apply **T-it**.)

3. S + was astonishing. **(T-sub, that)**: The trapeze artist could fly through the air gracefully. (Now apply **T-it**.)

4. The children were afraid + S **(T-rel, deletion** and **T-noun modifier)**: The children were young. **(T-rel, deletion)**: The children were in the park. **(T-sub, that)**: A storm was coming. **(T-rel, deletion** and **T-noun modifier)**: A storm was violent.

5. S + was remarkable. **(T-sub, how)**: The parrot could talk clearly. **(T-rel, deletion)**: The parrot was in the cage. (Now apply **T-it**.)

6. The girls were pleased. **(T-comp)**: The boys were pleased + S **(T-sub, that)**: The lady had provided an orchestra. **(T-rel)**: The lady gave the party.

7. **(T-neg)**: We are disappointed + S **(T-sub, that)**: The test has been postponed. **(T-rel)**: Miss Watkins had planned the test for tomorrow. (Now delete any relative pronoun you can.)

8. S + was amazing. **(T-sub, how)**: We heard the voice distinctly. **(T-poss)**: Tom has a voice. (Now apply **T-it**.)

9. S + was incredible. **(T-sub, how)**: The storm passed quickly. **(T-rel, deletion** and **T-noun modifier)**: The storm was sudden. (Now apply **T-it**.)

You have seen that many <u>ion</u> nouns have no underlying English verb, though most of them do have an underlying Latin verb. What has happened is that we have borrowed the noun from Latin, but we did not borrow the verb that goes with it. For example, we have the noun **section.** The **sect** of **section** comes from the Latin verb **secare,** which means to cut. We have in English no verb "sect" meaning to cut.

► Though words like **section** do not have underlying English verbs, they often have parts that we use in other verbs. For example, we have **bisect** and **intersect.** What do these verbs have to do with cutting? What nouns that end in <u>ion</u> can be made from them?

The first part of **position** comes from the Latin verb **ponere,** meaning to put. We have no verb "pone" with this meaning. But we do have the word **compose,** which means to put together.

You have noticed that there does not always appear to be a close similarity between an English word and a Latin word from which it is borrowed. For example, English **position** has **s** where Latin **ponere** has **n.**

You have seen that Latin verbs, like some English ones, had several forms. The participle form of the Latin verb **ponere** was **positus.** This was the form underlying the Latin <u>ion</u> form, **positionis.** And of course our word **position** comes from that.

■ One form of the noun-making morpheme <u>ion</u> is **ition,** as in **position.** Here are some familiar English verbs which contain the part **pose** from the Latin verb **ponere.** Make nouns from the verbs by adding **ition.** What letter will you drop from each of the English verbs?

compose	oppose	expose	suppose
propose	dispose	impose	transpose

What noun that names a word class can be made from the verb **prepose?**

■ Use each "pose" noun in a sentence. Look up any of them whose meaning you can't figure out.

► 1. So far, you have made **how** exclamations to match sentences like the following one, sentences that contain just one noun phrase, with an adjective or an adverb of manner in the predicate:

The day is amazingly beautiful.

The exclamation that matches this is "How beautiful the day is!" What word in the statement is dropped in making the exclamation? How is the position of the adjective in this statement changed?

■ 2. Write **how** exclamations to match the following:
   a. The dog was dangerously vicious.
   b. James spoke remarkably well.
   c. Alice works very effectively.

► 3. Study the following sentences:
   a. She is a very pretty girl.
   b. That collie is an unusually big dog.
   c. They are remarkably good men.

How many noun phrases does each sentence above contain?

■ 4. To write exclamations with **how** clauses from sentences that contain both a noun phrase subject and a noun phrase complement, like "She is a very pretty girl," we have to drop the intensifier, of course. But we can drop one of the noun phrases too. We could drop the subject, **she:**

How pretty the girl is!

Or, we could drop the complement, **a girl:**

How pretty she is!

Try writing two exclamations for **3b,** above, and two exclamations for **3c.**

■ 5. There is another way to make an exclamation for a sentence with a noun phrase in the predicate. It is done without dropping anything but the intensifier.

The word we use in asking questions about noun phrases is **what:** "What is she?" We can make noun clauses using **what** in the same way that we make them using **how:**

She is a very pretty girl. → what a pretty girl she is

We could then use the **what** clause in a noun phrase function:

What a pretty girl she is is amazing.

266

When we apply the **it** transformation to this sentence, we get the following: It is amazing what a pretty girl she is. Apply the **it** transformation to the following sentences:

    a. What a beautiful day it is is astonishing.

    b. What a shrill voice she has is incredible.

■ 6. Make exclamations from the following **it** transforms. Write the **what** part of the **it** transform, dropping the rest of the sentence. Begin the exclamation with a capital letter and put an exclamation mark after it to show that it expresses surprise or strong feeling.

    a. It is astonishing what a beautiful day it is.

    b. It is incredible what a shrill voice she has.

■ 7. Make exclamations from the following **it** transforms. Notice that the **how** clauses contain adjectives or adverbs after the **how,** and that the **what** clauses contain noun phrases after the **what.**

    a. It is surprising how clever she is.

    b. It is amazing how happily they play together.

    c. It is remarkable what a great curve the pitcher has.

    d. It is astonishing what a fine voice she has.

    e. It is ridiculous how silly he was.

    f. It is surprising what a goal-line stand they made.

    g. It is astonishing how angrily they argued.

    h. It is remarkable what a beautiful lawn Mr. Walker has.

■ 8. Now that you understand what an exclamation really means, you may simply write the **how** or **what** clause as an exclamation, without going through all the steps. You will have to decide for each of the following sentences whether to use **how** or **what.** Then write the exclamation to match the sentence. Begin it with a capital letter and put an exclamation mark after it.

    a. He is a very strong boy.

    b. This bus is very slow.

    c. She is a very attractive lady.

    d. Tom talks very slowly.

    e. That is a very hot fire.

    f. She is a very skillful cook.

    g. She cooks very skillfully.

    h. He seems very intelligent.

    i. Mr. Watson plays an excellent game of golf.

On pages 112 and 113, you wrote different types of sentences, all of which started with the same basic structures. Let's try this kind of sentence writing again, starting not with morphemes, but with the basic structures beneath the surface. Then we'll begin to make choices that will bring the structures nearer and nearer to the surface — to the actual sentence.

We start with the basic structures, **NP** and **VP:**

$$NP \quad + \quad VP$$

For the NP, we could choose any of the four types, but let's begin with a personal pronoun, abbreviated **pers.** The VP could also be any one of several types, but for this first exercise, let's choose tense, the word **be,** and a complement. We now add these choices to our basic structures. When we choose **be,** of course, we have already selected one of the surface morphemes.

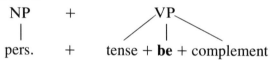

The only thing left to do before making choices of the actual morphemes is to decide which of the three possible kinds of complement after **be** to choose. Suppose we choose **adjective,** abbreviated **adj.,** and add it to the diagram.

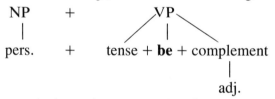

Now we are ready to choose exactly what morphemes we will use. To start the exercise, suppose we choose the following:

pers.: you   tense: pres.   adj.: careful

We now have this morpheme string:

$$\underline{you} + \underline{pres.} + \underline{be} + \underline{careful}$$

■ 1. Write a question based on the string.
■ 2. Write a negative statement, using these morphemes.
■ 3. Write a negative question, using a contraction.
■ 4. Write a command based on this string.
■ 5. Write an exclamation based on the string.

▶ 6. Suppose that you substitute another personal pronoun for **you** in the morpheme string on page 268. Which of the six kinds of sentences listed there could not be written with a different pronoun?

▶ 7. Study the diagram of basic structures below and then answer the questions:

NP   +   VP

det. + common n.   +   tense + verb + NP

(article)	(count)			(transitive) det.	+	common n.
	(singular)			(article)		(count)
	(nonhuman)					(singular)
	(abstract)					(human)

a. What choices are possible for **det.?**

b. From the diagram, tell what follows the kind of verb that is called **transitive.** Does a noun phrase object have to be a **det. + n.?** What choices are possible for **det.** in the noun phrase object of the verb?

■ 8. Here is a list of choices for the structures shown in 8:

det. (article): **the**

common n. (count, singular, nonhuman, abstract): **decision**

tense (present or past): **past**

verb (transitive): **bother**

det. (article): **the**

common n. (count, singular, human): **pitcher**

We have the following morpheme string at this point:

the + decision + past + bother + the + pitcher

a. Write a yes/no question for this string.

b. Write a negative statement.

c. Write a negative question.

d. Write an expanded noun phrase, using the relative clause transformation and expanding the first noun phrase.

e. Write a subordinate clause, using **T-sub, that.**

f. Write an expanded noun phrase using **T-rel** and expanding the second noun phrase.

■ 9. In the diagram above, substitute a different kind of NP for subject, and make other original choices. Then carry out **9a–f** for your new morpheme string.

1. Add the morpheme <u>ion</u> to the verbs in heavy black type and use the resulting nouns to complete the sentences.   If you make mistakes, study pages 247–48.

  a. **pronounce**   The word _____ comes from Latin.
  b. **decide**   The court handed down its _____.
  c. **omit**   The apostrophe may mark the _____ of a letter.
  d. **apply**   A driver must make an _____ for a license.
  e. **subtract**   The _____ of 17 from 36 leaves 19.
  f. **except**   The spelling of **does** is an _____.

2. Add the morpheme <u>ion</u> to the verbs in heavy black type and use the resulting nouns to complete the sentences.   If you make mistakes, study page 257.

  a. **describe**   The robber's _____ appeared in the papers.
  b. **receive**   The mayor's _____ was a splendid occasion.
  c. **absorb**   Plants get nourishment by the _____ of liquids.
  d. **assume**   When we take something for granted, we make an _____.
  e. **invent**   The _____ of the airplane is credited to the Wrights.

3. Write three English words that contain the suffix **ition.** If you make mistakes, study page 265.

4. Write the "how" questions that you could ask about these statements.   If you make mistakes, study pages 249–50.

  a. The gardener is lazy.
  b. The old lady walks slowly.
  c. The story is silly.
  d. The lesson seems challenging.

5. Make **how** noun clauses from the following "how" questions and use them as subjects of sentences like "How hot the room is is unbelievable."   If you make mistakes, study pages 249–50.

  a. How carefully does Mr. Wilkins drive?
  b. How pretty is his sister?
  c. How sick is the kitten?
  d. How exciting is that novel?

6. Apply the **it** transformation to the following sentences that contain **how** clauses. If you make mistakes, study pages 258–59.

a. How easy the work was is unbelievable.

b. How quickly he thinks is remarkable.

c. How stupid she was is amazing.

d. How thoughtless we were is astonishing.

7. Make exclamations with **how** from the following **it** transforms. If you make mistakes, study page 259.

a. It is ridiculous how poorly we spelled.

b. It is terrible how fierce the storm was.

c. It is outrageous how cruelly they treat their pets.

d. It is absurd how unbecoming that hat is.

Make **how** clauses from the **b** sentences below and embed them in the **a** sentences. If the **how** clause functions as subject, apply the **it** transformation. If you make mistakes, study page 263.

8. a. We know + S

   b. She tried hard.

9. a. S + was pitiful.

   b. He had become thin.

10. Make exclamations from the following **it** transforms, using **what** or **how**. If you make mistakes, study pages 259, 266–67.

a. It is incredible what a great game Jim played.

b. It is ridiculous how clumsily he threw the ball.

c. It is surprising what a handsome house they bought.

d. It is delightful how good-humored they are.

e. It is astonishing what a meal she turned out.

11. Make exclamations from the following statements. You will have to decide for each sentence whether to begin the exclamation with **what** or **how**. If you make mistakes, study pages 259, 266–67.

a. This is a very useful book.

b. The horse was very thin.

c. The man drove very slowly.

d. She is a very fine student.

e. His bulldog is a very gentle pet.

PART

10

A Poem

The black poet, Langston Hughes, writes of what dreams are made of.   Read the poem to yourself.   Listen as your teacher reads it or plays a recording of it.

Dream Variation

To fling my arms wide
In some place of the sun,
To whirl and to dance
Till the white day is done.
Then rest at cool evening
Beneath a tall tree
While night comes on gently,
   Dark like me —
That is my dream!

To fling my arms wide
In the face of the sun,
Dance! whirl! whirl!
Till the quick day is done.
Rest at pale evening . . .
A tall, slim tree . . .
Night coming tenderly
   Black like me.

LANGSTON HUGHES

Dream Variation

▶ What does **variation** mean?   Is the last stanza of the poem a variation on what is said in the first stanza?   How is the last stanza like the first?   How does it vary from it?

■ Start a sentence with the words "My dream is . . ." Then complete the sentence by writing the first stanza. Did you write a good English sentence? How did you change the punctuation? Does your sentence say the same thing as the first stanza of the poem?

► The poet contrasts the day with the evening and night. What adjective does he use to describe the day in the first stanza? What adjective does he use to describe the day in the second stanza?

► How does he contrast day and evening — what adjectives does he use to describe evening in the first and the last stanzas?

► How does he describe the coming of the night in the first stanza and the last stanza?

A Prefix from Latin

The morphemes we have been studying so far have been represented by suffixes — additions at the ends of words. English is a suffixing language. We indicate changes of word class by derivational morphemes, which are represented by word endings, such as **ly** or **ion.** We show possession, comparison, plural, and tense and other forms of verbs by inflectional morphemes, which are also represented by word endings, such as **ed** or **'s.**

A great many words which have come to us from Latin have beginning syllables which were prefixes in Latin. These Latin prefixes represented morphemes in Latin, but to us they may seem to be part of the basic word. For instance, the **ex** in **expel** may not look like a prefix to us. If we removed it, **pel** would be left, and there isn't any English word **pel.** But the Latin word **expellere,** from which **expel** comes, was made up of a Latin prefix and a Latin verb:

expel: ex out + **pellere** to put

■ Here are some other words which have the Latin prefix **ex,** meaning out. Study them. Then copy the definitions below and write each English verb beside its definition.

ex out + **clamare** to cry	exclaim
ex out + **emere** to take	example

274

Latin		English
ex out + **portare** to carry		export
ex out + **plaudere** to clap		explode
ex out + **habere** to hold		exhibit
ex out + **causa** accusation		excuse
ex out + **ciere** to arouse		excite
ex out + **haurire** to draw		exhaust
ex out + **claudere** to close		exclude
ex out + **capere** to take		except
ex out + **ponere** to put		expose
ex out + **pendere** to pay		expend
ex out + **torquere** to twist		extort
ex out + **trahere** to draw		extract
ex out + **tendere** to stretch		extend
ex out + **premere** to press		express
ex out + **planare** to make level		explain
ex out + **sistere** to be located		exist
ex out + **cedere** to go		exceed

a. To cause to blow up with a loud noise.
b. To obtain (money) from someone by threats.
c. To straighten or stretch out, as an arm or leg.
d. Something taken from a group to show what others in the group are like.
e. To shut out or keep from entering a place.
f. To put on view; to hold out for examination.
g. To be greater than.
h. To draw off, as gas or vapor.
i. To squeeze out or press out; to state or put into words.
j. To free from blame.
k. To draw out or pull out by force.
l. To arouse strong feeling or emotion in.
m. To put out in view or in an unprotected place.
n. To carry or send (goods) to other countries for sale.
o. To pay out or spend.
p. To take out of, or exempt from, consideration.
q. To cry out abruptly; to speak out with strong or sudden emotion.
r. To have actual being; to continue to live.
s. To give the reasons for; to give the meaning of.

275

You have studied these types of sentences this year:
statements — affirmative and negative
questions — "yes/no," affirmative and negative "wh"
commands — affirmative and negative
exclamations

■ Copy each sentence below, punctuate it correctly, and tell what type of sentence it is.
1. Please close the window
2. Isn't that lady your mother
3. What a magnificent painting that is
4. Remove your hat, please
5. Where did you put my coat
6. The beggar held a cup of pencils
7. How silly that girl was
8. The snow on Mt. McKinley doesn't melt all year
9. What did your brother say
10. Were the Williamsons at home
11. When will the party be
12. Don't forget your gloves

■ Write each affirmative statement below as a negative statement. If you prefer, use a contraction.
13. That actor will appear again in this play.
14. The package from your uncle has arrived.
15. The truck stopped at your house.
16. The toys were put away.
17. The men work on Saturday.

■ Write an affirmative "yes/no" question to match each of the following affirmative statements:
18. People can come to the park the year round.
19. That lady is the librarian.
20. Molly bakes pies.
21. He had been studying mathematics.
22. The gentlemen were on time.

■ Write a negative "yes/no" question to match each of the following negative statements. Use contractions.
23. That pony does not belong to Sally.
24. The girls will not wash the dishes.

276

25. Roses do not grow well in this climate.
26. The people were not pleased with the show.
27. Bob had not finished his homework.

■ Write a **wh** question to match each statement below.
28. Mr. Patrick will arrive at seven.
29. The farmer stored the hay in the barn.
30. The girls dance gracefully.
31. Mrs. Blanding has lived in Mexico.
32. They were in the balcony.
33. He studies at night.

■ Make affirmative commands of the following statements.
34. You are alert.
35. You think ahead.
36. You are thinking about the problem.
37. You walk more slowly.
38. You brush your teeth after meals.

■ Transform the following affirmative statements into negative commands.
39. You are impudent.
40. You trample the flowers.
41. You are silly.
42. You worry about the future.
43. You are late.

■ Make exclamations from the following **it** transforms.
44. It is astonishing how quiet she is.
45. It is amazing what a fine speaker he is.
46. It is surprising how carefully he works.
47. It is remarkable how quietly they play.
48. It is incredible what a modest girl she is.
49. It is astounding how tactful she is.

■ Make exclamations to match the following statements. You will have to decide whether to use **how** or **what.**
50. She is a very unusual woman.
51. He is a very strong man.
52. They are very courageous.
53. We were very lucky people.
54. Mr. Smith is a very happy person.
55. Miss Ellis is very kind.
56. Ralph plays the piano beautifully.

▶ Study the following examples of exclamations:
  a. How reckless he is!
  b. How recklessly he plays!
  c. What a reckless player he is!

Do the three exclamations have the form of statements or of subordinate clauses?   Can they be embedded in **it** transforms? Give an **it** transform for each of the three exclamations.

You remember that the exclamation mark after an exclamation means that the sentence shows surprise or astonishment. You have probably noticed that writers often use exclamation marks after sentences that do not have the form of an exclamation.   When an exclamation mark is used after a statement, question, or command, it means that the writer thinks that the sentence expresses surprise, astonishment, or strong feeling:

  d. He is so reckless!   (Statement)
  e. Isn't he reckless!   (Question)
  f. Don't be so reckless!   (Command)

Simply putting an exclamation mark after a sentence doesn't make it an exclamation.   To be an exclamation, a sentence must have the form of a noun clause beginning with **how** or **what.**   Of course, questions, too, can begin with **how** or **what.**

▶ All of the following sentences are punctuated with exclamation marks, but not all of them are exclamatory sentences. Pick out the exclamations.   Tell what type each of the other sentences is.

  1. She was being very foolish!
  2. How foolish she looked!
  3. Didn't she look foolish!
  4. What a foolish girl she was!
  5. Don't be foolish!
  6. How foolishly she acted!
  7. Weren't her actions foolish!
  8. How could she be so foolish!

Skillful writers use exclamation marks sparingly because they know that punctuation doesn't put much meaning into writing.   Writing should stand on its own feet a much as possible.

You have had some experience earlier in using the same structures to write sentences of different types. In every case you began with structures that lie deep beneath the surface. You started with what we call the **deep structure** of the sentence, and then, by making various decisions as to what precisely would represent these deep structures, you came closer and closer to the sentence. At last you wrote a string of morphemes — a sequence of specific structures that lies just beneath the surface of the actual sentence itself.

The exercises that follow will give you more experience of this kind, and show you how to embed one sentence in another.

► In every case we will start with the same deep structure arrangement that underlies a simple sentence: NP + VP. What does NP stand for? What does VP represent?

► For the NP, we could choose any one of four types. What are the four types? The VP, also, could be any one of several types. What are some possibilities?

For the first exercise, suppose we choose for NP a personal pronoun. For the VP, we must have tense. Suppose that instead of a verb we choose the word **be.** When we choose **be,** we must also have a complement. At this point our diagram looks like this:

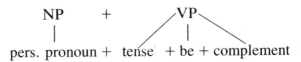

To develop this diagram still further, we must choose the actual morphemes. Suppose that we choose **you** for the personal pronoun, **present** for tense, **be,** and the adjective **quiet** for the complement. At this point, here is our diagram:

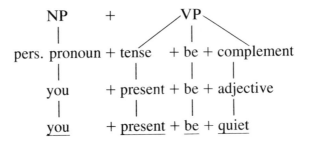

■ 1. The morpheme string in the last line of the diagram on page 279 is you + present + be + quiet. Write an affirmative statement based on this string.

■ 2. Write an affirmative command based on the string.

■ 3. Write an exclamation based on the string.

■ 4. Write an affirmative "yes/no" question, adding be + ing

■ 5. Write a negative statement, adding be + ing.

■ 6. Write an affirmative statement, adding have + part.

■ 7. Write a negative statement, adding have + part.

■ 8. Write a negative "yes/no" question, adding have + part.

Now suppose we begin a new diagram, this time choosing a proper noun for NP. We must, of course, have tense in the VP. We might also choose a verb.

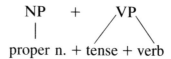

Now all that we need to do is to decide on the proper noun, the tense, and the verb. Suppose we choose **Nancy** for the proper noun and **past** for the tense. For the verb, we could choose one that does not require an object or one that does. We say that a verb which does not require an object is **intransitive.** What do we call the verb if it does require an object? Suppose we make our diagram as simple as possible by choosing an intransitive verb, say **cry.** Now we have the following:

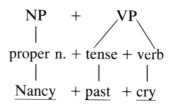

■ 9. Write an affirmative statement based on the string Nancy + past + cry.

■ 10. Write a negative statement for the string.

■ 11. Write an affirmative "yes/no" question for the string.

■ 12. Write a negative "yes/no" question.

Now let's keep in mind that we could add an adverbial to this string, although we don't have to. Suppose we want to add the information that she cried at the wedding. What kind of adverbial is **at the wedding?**

We could add this further information to our diagram:

$$
\begin{array}{ccc}
\text{NP} & + & \text{VP} \\
| & & /|\backslash \\
\text{proper n.} & + & \text{tense} + \text{verb} \\
| & | & | \\
\textbf{Nancy} & + \text{past} + & \text{cry} + \text{adv p} \\
| & | & | \\
\underline{\text{Nancy}} & + \underline{\text{past}} + & \underline{\text{cry}} + \text{S}
\end{array}
$$

▶ Here is a string from which you make an affirmative statement telling the place where Nancy cried. We will not go through all the steps of diagramming it from the structures NP + VP, although this could easily be done.

   the + place + past + be + at + the + wedding

Now the two strings can be combined into a single string:
a. <u>Nancy</u> + <u>past</u> + <u>cry</u> + S
b. <u>the</u> + <u>place</u> + <u>past</u> + <u>be</u> + <u>at</u> + <u>the</u> + <u>wedding</u> } →
c. <u>Nancy</u> + <u>past</u> + <u>cry</u> + <u>at</u> + <u>the</u> + <u>wedding</u>

▶ What structure from the **b** sentence was used to replace the **S** in the **a** sentence?

■ 13. Write an affirmative statement based on the string <u>Nancy</u> + <u>past</u> + <u>cry</u> + <u>at</u> + <u>the</u> + <u>wedding</u>.

■ 14. Write a negative statement based on the string.

■ 15. Write an affirmative "yes/no" question.

■ 16. Write a "wh" question for the string.

■ 17. Write a negative "yes/no" question.

▶ Finally, let's add another bit of information — that she cried at the wedding yesterday. What kind of adverbial would we add? Here is the morpheme string about Nancy, a string for a new **b** sentence, and the resulting **c** string:
a. <u>Nancy</u> + <u>past</u> + <u>cry</u> + <u>at</u> + <u>the</u> + <u>wedding</u> + S } →
b. <u>the</u> + <u>time</u> + <u>past</u> + <u>be</u> + <u>yesterday</u>
c. <u>Nancy</u> + <u>past</u> + <u>cry</u> + <u>at</u> + <u>the</u> + <u>wedding</u> + <u>yesterday</u>

■ 18. Write an affirmative statement based on this **c** string.

■ 19. Write a "wh" question using **when.**

■ 20. Write a different "wh" question.

■ 21. Write a negative statement.

■ 22. Write a "yes/no" question.

A Fatal Journey

The discovery of the North Pole was a triumph, but the discovery of the South Pole was a tragedy. In late 1911, two expeditions were trying to reach the South Pole. One was led by the Norwegian Roald Amundsen, the other by the Englishman Robert Falcon Scott. Scott and four companions reached the Pole on January 18, 1912, to find that Amundsen had been there before them. Because the weather was bad, the Scott group had made slow progress. The southern summer ended before they could get back, and they perished. When Scott's body was found, the diary from which the following is taken was found with it.

Captain Scott's Last Expedition

Sunday, March 11 (1912). The sky completely overcast when we started this morning. We could see nothing, lost the tracks, and doubtless have been swaying a good deal since — 3.1 miles for the forenoon — terribly heavy dragging — expected it. Know that 6 miles is about limit of our endurance now, if we get no help from wind or surfaces. We have 7 days' food and should be about 55 miles from One Ton Camp tonight, $6 \times 7 = 42$, leaving us 13 miles short of our distance, even if things get no worse. Meanwhile the season rapidly advances.

Monday, March 12. We did 6.9 miles yesterday, under our necessary average. Things are left much the same, Oates not pulling much, and now with hands as well as feet pretty well useless. We did 4 miles this morning in 4 hours 20 minutes — we may hope for 3 this afternoon, $7 \times 6 = 42$. We shall be 47 miles from the depot. I doubt if we can possibly do it. The surface remains awful, the cold intense, and our physical condition running down. God help us! Not a breath of favorable wind for more than a week, and apparently liable to head winds at any moment.

Wednesday, March 14. . . . This morning started with southerly breeze, set sail and passed another cairn at good speed; halfway, however, the wind shifted to W. by S. or W.S.W., blew through our wind clothes and into our mits. Poor Wilson horribly cold, could not get off ski for some time. Bowers and I practically made camp, and when we got into the tent at last we were all deadly cold. Then temp. now midday down −43° and the wind strong. We *must* go on, but now the making of every camp must be more difficult and dangerous. It must be near the end, but a merciful end. Poor Oates got it again in the foot. I shudder to think what it will be like tomorrow. . . .

Friday, March 16, or Saturday 17. Lost track of dates, but think the last is correct. Tragedy all along the line. At lunch, the day before yesterday, poor Titus Oates said he couldn't go on; he proposed we should leave him in his sleeping bag. That we could not do, and we induced him to come on, on the afternoon march. In spite of its awful nature for him, he struggled on and we made a few miles. At night he was worse and we knew the end had come.

Should this be found I want these facts recorded. Oates' last thoughts were of his Mother, but immediately before he took pride in thinking that his regiment would be pleased with the bold way in which he met his death. We can testify to his bravery. He has borne intense suffering for weeks without complaint, and to the very last was able and willing to discuss outside objects. He did not — would not — give up till the very end. He was a brave soul. This was the end. He slept through the night before last, hoping not to awake; but he woke in the morning — yesterday. It was blowing a blizzard. He said, "I am just going outside and may be some time." He went out into the blizzard and we have not seen him since. . . .

Sunday, March 18. Today, lunch, we are 21 miles from the depot. Ill fortune presses, but better may come. We have had more wind and drift from ahead yesterday; had to stop marching; wind N.W., force 4, temp. −35°. No human being could face it, and we are worn out *nearly.*

My right foot has gone, nearly all the toes — two days ago I was proud possessor of best feet. . . .

Monday, March 19. Lunch. We camped with difficulty last night, and were dreadfully cold till after supper of cold pemmican and biscuit and half a pannikin of cocoa cooked over the spirit. Then, contrary to expectation, we got warm and slept well. Today we started in the usual dragging manner. Sledge dreadfully heavy. We are $15\frac{1}{2}$ miles from the depot and ought to get there in three days. What progress! We have two days' food but barely a day's fuel. All our feet are getting bad — Wilson's best, my right foot worst, left all right. There is no chance to nurse one's feet till we can get hot food into us. Amputation is the least I can hope for now, but will the trouble spread? That is the serious question. The weather doesn't give us a chance — the wind from N. to N.W., and $-40°$ temp. today.

Wednesday, March 21. Got within 11 miles of depot. Monday night, had to lay up all yesterday in severe blizzard. Today forlorn hope. Wilson and Bowers going to depot for fuel.

Thursday, March 22 and 23. Blizzard bad as ever. Wilson and Bowers unable to start — tomorrow last chance — no fuel and only one or two of food left — must be near the end. Have decided it shall be natural — we shall march for the depot with or without our effects and die in our tracks.

Thursday, March 29. Since the 21st we have had a continuous gale from W.S.W. and S.W. We had fuel to make two cups of tea apiece and bare food for two days on the 20th. Every day we have been ready to start for our depot 11 *miles* away, but outside the door of the tent it remains a scene of whirling drift. I do not think we can hope for any better things now. We shall stick it out to the end, but we are getting weaker, of course, and the end cannot be far.
    It seems a pity, but I do not think I can write more. — R. Scott.

For God's sake, look after our people.

R. SCOTT

► How much time had passed between the date when the expedition reached the South Pole and the beginning of the diary entries given here? You know, of course, that the seasons of the Southern Hemisphere reverse those of the Northern: their summer is our winter, etc. About what season would March 11 be at the South Pole?

► What is Scott multiplying when he writes "6 × 7 = 42"? One Ton Camp was a place between them and their base camp where a ton of supplies had been left for them. If they could reach that camp they would be safe. How much will they fall short when their food runs out, at the rate they are going?

► Scott says "if we get no help from wind or surfaces." The sledge had sails to help push it along if the wind was blowing from the right direction. What do you think he means by **surfaces?**

► Why, in the entry for March 12, has "6 × 7" become "7 × 6"? What is meant by **head winds?**

► How did the weather improve for them on March 14? Look up **cairn** in a dictionary. How cold was it?

► Oates was at this time the weakest of the group. What did he suggest that the others do? What was their response to his suggestion? What did Oates take pride in thinking as he neared his death? What did he hope when he went to sleep that night? What did he do when he woke up? Why do you think he did that instead of just waiting to die in the tent?

► How far were they from One Ton Camp on March 18? What is meant by "two days ago I was proud possessor of best feet"?

► How far were they from the camp on March 19? How much food and fuel had they left? What did Scott think about his feet?

► On March 19 they had a two days' supply of food and one of fuel left. How long, at least, did they live after that? What final desperate plans did they make that they were unable to carry out?

The Antarctic Continent is so far from Europe, its climate is so severe, and the seas surrounding it are so stormy and clogged with ice, that it was the last great land mass on earth to be discovered. The coast was first sighted by navigators about a century and a half ago. Since that time many brave men have explored that rugged, uninhabited land, and a number of them have lost their lives in the attempt, as Captain Scott and his men did.

Write a report describing the Continent of Antarctica.

To do this, you will need to use dictionaries, encyclopedias, histories, or accounts of polar exploration. It will be necessary to study a map of Antarctica, which you can find in a book of maps called an **atlas.** If there are geography textbooks in your classroom or library, you may be able to find considerable information in one of these. A globe will be useful, also, in picturing the distance from Europe to the Antarctic Continent.

As you collect your information, make notes to help you remember the points you have discovered. Here is an example of notes that one might take on the location of Antarctica:

Antarctica

Location

The southernmost part of Atlantic, Pacific, Indian Oceans. Surrounding water called Antarctic Ocean. South Pole roughly in the center of the land mass. Coast surrounded by masses of floating ice. Nearest land, 600 miles, Cape Horn in S. America. Africa, Australia and New Zealand farther away.

When you have collected your information in the form of notes, organize them into an outline under main topics. The following is an example of possible topics:

I. Where Antarctica is
II. Difficulty of exploration
III. What the continent is like

You might write one or more paragraphs under each topic.

You have studied some words from Latin that begin with the prefix **ex,** meaning out. One of these is **expose,** which means to put out (where it can be seen).

▶ The prefix **ex** is only one of several very common prefixes from Latin. Another is **sub,** which means under, beneath, below, or away.

subtract: **sub** away + **trahere** to draw

The meaning of the English word **way** is road. So what does **subway** mean?

■ Here are some other words which have the Latin prefix **sub.** Study them. Then copy the definitions below and write each English word beside its definition. Notice that **sub** may be prefixed to English words as well as Latin.

Latin Origin	English Word
sub under + **dividere** to separate	subdivide
sub under	subfloor
sub under + **jacere** to throw	subject
sub under	sublet
sub under + **mare** the sea	submarine
sub under + **mergere** to plunge	submerge
sub under + **mittere** to send	submit
sub under + **scribere** to write	subscribe
sub under + **sidere** to settle	subside
sub under	substandard
sub under + **terra** the earth	subterranean

a. Being below the surface of the earth; underground.
b. A rough floor under the finished floor.
c. To sign an agreement or make an agreement.
d. To let (or rent) a rented property to someone else.
e. One who is under the governing power of a monarch.
f. A ship that operates below the surface of the sea.
g. To become quiet; to settle down.
h. To plunge under the surface of the water.
i. To divide (land) into lots for sale.
j. To place under the authority of someone; to surrender.
k. Below or under the standard.

REVIEW: The Comparative and Superlative Transformations

▶ The morpheme of comparison, which you studied earlier in the year, is abbreviated <u>comp</u>. It is used to compare one person or thing with one other person or thing. You may remember that this morpheme is expressed in more than one way. Study the following example, in which it is said that Bill has the same amount of wit as Joe does:

    a. Bill is witty + <u>comp</u>. + S   }→

    b. Joe is witty.

    c. Bill is as witty as Joe is witty. →

       Bill is as witty as Joe is.   **or**

       Bill is as witty as Joe.

What word in the verb phrase of **c** must be omitted? Can the whole verb phrase of **b** be deleted from the **c** sentence?

■ Apply the comparison transformation to the following, using **as . . . as** to express the morpheme <u>comp</u>., and deleting the entire verb phrase of the **b** sentence.

  1. a. Jean is friendly + <u>comp</u>. + S

     b. Jane is friendly.

  2. a. The creek is wide + <u>comp</u>. + S

     b. A river is wide.

  3. a. The motorboat is fast + <u>comp</u>. + S

     b. An automobile is fast.

▶ To tell how witty Bill is, we could also compare him to someone who isn't as witty as he is. For this kind of comparison we may use **er than** to represent the morpheme <u>comp</u>., as shown in the following example:

    a. Bill is witty + <u>comp</u>. + S   }→

    b. Tom is witty.

    c. Bill is witty + er than + Tom is witty

What is witty + er? What is the finished **c** sentence? What word must you drop? What else may you drop?

■ Apply the comparison transformation, using **er than** and dropping the verb phrase of the **b** sentence.

  4. a. The horse is strong + <u>comp</u>. + S

     b. The ox is strong.

  5. a. Gold is scarce + <u>comp</u>. + S

     b. Silver is scarce.

6. a. Mr. Wilkins is wise + comp. + S

   b. Mr. Thompson is wise.

▶ A number of adjectives don't take **er than** to express the morpheme comp. This is especially true of longer adjectives. For these, we use **more . . . than** to replace comp.

   a. Alfred is original + comp. + S ⎫
                                    ⎬ →
   b. Wally is original. ⎭

   c. Alfred is + more + original + than + Wally is original.

What is the finished **c** sentence with the verb phrase of **b** omitted?

■ Make comparisons by using **more . . . than** to replace comp. Drop the entire verb phrase of the **b** sentence.

  7. a. The first poem seemed familiar + comp. + S

     b. The second poem seemed familiar.

  8. a. The rapids are dangerous + comp. + S

     b. The waterfall is dangerous.

If we want to compare more than two persons or things, we use the superlative morpheme, sup. With adjectives that take the **er than** form of comp., we use **the . . . est of** form of sup.:

   a. Tom is strong + sup. + S ⎫
                           ⎬ →
   b. The five boys are strong. ⎭

   c. Tom is + the + strong + est of + the five boys are strong.

With sup. we must omit the verb phrase of the **b** sentence. What is the finished form of the **c** sentence?

▶ With adjectives that require the **more . . . than** form of comp., we use **the most . . . of** to represent sup.:

   a. Alice is faithful + sup. + S ⎫
                          ⎬ →
   b. The students are faithful. ⎭

   c. Alice is + the most + faithful + of + the students are faithful.

What is the finished **c** sentence?

■ Apply the superlative transformation to each of the following. Use **the most . . . of** with one and **the . . . est of** with the other to replace sup.

  9. a. Janet is popular +   10. a. Harry is tall + sup. + S
       sup. + S   b. The three boys are tall.

    b. The girls in the class
      are popular.

▶ A sentence that contains the verb **have** shows possession:

The dog has a collar.

Of course, we can show possession by adding an apostrophe and **s** to a regular noun like **dog: dog's.** By using this possessive form of **dog,** we can rewrite the "have" sentence as a possessive noun phrase:

the dog's collar

A determiner plus noun, like **the collar,** is one type of noun phrase. We say that **the dog's collar** is an **expanded noun phrase.** What word was added to **the collar** to expand it?

▶ Having changed the "have" sentence, "The dog has a collar," to the possessive noun phrase **the dog's collar,** we are ready to replace the noun phrase **the collar** in another sentence with the expanded noun phrase:

    a. The collar is too tight. → NP + is too tight⎫
                                                      ⎬ →
    b. The dog has a collar. → the dog's collar ⎭
    c. The dog's collar is too tight.

Where does the last part of the **c** sentence come from? What does the expanded noun phrase, **the dog's collar,** replace?

■ Apply the possessive transformation to the following pairs of sentences. Replace a noun phrase in the **a** sentence each time with an expanded noun phrase made from the **b** sentence — the sentence that contains the verb **have.**

  1. a. The coats are upstairs.
      b. The ladies have coats.
  2. a. The bib fell on the floor.
      b. The baby has a bib.
  3. a. The saddle is trimmed with silver.
      b. The cowboy has a saddle.
  4. a. The golf bags are stored in lockers.
      b. The men have golf bags.
  5. a. The jacket is red and white.
      b. She has a jacket.
  6. a. Nobody could guess the secret.
      b. We have a secret.
  7. a. Crows robbed the nest.
      b. The robins have a nest.

A Poem

The noted black poet Langston Hughes speaks of the antiquity and dignity of the Negro race in this poem.

The Negro Speaks of Rivers

I've known rivers:
I've known rivers ancient as the world and older than the
   flow of human blood in human veins.

My soul has grown deep like the rivers.

I bathed in the Euphrates when dawns were young.
I built my hut near the Congo and it lulled me to sleep.
I looked upon the Nile and raised the pyramids above it.
I heard the singing of the Mississippi when Abe Lincoln
   went down to New Orleans, and I've seen its
   muddy bosom turn all golden in the sunset.
I've known rivers:
Ancient, dusky rivers.

My soul has grown deep like the rivers.

LANGSTON HUGHES

The Negro Speaks of Rivers

▶ The poet uses the first person throughout this poem. Do you think he is really speaking of himself, or is he speaking of the Negro race in general?

▶ What line is repeated at the end of the poem?

▶ The Euphrates and, near it, the Tigris are rivers of Iraq. Some of the world's earliest great civilizations arose in the Tigris and Euphrates valleys. Where is Iraq? Where is the Congo River? Where is the Nile?

▶ What river in the United States does the poet identify with the black race? How does the poet describe the majesty of the Mississippi? What has Abe Lincoln to do with the theme of this poem?

REVIEW: The Subordinate Clause Transformation

You have learned that any statement at all can be made into a subordinate clause by simply putting the word **that** before it.

The sailboat heeled over before the breeze. →

that the sailboat heeled over before the breeze

The subordinate clause can then be embedded in another sentence:

We saw that the sailboat heeled over before the breeze. Study the clauses which begin with **that** in the following sentences:

a. We noticed that the girl had left the house.

b. We noticed the girl that had left the house.

▶ 1. If we remove **that** from the clause in Sentence **a,** is what is left a complete sentence? Then is the **that** clause in the first sentence a subordinate clause or a relative clause?

▶ 2. If we remove **that** from the clause in Sentence **b,** is what is left a complete sentence? Then is the **that** clause in the second sentence a subordinate clause or a relative clause?

▶ Tell whether the **that** clause in each of the following sentences is a subordinate clause or a relative clause.

3. The statement that he made was held against him.

4. That he made the statement was held against him.

5. We remembered that the man had fixed the motor.

6. We remembered the man that had fixed the motor.

7. The girl that we knew helped Mr. Otis.

8. That we knew the girl helped Mr. Otis.

9. He understood that the carpenter had built the porch.

10. He understood the carpenter that had built the porch.

11. We saw the man that lives next door.

12. We saw that the man lives next door.

▶ 13. In the subordinate clause transformation, we replace S in the **a** sentence with a subordinate clause from the **b** sentence:

a. S + was held against him.

b. He made the statement. → that he made the statement ⎫
⎬ →
c. That he made the statement was held against him. ⎭

What replaces S in Sentence **a** to make Sentence **c?**

■ Apply the subordinate clause transformation to the following sets of **a** and **b** sentences:

14. a. Mr. Wilson suspected + S
    b. Somebody was taking his strawberries.
15. a. Janet said + S
    b. She would not agree to the suggestion.
16. a. S + was not clearly understood.
    b. The girls would bring the dessert.
17. a. Nobody knew + S
    b. The Watsons were in town.
18. a. The man in the car feared + S
    b. Children would dart into the street.
19. a. S + was widely predicted.
    b. The new factory would fail.
20. a. The mayor was surprised + S
    b. The bond issue was passed by the voters.

► 21. When a **that** subordinate clause functions as subject of the sentence in which it is embedded, we usually apply the **it** transformation:

a. S + helped Mr. Otis. ⎫
b. We knew the girl. ⎬ (by **T-sub, that**) →

c. That we knew the girl helped Mr. Otis. (by **T-it**) →
   It helped Mr. Otis that we knew the girl.

Where does the **it** come when **T-it** is applied to the **c** sentence? What structure in the **c** sentence follows the **it**? Did this structure originally come from the **a** sentence or the **b** sentence?

■ Apply **T-sub, that** to each of the following and write the **c** sentence. Then apply **T-it** to the **c** sentence.

22. a. S + annoyed the bus driver.
    b. We sang all the way to school.
23. a. S + surprised everybody.
    b. Our school won the safety award.
24. a. S + offended the speaker.
    b. Everybody laughed.
25. a. S + pleased the gardener.
    b. His employers loved flowers.
26. a. S + startled the landlord.
    b. His tenants threatened to sue him.

■ Use transformations according to the directions to combine each group of sentences below into a single sentence. The abbreviations used in the directions are explained on pages 245 and 264. You may add to the list (**T-sub, what**) now that you have made subordinate clauses and exclamations with **what.**

1. I was thinking + S (**T-sub, what**): It is a pity. (**T-sub, that**): The weather is stormy.

2. (**T-neg**): You know + S (**T-sub, how**): You are lucky + S (**T-sub, that**): You missed the train. (**T-rel**): The train stalled in the tunnel.

3. The lady said + S (**T-rel**): The lady lost the purse. (**T-rel, deletion** and **T-noun modifier**): The purse was brown. (**T-sub, that**): She would put an ad in the paper.

4. S + was remarkable. (**T-sub, that** and **T-neg**): The girl broke a bone. (**T-rel**): The girl fell into the swimming pool. (**T-rel** and **T-noun modifier**): The swimming pool was empty. (Now apply **T-it.**)

5. The fisherman cast a fly so skillfully + S (**T-rel**): The fisherman had waded into the water. (**T-rel, deletion** and **T-noun modifier**): The water was fast. (**T-rel, deletion**): The water was below the pool. (**T-sub, that** and **T-neg**): It disturbed the water.

6. S + pleased Miss Ellis. (**T-sub, that**): The ladies told everybody + S (**T-rel**): The ladies had heard her sing. (**T-sub, what**): She had a voice. (**T-rel, deletion** and **T-noun modifier**): The voice was remarkable. (Now apply **T-it.**)

7. A heron caught something. (**T-rel, deletion**): A heron was wading in the water. (**T-rel, deletion** and **T-noun modifier**): The water was shallow. (**T-rel**): Something resembled a turtle. (**T-rel, deletion** and **T-noun modifier**): A turtle was small.

8. (**T-neg**): The girl suspected + S (**T-rel, deletion**): The girl was at the door. (**T-sub, that**): Something had gone wrong inside the house.

9. We all said + S (**T-sub, what**): It was a shame. (**T-sub, that** and **T-neg**): Paula could be there.

▶ 1. You may remember that the definite article is **the,** and the nondefinite articles are **a, some,** and **null** (∅). When **a** is used before a noun that begins with a vowel sound, what form of the article is used? What kinds of nouns may have the null article before them as determiner?

▶ 2. Study the following sentence. Is **robin** a count or a noncount noun? What article functions as determiner before **robin?** Think what the nondefinite article means.

A robin was on its nest.

In this sentence does **a** refer to one robin?

▶ 3. Now study the sentence and think what the article **a** before **robin** means:

A robin has a red breast.

Does this **a** mean that just one robin has a red breast, or does it mean that all robins have red breasts?

As you see, the article **a** has two meanings when it is used as a determiner. In the first example it refers to one robin and has the meaning **one.** In the second example it does not refer to one robin, but to robins in general.

▶ 4. Would you say that the article **a** functions as determiner for singular count nouns or for plural count nouns?

▶ 5. Now study the following sentence with a plural noun phrase. Is the noun in the noun phrase count or noncount?

Some robins are on the lawn.

In this sentence does **some** refer to a certain group of robins? When a determiner refers to one or a group that can be identified, we say that it is a **referring** determiner. So the referring article **a** means one and is used before singular count nouns. The referring article **some** refers to a group that can be identified and goes with plural count nouns.

▶ 6. At this point, study **some** in these sentences:
   a. Some robins are on the lawn.
   b. Some people dislike parsnips.

Which **some** is pronounced (səm)? The **some** in Sentence **a,** with the vowel /ə/, is an article. The other **some** has the vowel /u/. It is pronounced (sum). It is not the article **some.**

► 7. Here is another sentence that contains a count noun in the noun phrase subject. Is the noun singular or plural? What is the determiner?

    a. Robins have red breasts.

Which of the following sentences means about the same as Sentence **a?**

    b. A robin was on its nest.

    c. A robin has a red breast.

Since the **a** in Sentence **c** is general, not referring, would you say that the null determiner, Ø, is general or referring?

► 8. Now let's look at noncount nouns with the nondefinite articles. Study the following sentence in which the article **some** (səm) is used with the noncount noun **mud:**

Some mud got on the rug.

Does the **some** refer to a particular quantity of mud? Then is the article **some** in this sentence referring or general?

► 9. In the following sentence, the article before the noncount noun is Ø:

Mud is dirty.

In this sentence, does the nondefinite article Ø mean some particular quantity of mud, or mud in general? Then is Ø before noncount nouns referring or general?

► 10. The article **a** is rarely used before noncount nouns, but it does appear in sentences like the following:

A mud that is found in Canada is radioactive.

Does this **a** mean one kind of mud or mud in general? Then is the **a** that is used in sentences like this the referring **a** or the general **a?**

► 11. Now let's look again at the definite article **the.** Study the following sentences in which **the** is used with count nouns:

    a. The robin was on its nest.

    b. The robins were on the lawn.

Can **the** be used with both singular and plural count nouns? In **a** and **b,** does it refer or is it general?

► 12. Here is another sentence in which **the** is used with a noun that means members of a kind or class in general:

The hippopotamus is a river animal.

Does the sentence "The hippopotamus is a river animal" mean that just one hippopotamus is a river animal, or that all hippopotamuses are river animals? Then can **the** in some cases be general, rather than referring?

▶ 13. Now study the following sentence and notice the determiner and noun that function as subject:

The mud is ten inches deep.

Is the noun **mud** count or noncount? Does the article **the** refer to mud in general or to a particular quantity of mud? Then when **the** is used with a noncount noun, do you think it is referring or general?

The following chart summarizes what you have discovered about the meaning of the article:

Count Nouns	**Nondefinite Articles**	Referring — Singular: A horse (threw me)
		General — Singular: A horse (whinnies)
		Referring — Plural: Some horses (are in that barn)
		General — Plural: Ø Horses (whinny)
	Definite Article	Referring — Singular: The horse (threw me)
		Plural: The horses (galloped)
		General — Singular: The horse (is a mammal)
Noncount Nouns	**Nondefinite Articles**	Referring: Some mud (got on the rug)
		A mud (that is radioactive . . .)
		General: Ø Mud (is dirty)
	Definite Article	Referring: The mud (is ten inches deep)

▶ Tell whether the articles in the following sentences are referring or general.

14. Some children were riding a pony.

15. A philatelist collects stamps.

16. The snow is melting.

17. Vinegar is sour.

18. The conductor collected the tickets.

19. The sea otter depends on a seaweed that grows along the coast.

20. Some soap got into my eyes.

21. An eagle nested beside the river.

22. Seals eat fish.

23. A child built the wall with some stones.

1. Copy the sentences below and complete them with these words that have the Latin prefix **ex: exhaust, exhibit, export.** If you make mistakes, study page 275.

    a. You _____ something when you send it abroad.

    b. You _____ gas from a room when you draw it out.

    c. You _____ something when you show it to people.

2. Copy the sentences below and complete them with these words that have the Latin prefix **sub: submerge, subside, subscribe.** If you make mistakes, study page 288.

    a. You _____ to an agreement when you write your name under it.

    b. You _____ when you plunge beneath the surface of the water.

    c. Disturbances _____ when they settle down.

3. Copy each sentence below, punctuate it correctly, and tell whether it is an affirmative or a negative statement, "yes/no" question, or command, or whether it is an exclamation, or whether it is a "wh" question. If you make mistakes, study pages 276–77.

    a. What a glorious view this is

    b. Please don't disturb the students

    c. The crackers are on the second shelf

    d. Can't you give me the answer

    e. Work hard

    f. How did Jack behave

    g. How skillfully he throws the ball

    h. John hasn't completed his report

    i. When will they deliver the new chair

    j. How beautiful the flowers look

    k. Were the peaches ripe

    l. Where have the ladies gone

4. Although the following sentences are punctuated with exclamation marks, they aren't exclamations in structure. Tell what type of sentence each one is. If you make mistakes, study page 278.

    a. Look out!

    b. Isn't his haircut terrible!

    c. This is so embarrassing!

Apply the comparison transformation, using **as . . . as** for the first comp. morpheme, **er than** for the second, **more . . . than** for the third.   If you make mistakes, study pages 289–90.

5. a. The girl is tall + comp. + S
   b. The boy is tall.
6. a. The wrestler is strong + comp. + S
   b. The weight lifter is strong.
7. a. The thunderstorms are frequent + comp. + S
   b. The hailstorms are frequent.

Apply the possessive transformation to the following pairs of sentences.   If you make mistakes, study page 291.

8. a. The gloves are lost.
   b. Jenny has gloves.
9. a. The man found the beads.
   b. The lady has some beads.
10. a. Spotlights play on the kennels at night.
    b. The dogs have kennels.

For each sentence below, write **subordinate** if the **that** clause is a subordinate clause.   Write **relative** if it is a relative clause.   If you make mistakes, study page 294.

11. That the lawyer took the case reassured Mr. Wilks.
12. The lawyer that took the case reassured Mr. Wilks.
13. We forgot that the plumber was on his way.
14. We forgot the plumber that was on his way.

Apply the subordinate clause transformation to the following.   If you make mistakes, study pages 294–95.

15. a. S + made us sad.
    b. The children were hungry.
16. a. We had guessed + S
    b. The play wouldn't start on time.
17. a. S + was unusual.
    b. Miss Allen came late.

Apply the **it** transformation to the following.   If you make mistakes, study page 295.

18. a. S + angered the hostess.
    b. Her guests were an hour late.
19. a. S + astonished me.
    b. The prize was awarded to Jean.
20. a. S + upset our cat.
    b. The cat food was full of cereal.

Essentials of the Grammar Taught in Grades Three, Four, and Five

1. Simple sentences like "The night is dark" have two main parts — a subject and a predicate. The subject is what the sentence is about, and it comes first in a simple sentence:

Subject	Predicate
a. The night	is dark.
b. Mr. Peters	was the umpire.
c. They	were in the water.
d. Somebody	broke the window.

The words or groups of words used as subjects are called noun phrases. There are four kinds of noun phrases that can act, or function, as subjects of simple sentences:

the night:	determiner plus common noun
Mr. Peters:	proper noun
they:	personal pronoun
somebody:	indefinite pronoun

2. In the noun phrase **the night, the** is a determiner. Determiners are words like **the, a, many, my, this,** which come before common nouns. They determine, or decide, something about the noun that follows them. In **the night,** the determiner **the** determines that we are talking about some special night.

Common nouns are words like **night, dog, city, boy.** They may have words as determiners before them, but they do not always have them. The subjects of the following sentences are nouns without determiners:

> Nights are dark.
> Ice is cold.

In the sentence "The night is dark," the determiner **the** showed that we were talking about some special night. But in "Nights are dark," **nights** just means nights in general. In the sentence "That ice is melting," the determiner **that** shows that we mean the quantity of ice in some special place. But in "Ice is cold," ice just means ice in general.

3. One group of determiners is made up of the four words **the, a, an, some.** These words are called **articles.** The

word **the** is called the **definite** article. The others are **non-definite** articles. The nondefinite articles **a** and **an** are two forms of the same word.

The nondefinite determiner **some** is used with plural subjects that refer to a group or with subjects that refer to a quantity of something, but we don't have a nondefinite article to use with subjects that don't refer to some group or quantity.

> Some ducks flew overhead. Some mud splattered the
> windshield.

> Ducks fly south in the fall. Mud is dirty.

It is useful to have a determiner for subjects like **ducks** and **mud.** For this reason a nondefinite determiner called null (∅) has been invented. The subjects **ducks** and **mud** above are said to have the null determiner, even though there is no word before them.

4. Noun phrases of the determiner + common noun type are either **singular** or **plural.** They are singular if they mean one person or thing. They are plural if they mean more than one.

> **Singular:** The dog barks at the moon.
> **Plural:** The dogs bark at the moon.

The common nouns in such noun phrases are also singular or plural. **Dog** is singular. **Dogs** is plural.

5. The most usual way to write the plural of a noun is to add the letter **s** to the singular form: **dog, dogs; boy, boys; book, books.**

When a word ends with the sound / sh /, / ch /, / j /, / s /, or / z /, we cannot simply add the sound / s / or / z / when we say the plural form. We have to add a syllable to the word. This syllable ends with the sound / əz / and is spelled **es:**

ashes	matches	arches	cages	judges
noses	boxes	blazes	kisses	faces

To spell the syllable **es** when a word already ends in **e,** we just add **s.**

When the singular form ends in consonant + **y,** we change **y** to **i** and add **es: sky, skies.** If a vowel letter precedes **y,** we just add **s: boy, boys.**

About a dozen common nouns that end in the letter **f** make their plurals in irregular ways. They change **f** to **v** and add **es: leaf, leaves.**

Some common nouns form their plurals by changing the vowel or making other changes in sound and spelling:

man — men   foot — feet   goose — geese
mouse — mice   tooth — teeth   woman — women
child — children   ox — oxen

A few nouns have the same form in the plural that they do in the singular:

sheep — sheep   deer — deer   moose — moose

6. In "Mr. Peters was the umpire," the noun phrase subject, **Mr. Peters,** is the name of a special person. Like **night, Mr. Peters** is a noun, but we call special nouns like this **proper nouns.** Proper nouns are written with capital letters, and they usually do not have determiners before them.

Names of persons are proper nouns, but there are other kinds, too:

Names of pets: Rover, Spot
Names of cities: San Diego, Chicago
Names of countries: Mexico, the United States
Names of states: Virginia, South Dakota
Names of days of the week: Tuesday, Sunday
Names of months of the year: May, December

Proper nouns often include the words **Mr., Mrs.,** or **Miss: Mr. Curtis, Mrs. Jones, Miss Wilkins. Mr.** and **Mrs.** are abbreviations. Like other parts of proper nouns, they are written with capital letters. We put periods after **Mr.** and **Mrs.** to show that they are abbreviations. **Miss** is not an abbreviation, so we do not put a period after it.

7. Another kind of noun phrase is a **personal pronoun.** A personal pronoun is one of the seven words **I, he, she, it, we, you, they.**

Like other noun phrases, personal pronouns may be used as subjects:

I am glad.   They are here.

Four of the personal pronouns, **he, she, it, they,** take the place of other noun phrases:

The boy studied.   → He studied.
Miss White laughed.   → She laughed.
The dog barked.   → It barked.
Some kittens live there. → They live there.

The personal pronouns **I, we,** and **you** don't take the place of other noun phrases. They just refer to the person speaking or the person spoken to.

8. Determiner + common noun, proper noun, and personal pronoun are three kinds of noun phrases. A fourth kind is the **indefinite pronoun.**

Indefinite pronouns are words made up of **every, some, any, no,** and **body, one,** or **thing.**

There are twelve indefinite pronouns:

everybody	everyone	everything
somebody	someone	something
anybody	anyone	anything
nobody	no one	nothing

All of the indefinite pronouns except **no one** are written as single words.

In the sentences below, the noun phrases used as subjects are indefinite pronouns:

Everyone enjoyed it.   No one left early.

Indefinite pronouns do not refer to definite people or things as the personal pronouns do. In simple sentences, they do not replace other noun phrases.

9. The predicate of a simple sentence is made up of a form, or structure, called a **verb phrase.** The verb phrase that functions as predicate **may** contain a noun phrase or other kinds of words or groups of words. But it **must** contain either a form of the word **be** or of a verb.

The word **be** is itself used in predicates like the ones in this sentence:

The day may be cloudy.

If we take away the word **may,** we use another form of **be** — the word **is:**

The day is cloudy.

Besides **be** itself, the forms of **be** which show tense are **is, are, am, was,** and **were.** If the predicate of a simple sentence has a form of **be** in it, then it must have another word or other words after it to complete the sentence. Each of the following sentences has a form of **be** in the predicate:

Bob is outside.   The girls are pretty.

I am the leader.   He was on the porch.

They were happy.

10. If a predicate does not have a form of **be** in it, it must have a verb. Verbs are words like **bark, walk, see, teach, drive.**

In a simple sentence that has a verb, the verb may be the first word in the predicate:

Mr. Waters drives a truck.

The first word in the predicate **drives a truck** is a form of the verb **drive.** In predicates that have verbs, other words or groups of words usually follow the verb. But the predicate may also be made up of just a verb alone:

Jenny sings.

11. A word or group of words that follows a form of **be** in a simple sentence and completes the sentence is called a **complement.** In the following sentence, a noun phrase functions as complement after **be:**

The girls were the winners.

One function of a noun phrase is **subject.** Another function that a noun phrase may have is that of **complement** after **be.**

12. Another kind of complement that may follow a form of **be** is a word called an **adjective.** Adjectives are words like **happy, large, cold, rainy, playful.** In the following sentence, a form of **be** is followed by an adjective:

The kittens are playful.

The word **very** can be used before an adjective, but not before a noun phrase.

13. An adjective may also function as complement after a very few verbs, like **seem, look, feel, taste, sound, smell:**

He seems happy.

14. Noun phrases may function as subjects and as complements after **be.** They may also function as complements after certain verbs, as in the following sentence:

George found a button.

When noun phrases are used as complements after verbs like **find, help, see, bite,** we say they function as **objects** of the verbs.

15. Most noun phrases have the same form no matter how they are used. But five of the personal pronouns have one form when they function as subject and another when they function as object:

Subject:	I	he	she	we	they
Object:	me	him	her	us	them

Tom found me.   Mary helped him.

Sam saw her.   Miss Ellis called us.

Our dog bit them.

You and **it** have the same form as both subject and object:

You saw Tom.   Tom saw you.

It growled at the cat. The cat scratched it.

16. Noun phrases and adjectives function as complements after forms of **be.** A third kind of complement after **be** tells where something is. A word or group of words that does this is an **adverbial of place:**

Sally is upstairs.

Bill is in the boat.

A single-word adverbial of place, like **upstairs,** is called an adverb. A group of words that function as an adverbial of place, like **in the boat,** is called a **phrase.** It begins with a word called a **preposition,** like **in, on, under, near, behind.** Since these phrases begin with prepositions, they are called **prepositional phrases.**

17. These adverbials of place are prepositional phrases:

in this room   beside Mr. Smith

near him   behind someone

The words **this room, Mr. Smith, him, someone** are noun phrases that follow the prepositions **in, beside, near, behind.** Noun phrases within prepositional phrases function as **objects of prepositions.** So noun phrases can function as objects of prepositions, as well as objects of verbs, complements after **be,** and subjects. When a personal pronoun functions as the object of a preposition, it has the object form: **me, him, her, us, them.** Of course, **you** and **it** have the same form as subject and as object.

18. Some sentences have verbs alone in the predicate:

Jenny sings.   They study.

These verbs do not have to be followed by an adverbial of place, but they may be:

Jenny sings at church.   They study in the library.

A verb like **find** must have a noun phrase object:

We found a quarter.

Such verbs do not have to be followed by an adverbial of place, but they may be:

We found a quarter on the sidewalk.

19. Each of these sentences tells how the subject felt at a time in the past:

Sally was hungry yesterday.

The men were thirsty last week.

The words **was** and **were** are the forms of **be** that refer to time in the past. **Was** and **were** are the **past tense** forms of **be.**

These sentences tell how the subject feels at this time:

Sally is hungry.   I am cold.   The men are thirsty.

Is, are, and **am** are the forms of **be** which do not refer to time in the past. **Is, are,** and **am** are the present tense forms of **be.**

20. Verbs, like the word **be,** have present and past tense forms. **Be** has two past tense forms — **was** and **were.** But verbs have only one past tense form, such as **walked,** or **spoke.**

Be has three present tense forms — **am, is, are.** But verbs have only two present tense forms:

walk, walks   speak, speaks

21. The two present tense forms of verbs are called the **s** form and the simple form. **Walks, speaks, hopes** are **s** forms. **Walk, speak, hope** are simple forms.

The rules for spelling the **s** form of verbs are the same as the rules for spelling noun plurals. A very few verbs make the **s** form in irregular ways:

have, has   go, goes   do, does

22. The **s** form of the present tense of verbs is used when the subject is a singular noun phrase:

The dog barks at noon.

The personal pronouns **he, she,** and **it** stand for singular noun phrases, and so the **s** form is used after them too:

It barks at the moon.

Indefinite pronouns and most proper nouns are followed by the **s** form:

Everyone likes Ed.   Jenny sings.

23. The simple form of verbs is used in the present tense when the subject is a plural noun phrase:

The dogs bark at the moon.

The personal pronoun **they** stands for plural noun phrases, and so the simple form of verb is used after **they** too:

> They bark at the moon.

The simple form of verbs is used also after the remaining personal pronouns — **I, we,** and **you:**

> I work.   We work.   You work.

24. The present tense forms of **be** are **am, is,** and **are.** The form **am** is used when the subject is the personal pronoun **I:**

> I am hungry.

Apart from this, the form **is** is used after subjects that take the **s** form of verbs and the form **are** is used after those that take the simple form:

is

Singular noun phrase:	The boy is happy.
He, she, or it:	He is happy.
Indefinite pronoun:	Somebody is happy.
Proper noun:	James is happy.

are

Plural noun phrase:	The boys are happy.
We, you, they:	We are happy.

25. When we say or write a sentence with a personal pronoun as subject and a present tense form of **be** in the predicate, we often put the pronoun and the form of **be** together as a contraction:

> a. She is late.   She's late.
> b. They are cold.   They're cold.

The apostrophes in **she's** and **they're** show that something has been left out. In **she's,** the **i** of **is** has been left out. In **they're,** the **a** of **are** has been left out.

Here are the contractions of the personal pronouns with **is, are,** and **am:**

> he is → he's   she is → she's   it is → it's
> we are → we're   you are → you're   they are → they're
> I am → I'm

26. The past tense forms of **be** are **was** and **were.** We use **was** when the subject is a singular noun phrase; **he, she, it,** or **I;** an indefinite pronoun; or, usually, a proper noun:

> The boy was busy.   Everybody was busy.
> He was busy.   Mr. Clark was busy.

We use **were** when the subject is a plural noun phrase or **we, you,** or **they:**

    The boys were busy. You were busy.

27. Verbs have just one past tense form. Each verb has the same form in the past tense, no matter what the subject is.

Most verbs make the past tense by adding a sound that is spelled **ed:**

    jump — jumped   fill — filled

Here is the rule for writing the past tense of regular verbs:

 a. If the simple form ends in consonant **y,** change the **y** to **i** and add **ed.**

 b. If the verb ends in a single consonant letter preceded by a simple vowel, double the final consonant and add **ed.**

 c. If the simple form ends in **e,** add **d.**

 d. For other verbs, add **ed.**

28. A good many verbs have irregular past tense forms:

    see — saw eat — ate drink — drank

Some irregular verbs have the same form in the past tense as the simple form of the present tense: **hit — hit.**

    They hit golf balls every day.
    They hit golf balls yesterday.

29. Possession means having. We can show possession by using a sentence with a form of the verb **have:**

 a. Jerry has a pony.   b. I have a bike.

 c. Somebody has a hammer. d. The man has balloons.

We can also show possession by using the possessive form of noun phrases:

 a. Jerry's (pony)   b. my (bike)

 c. Somebody's (hammer)   d. the man's (balloons)

When the noun phrase is a determiner + common noun, a proper noun, or an indefinite pronoun, we usually add an apostrophe and the letter **s,** as shown above.

When the noun phrase is plural and the noun ends in **s,** as all regular noun plurals do, we do not add another **s.** We add just an apostrophe:

    The ladies have canaries. → the ladies' (canaries)

When the noun phrase is plural but the plural noun does not end in **s,** we add an apostrophe and **s** just as we do with singular noun phrases:

    The men have balloons. → the men's (balloons)

The plural, the singular possessive, and the plural possessive of regular noun phrases all sound alike: **the girls, the girl's, the girls'.** But they are all spelled differently.

30. The personal pronouns have special forms for the possessive. We do not use the apostrophe with them, but show the possessive by using different words:

a. I have a dog. → my (dog)
b. He has a nickel. → his (nickel)
c. She has a hat. → her (hat)
d. It has a kennel. → its (kennel)
e. We have a boat. → our (boat)
f. You have a sister. → your (sister)
g. They have a tent. → their (tent)

The possessive of **it** is **its.** It has no apostrophe. The word **it's** is the contraction of **it is.**

31. A **morpheme** is a single unit of meaning expressed by a word or part of a word.

Girl is just one morpheme. It means "a female child."
Girl's is two morphemes: girl + possessive
Girls is two morphemes: girl + plural
Girls' is three morphemes: girl + plural + possessive

32. The tenses, present and past, are morphemes. The past tense morpheme is whatever we do to a verb to make it past tense. Usually, we add a sound that is spelled **ed:** past + jump → **jumped.** But the past morpheme is not always shown by the spelling **ed:** past + buy → **bought.**

The sentence "She wrote a note" is made up of the following string, or set, of morphemes:

$$she + past + write + a + note$$

The present tense is also a morpheme.

the + boy + present + work   **(The boy works.)**

the + boy + plural + present + work   **(The boys work.)**

For plural noun phrase subjects, the morpheme **present** is null; that is, we don't add anything to the simple form of the verb.

The tense morphemes apply to what comes after them in a string of morphemes.

33. We can expand a predicate by adding the morphemes be + ing. In a string of morphemes this is shown this way:

Sally + past + sing   **(Sally sang.)**

311

Sally + past + be + ing + sing   (**Sally was singing.**)
George + present + grow   (**George grows.**)
George + present + be + ing + grow   (**George is growing.**)
Like the tense morphemes, ing applies to what follows it.

34. Another morpheme that is applied to verbs is the participle morpheme, abbreviated part. This makes a verb into the participle form, which is what we use after have in a simple sentence: "He has **worked**"; "They have **eaten.**"

   past + work → **worked**   part. + work → **worked**

We can expand a predicate by adding have + part.:

   he + present + walk   (**He walks.**)
   he + present + have + part. + walk   (**He has walked.**)
   she + past + drive   (**She drove.**)
   she + past + have + part. + drive   (**She had driven.**)

Like the tense morphemes and **ing,** the morpheme **part.** applies to whatever follows it.

35. The **principal parts** of verbs are the simple form, the past tense form, and the participle form:
   a. The simple form: **look, bring, throw, put**
   b. The past tense form: **looked, brought, threw, put**
   c. The participle form: **looked, brought, thrown, put**

36. We must have tense in a predicate, and we may also have be + ing or have + part. Another thing we may add to a predicate is a modal — a word like **may:**

   He walks to school.   He may walk to school.

Modals do not have an **s** form, and they are followed by the simple forms of verbs or **be.**

There are five modals: **may, can, will, shall, must.** These are the present tense forms of the modals. When we speak of tense, we mean the form of the word — present tense form or past tense form.

The modal **must** has no past tense form — only a present tense form. But the other four modals do have past tense forms: **might, could, would, should.**

Modals have many meanings. We use them to predict, to promise, to suggest that something is possible, and for many other purposes.

37. We can express the idea of a "have" sentence by writing it in the form of a possessive phrase. To do this, we use the possessive form of the noun phrase subject of the "have" sentence, and drop the verb **have** and any determiner that comes after the **have:**

The boys have some candy. → the boys' candy

They have a pony. → their pony

The girl has a book. → the girl's book

Mr. White has flowers. → Mr. White's flowers

Somebody has a pocketbook. → somebody's pocketbook

We can now use the possessive phrase we made from the "have" sentence as part of a different sentence. When we put together a "have" sentence and another sentence in this way, we are using what is called the **possessive transformation.**

We begin with a "have" sentence and another sentence:

a. The boys have some candy.

b. The girls ate the candy.

First, we rewrite the "have" sentence as a phrase that expresses the meaning of possession:

a. The boys have some candy. → the boys' candy

Next, we replace the phrase **the candy** in Sentence **b** with the possessive phrase **the boys' candy:**

The girls ate **the boys' candy.**

The sentence "The girls ate the boys' candy" expresses the meaning of two sentences, Sentence **a** and Sentence **b.** It is called a **transform.**

The possessive phrase **the boys' candy** could be used instead of **the candy** in other sentences like the following:

The candy was sticky. → **The boys' candy** was sticky.

There were flies on **the candy.** → There were flies on **the boys' candy.**

The possessive transformation works the same way no matter what the subject of the "have" sentence is.

38. Sentences like "The water is warm" or "That cat is a tiger" say that something is so. A sentence like this is called an **affirmative** sentence.

Sentences like "The water is not warm" and "That cat is not a tiger" say that something is not so. A sentence which says that something is not so is called a **negative sentence.**

When the predicate of an affirmative sentence contains a form of **be,** we make the sentence negative by simply putting in the word **not:**

I am sleepy. → I am **not** sleepy.

She is a singer. → She is **not** a singer.

They were tired. → They were **not** tired.

When the predicate of an affirmative sentence begins with a modal, we simply add the word **not,** just as we do with forms of **be:**

The man will forget. → The man will **not** forget.

The ladies can win. → The ladies **cannot** win.

The guests may come. → The guests may **not** come.

Notice that when **not** follows **can,** we unite the two words as one word: **cannot.**

When the predicate begins with a form of **have,** followed by a verb or **be,** we add **not** in the same way:

He has been busy. → He has **not** been busy.

They have worked hard. → They have **not** worked hard.

But when the predicate begins with a verb, we can't just put in **not** to make the sentence negative. We must put the right form of **do** after the subject. Then we put in the word **not:**

Bill likes Mabel. → Bill **does not** like Mabel.

Jenny worked hard. → Jenny **did not** work hard.

The children play in the yard. → The children **do not** play
   in the yard.

39. We usually contract modals, **have, be,** and **do** with the word **not** in negative sentences. Here are the most commonly used contractions of **not** with **be:**

is + not → isn't	are + not → aren't
was + not → wasn't	were + not → weren't

Instead of contracting **am** and **not,** we contract **I** and **am:** "I'm not ready."

The contractions of **have, do,** and the modals with **not** are these:

have + not → haven't	can + not → can't
has + not → hasn't	will + not → won't
had + not → hadn't	must + not → mustn't
do + not → don't	could + not → couldn't
does + not → doesn't	should + not → shouldn't
did + not → didn't	would + not → wouldn't

The contractions **mayn't** and **mightn't** are seldom used, and **shan't** is not used very often.

40. An affirmative statement like "The water is warm" is the answer to the affirmative question "Is the water warm?" In the statement, the noun-phrase subject comes first. In the question, the form of **be** comes before the subject. We call such questions "yes/no" questions because one answer to them can be **yes** or **no.**

When the predicate of an affirmative statement begins with a modal, a form of **be,** or a form of **have** followed by a verb or **be,** the matching "yes/no" question begins with that word and the noun-phrase subject of the statement comes next:

modal: The child can skate. → Can the child skate?

be: The train was late. → Was the train late?

have: Mr. Watson has arrived. → Has Mr. Watson arrived?

When the first word in the predicate of the statement is a verb, however, we change the verb to its simple form. Then we begin the matching "yes/no" question with a form of **do** which carries the tense:

Verb: Janet won the game. → **Did** Janet **win** the game?

Arthur builds boats. → **Does** Arthur **build** boats?

The ladies cook breakfast. → **Do** the ladies **cook** breakfast?

Notice that both negative statements and "yes/no" questions require a form of **do** when the predicate of the matching affirmative statement begins with a verb.

41. For each affirmative sentence there is a matching affirmative "yes/no" question also. For each negative statement there is a negative "yes/no" question:

Negative statement: he + past + do + not + wait (**He did not wait.**)

Negative question: past + do + not + he + wait (**Didn't he wait?**)

When the predicate of a negative statement begins with a modal, form of **be** or form of **have,** we simply put tense of the modal, **be,** or **have,** and **not** at the beginning of the negative "yes/no" question. We usually use contractions to begin the negative question:

modal: They are not happy. → Aren't they happy?

be: She is not there. → Isn't she there?

have: He has not arrived. → Hasn't he arrived?

42. When a statement contains an adverbial of place, there is a matching "yes/no" question. But there is also another question that can be asked which begins with the word **where:**

Statement: The principal works in this office.

Where question: Where does the principal work?

In the "where" question, the word **where** replaces the adverbial of place, and begins the question. When the statement begins with a verb, tense and **do** follow the word **where** at the beginning, and the simple form of the verb is used. The adverbial of place is dropped.

When a modal, **be,** or **have** begins the predicate of the statement, the "where" question begins with **where,** followed by the modal, **be,** or **have:**

modal: She will wait upstairs. → Where will she wait?

be: John was working outside. → Where was John working?

have: He has gone to the store. → Where has he gone?

We call questions that begin with words like **where** "wh" questions.

43. An **adverbial of place** answers "where" questions. Another kind of adverbial is called an **adverbial of time** because it answers "when" questions:

Max left **yesterday.** John will come **at three o'clock.**

We ask "wh" questions beginning with **when** just as we do "where" questions. **When** takes the place of the adverbial of time and comes first. Then comes the tense and the modal, **be,** or **have.** If there is a verb, instead of modal, **be,** or **have,** **do** follows the word **when,** and the simple form of the verb is used:

modal: She will arrive tonight. → When will she arrive?

be: He was sick last week. → When was he sick?

have: They had finished before noon. → When had they finished?

verb: She worked yesterday. → When did she work?

44. Another kind of adverbial is a word like **carefully,** or a phrase like **with caution,** that tells the way or manner in which something is done. We call them **adverbials of manner.** They answer "how" questions. Most adverbials of manner are single words. We make them by adding **ly** to adjectives:

thoughtful + ly → thoughtfully   pretty + ly → prettily

Although **how** doesn't begin with **wh,** we call it a **wh** word, and begin "wh" questions with the word, just as we use **where** and **when.** **How** replaces the adverbial of manner and comes first. The modal, **be,** or **have** carries the tense. If the predicate of the statement begins with a verb, **do** carries the tense and the verb is changed to the simple form:

modal: He can work quickly. → How can he work?

be: She was sleeping peacefully. → How was she sleeping?

have: They have studied faithfully. → How have they studied?

verb: Bob speaks quietly. → How does Bob speak?

45. When an adverbial is added to a sentence that is complete without it, the adverbial represents an additional sentence put into, or **embedded** in, the first one. "The plane landed," for example, is complete in itself, but we can put additional information in it by replacing the symbol S, for Sentence, with an adverbial of place, like **at Kennedy Airport,** an adverbial of time, like **yesterday,** an adverbial of manner, like **smoothly,** and so on. We thus make a third sentence that expresses the meaning of the first two:

    a. The plane landed + S

    b. It happened at Kennedy Airport.

    c. The plane landed at Kennedy Airport.

46. If we say "Tom is very lucky," the word **very** tells how much. But if we want to compare the degree of luck Tom has with the luck Ed has, we use the morpheme of comparison, comp., instead of **very,** and add a sentence about Ed's luck:

    a. Tom is lucky + comp. + S ⎱ →

    b. Ed is lucky.   ⎰

The suffix **er** and the word **than** often represent the morpheme comp., so we can use them here to replace comp.

            Tom is lucky + **er** + **than** + S

Lucky + **er** is **luckier.** The sentence to replace S is Sentence **b.** "Ed is lucky." So we can write Sentence **c** as follows:

    c. Tom is luckier than Ed is lucky.

Now we must remove the extra "lucky," and we may remove the entire predicate of Sentence **b.** So we get either **d** or **e:**

    d. Tom is luckier than Ed is.

    e. Tom is luckier than Ed.

In making comparisons with some adjectives, we use **more ... than** for comp. instead of **er than:**

    a. Tom is furious + comp. + S ⎫
                                 ⎬ →
    b. Ed is furious. ⎭
    c. Tom is more furious than Ed is furious.

This gives us either "Tom is more furious than Ed is" or "Tom is more furious than Ed."

There is still a third way of representing the morpheme comp. When we want to show that something is the same as something else, we replace comp. with **as ... as:**

    a. The soup was cold + comp. + S ⎫
                                  ⎬ →
    b. The meat was cold. ⎭

We use **as ... as** to replace comp.:

The soup was as cold as + S

Now we replace S with the **b** sentence and get this **c** sentence:

    c. The soup was as cold as the meat was cold.

For our result sentence, we can use either of the following: "The soup was as cold as the meat was," or "The soup was as cold as the meat."

47. When we compare one thing with two or more other things, we use the superlative morpheme, which we abbreviate sup. The morpheme sup. adds the meaning **most.**

Usually, sup. is represented by the word **the** placed before the adjective, the suffix **est** added to the adjective, and the word **of:**

    a. Sally was shy + sup. + S ⎫
                                 ⎬ →
    b. The girls in the room were shy. ⎭
    c. Sally was the shyest of the girls in the room.

In this transformation, it is the rule that the entire predicate of the **b** sentence must be dropped, not just the repeated adjective. However, we may substitute **girl** for the phrase **of the girls** if we wish. This would give us the result sentence: "Sally was the shyest girl in the room."

The adjectives **good** and **bad** are irregular both in the comparative and the superlative form:

good + comp. → better than   bad + comp. → worse than
good + sup. → the best of   bad + sup. → the worst of

With some adjectives, the morpheme sup. is represented by **the most ... of.**

a. Bill is careful + <u>sup.</u> + S ⎫
b. The boys in the pool are careful. ⎭ →

c. Bill is **the most** careful **of** the boys in the pool.

The result sentence, **c,** can be changed by substituting **boy** for **of the boys:** "Bill is the most careful boy in the pool."

48. Although the morpheme <u>comp.</u> is expressed in three ways, we usually use only two of them with adverbs. We may say that something was done **more thoroughly than** something else, or **as thoroughly as** something else:

a. Jean walked swiftly + <u>comp.</u> + S ⎫
b. Jane walked swiftly. ⎭ →

c. Jean walked more quickly than Jane.

There are four words that have the same form as adverbs that they have as adjectives: **fast, straight, hard, high.** We use **er than** with those adverbs to express the morpheme <u>comp.</u>

With these four adverbs we also use **the . . . est of** to express the morpheme <u>sup.</u> With adverbs that end in **ly,** we express sup. with **the most . . . of.**

The adverb **well** is another adverb that does not add **ly.** The comparative and the superlative of **well** are the same as the comparative and superlative of the adjective **good:** "Tom plays **better** than I do"; "Bill plays **best** when the team is behind."

Vowel Sounds Studied in Grade Five
With Their Usual Spellings

Simple Vowels	Usual Spellings
/i/	**i:** tip (also **ui:** build)
/e/	**e:** let; **ea:** head (also **ie:** friend)
/a/	**a:** bat (also **au:** laugh)
/u/	**u:** but; **o:** son
/o/	**o:** top

VCe Vowels	Usual Spellings
/ī/	**VCe:** line; **igh:** high; **y:** try; **ie:** die (also **I** and **eye**)
/ē/	**VCe:** these; **ee:** deed; **ea:** heat; **e:** he
/ā/	**VCe:** lame; **ay:** pay; **ai:** wait
/ū/	**VCe:** rude; **oo:** root; **ew:** dew; **ue:** true; **o:** to
/ō/	**VCe:** lone; **oa:** goal; **ow:** slow; **oe:** hoe; **o:** no

Complex Vowels	Usual Spellings
/ᴔ/	**oo:** look; **u:** push; **ou:** could
/aɪ/	**au:** haul; **aw:** flaw; **a:** ball, walk; **o:** song; **ou:** cough
/ɑʊ/	**ou:** mouse; **ow:** crowd
/ɔi/	**oi:** oil; **oy:** toy

The Vowel Sound Schwa / ə /

	i	e	ea	u	o
1 Syllable Words	stir girl	were her	learn earth	burn spur	world worse

	er	or	ar			
/ə r/	runner maker	actor orator	beggar liar			

	al	le	el	ul	ile	il
/ə l/	legal moral	steeple battle	camel satchel	beautiful useful	fertile juvenile	April evil

	en	an	ain	in		
/ə n/	frozen deepen	Mexican orphan	captain curtain	robin cabin		

Consonant Sounds Studied in Grade Five
With Their Usual Spellings

Sound	At the Beginning	At the End
/p/	**p:** pie	**p:** rip; **pe:** ripe
/t/	**t:** ten	**t:** pet; **te:** date
/k/	**k:** kit, kettle;	**ck:** lick; **ke:** like;
	c: cold	**k:** leak
/ch/	**ch:** chin	**tch:** witch; **ch:** reach
/b/	**b:** bed	**b:** tub; **be:** tube
/d/	**d:** do	**d:** rid; **de:** ride
/g/	**g:** get	**g:** big; **gue:** league
/j/	**j:** jet; **g:** gentle	**dge:** judge; **ge:** cage
/f/	**f:** fun; **ph:** phrase	**ff:** stuff; **fe:** life;
		f: beef; **ph:** paragraph
/v/	**v:** very	**ve:** save
/s/	**s:** see; **c:** city	**ss:** glass; **s:** bus;
		se: case; **ce:** rice
/z/	**z:** zoo	**z:** quiz; **zz:** buzz;
		se: rose; **ze:** sneeze
/sh/	**sh:** ship	**sh:** push
	(**Medial-ss:** pressure)	
/zh/	**j:** Jacques	**ge:** rouge
	(**Medial-s:** treasure)	
/r/	**r:** run; **wr:** write	**r:** car; **re:** care
/l/	**l:** lose	**ll:** pill; **l:** pal; **le:** pale
/m/	**m:** move	**m:** Sam; **me:** same;
		mb: tomb
/n/	**n:** nose; **gn:** gnaw;	**n:** pin; **ne:** pine
	kn: know	
/ng/		**ng:** strong; **n:** trunk
/ngk/		**nk:** plank
/th/	**th:** thick	**th:** path
/th/	**th:** then	**th:** smooth; **the:** bathe
/w/	**w:** will; **o** /w u/: one;	
	qu: /k w/: quick	
/y/	**y:** you; **u**	
/y/	**y:** you; **u** /y ū/: use	
/h/	**h:** hat; **wh:** who	

abbreviation   A short way of writing words: **Mr., Mrs.**

adjective   A word like **happy, hungry, friendly, new.** Adjectives may occur in predicates after **be** and after verbs like **seem,** as well as before nouns.

adverb   A single-word adverbial. (See the next three entries).

adverbial of manner   A word or group of words that tells how something is done. It occurs only in verb phrases that contain verbs. It can be replaced by **how** in questions: "Bob runs fast." → "How does Bob run?"

adverbial of place   A word or group of words that tells where something is or is done. They occur after **be** in the predicate or after certain verbs. Single-word adverbials of place — **outside, upstairs, there** — are called adverbs. Groups of words — **in the house, near a car** — are prepositional phrases.

adverbial of time   A word or group of words that tell when something happens or is done. An adverbial of time can be replaced by **when** in questions: "The bus left at eight." → "When did the bus leave?" An adverbial of time may be a single-word adverb like **tomorrow,** or a phrase like **in the morning.**

affirmative sentence   A sentence which does not have a form of **not** in the predicate. An affirmative sentence may be a statement, question, or command.

apostrophe   This mark: '. Used in contractions like **he's, we're** to show that something is left out. Used also in the possessive form of most noun phrases: **John's, the man's.** Not used in the possessive form of personal pronouns: **his, theirs.**

articles   These are the most important kind of determiner. There are two kinds of articles — definite and nondefinite. There is one definite article: the word **the.** There are three nondefinite articles: **a/an, some,** and **null.** Some nouns can occur as noun phrases with no word before them: **pie, boys.** We then say that they have the nondefinite article null, which has the symbol Ø.

comma   This mark: ,. Used between day and year in dates; after greetings and closings in friendly letters.

common noun A word like **boy, teacher, school.** Not a proper noun.

comparative A morpheme, abbreviated comp., which is used in comparing something to something else. The morpheme comp. is expressed in these ways: **er than,** as in **prettier than; more ... than,** as in **more beautiful than** or **more carefully than;** and **as ... as,** as in **as shy as** or **as effectively as.**

complement A noun phrase, adjective, or other structure used after a form of **be** or a verb in the predicate of a simple sentence to complete the sentence.

complex sentence Any sentence that is not simple. Those sentences that result from transformations are complex.

complex vowel One of the four vowel sounds symbolized as follows: /ɑu/, /aɪ/, /ɑi/, /ɔo/. These are the vowels of **shout, hall, boil, book.**

consonant A sound made by stopping the breath in some way. Consonant sounds are usually spelled by consonant letters — **b, c, d, f,** etc.

consonant cluster A set of two or three consonant sounds in sequence without intervening vowels. The two sounds at the beginning of **clear** and the three at the end of **thirst** are consonant clusters. They are represented in writing by clusters of consonant letters.

contraction A form like **its, he's, we're,** made by putting together two words such as **it** and **is.**

determiner A word like **a, the, this** that forms part of a noun phrase with a common noun. It determines something about the meaning of the noun.

embedding Replacing a symbol such as S or NP in one sentence with another sentence or with part of another sentence.

function The use to which a word or group of words is put.

grammar The study of sentences.

homophone One of two words pronounced alike but spelled differently and having different meanings: **meet, meat pain, pane.**

indefinite pronoun One of the twelve English words made up from the words **some, every, any, no** combined with **one, body,** or **thing: someone, everybody, anything, no one,** etc. All the indefinite pronouns but **no one** are written solid.

323

indent   To put the first line of a paragraph farther in than the others.

irregular   Not formed according to the general rule. An irregular verb is one that does not form its past tense by adding a sound spelled **ed.**

margin   The unused spaces at the sides and top and bottom of a written page.

morpheme   The smallest unit of meaning. This may be a word or a part of a word. **Car** is one word and one morpheme. **Cars** is one word made up of two morphemes: car + plural. A sequence, or string, of morphemes, some of which may combine to form words, is a useful means of showing the surface structure of a sentence. Thus the + car + plural + past + be + use + ful represents the sentence "The cars were useful."

negative sentence   A sentence which has a form of **not** in the predicate. A negative sentence may be a statement, question, or command.

noun   A word like **Jerry, Mr. Dean, boy.** Proper nouns are also noun phrases. Common nouns are parts of noun phrases. Nouns usually indicate persons, places, things.

noun phrase   The word or group of words used as subject of a simple sentence and in certain functions in the predicate. **Jerry, he, everybody, the boy** are all noun phrases.

object of preposition   A function of a noun phrase. A prepositional phrase ("near the desk") is made up of a preposition ("near") and a noun phrase functioning as its object ("the desk").

object of verb   A function of a noun phrase. In "He hit the ball," **the ball** functions as the object of the verb **hit.**

past tense   One of the two tenses of verbs and **be.** The past tense form of **walk** is **walked.** The past tense forms of **be** are **was** and **were.** Past tenses usually indicate something occurring in past time.

personal pronoun   One of the words **I, he, she, it, we, you, they.** Four of these — **he, she, it,** and **they** — may replace other subjects. All seven may function as subjects.

phrase   A group of words used as a unit. Here the term is used also in the expressions noun phrase and verb phrase, which sometimes consist of single words.

324

plural More than one. The term applies to noun phrases, particularly those composed of determiners and common nouns. **The boy** is singular; **the boys** is plural.

possessive The form of a noun phrase that expresses the meaning of having something: **John's, the man's, his.**

predicate The second of the two main parts of a simple sentence. In a simple sentence, predicate is a function of the verb phrase.

preposition A word like **in, on, by, near, with.**

prepositional phrase A construction like **in the house, to the store,** formed by a preposition and a noun phrase functioning as its object.

present tense One of the two tenses of verbs and **be.** The present tense forms of **walk** are **walk** and **walks,** and of **be** are **am, is,** and **are.** The present tense usually indicates something not occurring in the past.

proper noun A particular name for someone or something, like **Joe, Denver.** The proper noun is one kind of noun phrase.

regular Formed according to the general rule. **Boy** and **table** are regular nouns. **Man** and **child** are irregular nouns because their plural forms — **men** and **children** — are irregular.

rhyme The sameness of sound of words or parts of words, especially at the end of lines of poetry.

s form The present tense form of verbs that goes with singular subjects: **eats, wins, goes.**

sentences The groups of words that express our thoughts when we speak or write.

simple form The form of the verb that has no additions and is used as the present tense with **I, we, you, they,** or plural subjects: **walk, hurry.**

simple sentence An unmodified statement such as "The train was early," "He might have been there," or "The cook spoiled the roast."

simple vowel One of the five vowel sounds shown in the words **pit, pet, pat, putt,** and **pot.** These are indicated by the symbols /i/, /e/, /a/, /u/, and /o/.

singular Meaning one. A noun phrase that means one person or thing is singular.

stanza   One of the parts of a poem.   Each stanza is set off from the other stanzas by extra space.

statement   A sentence which declares that something is or is not so.

stress   The degree of loudness with which a syllable in a word or sentence is pronounced.   English words may have as many as three degrees of stress.   Thus, **incinerator** has first stress on the syllable **cin,** middle stress on the syllable **a,** and weak stress on the syllables **in, er,** and **tor.**

subject   The first of the two main parts of a simple sentence.   Subject is one of the functions of a noun phrase.   It indicates someone or something about which the predicate makes a statement.

suffix   A letter or letters added at the end of a word to change its meaning.   For example, **ly** is a suffix in **quickly.**

superlative   A construction which compares something to two or more other things.   In "John is the tallest of the brothers," **tallest** compares John to his unnamed brothers, of whom there are two or more.   Adjectives form the superlative by adding the suffix **est (tall/tallest)** or by using the word **most (innocent/most innocent).**

tense   A form of verbs, **be,** and certain other structures, including modals and the tense-expressing dummy **do** used in questions.   There are two English tense forms, **present** and **past.**   Past tense generally refers to time in the past, and present tense generally does not.

transform   A sentence that has been made by changing a simple sentence in some way or by combining two or more simple sentences.

transformation   The process by which structures underlying simple sentences are modified, reordered, or combined to produce transforms.

VCe pattern   A system by which complex vowels are distinguished from simple ones by the letter **e** following a vowel (**V**) letter and a consonant (**C**) letter.   Thus the vowel of **pine** ($/\bar{\imath}/$) is distinguished from that of **pin** ($/i/$) by the **e** at the end of **pine.**

VCe vowel   One of the five vowels that occur in the **VCe** pattern — the vowels of **pine, these, lake, hope, duke.**   The **VCe** vowels are symbolized thus: $/\bar{\imath}/, /\bar{e}/, /\bar{a}/, /\bar{o}/, /\bar{u}/.$

326

verb   A verb or a form of **be** is often the first word in the predicate of a simple sentence.   Verbs are words like **go, eat, win, think, seem.**

vocabulary   A set of words a person knows.

vowel   A sound made without stopping the breath.   Different vowel sounds are made by changing the shape of the mouth. The vowel letters are **a, e, i, o, u,** but there are more vowel sounds than vowel letters.

yes/no question   A question that may be answered **yes** or **no** and that begins with a form of **do,** a form of **be,** one of the forms of the modals, or a form of **have.**

Index

329

It transformation, 204–05, 258–59, 266
  tests, 209, 271, 301
ity, 92, 101, 140

J

/j/ (sound), 163, 193
"Jabberwocky" (Carroll), 117
Jeffers, Robinson, 89

K

/k/ (sound), 193
Kirwan, L. P., 9–11

L

Latin, words from, 51, 63, 71–72, 92, 172,
  173, 182–83, 193–94, 203, 215, 247–
  48, 257, 265, 274–75, 288
Limericks, 50
Lincoln, Abraham, 189–90
Lincoln's Second Inaugural Address, 189–
  90
Longfellow, Henry Wadsworth, 45, 77–78
ly, 82–83, 140
"Lyonesse" (Hardy), 219

M

Margin, *326*
Metaphor, 26
Modals, 46–47, 216, 224–25
  be plus **ing** and, 52–53
  have plus part. and, 52–53
  negative contractions of, 67
  past tense, 46–47
  present tense, 46–47
  review, 313–14
Monkhouse, Cosmo, 50
Morphemes, 21–23, *324*
  able, 163, 173
  adjective forming, 43, 51, 63, 92, 140,
    163, 172, 182–83
  adverb forming, 140
  al, 51, 63, 92, 140
  ance, 203
  ant, 182-83, 193–94, 222
  ar, 22, 33
  ate, 215, 222–23, 233
  ation, 223, 233
  base words, 21–22
  comp. (comparison), 26–27, 33, 101,
    317–18, *323*

derivational, 101
en, 43, 140, 153
ence, 203
ent, 182–83, 193–94
er, 22, 33, 140
ible, 172, 173
inflectional, 101
ing, 35–36, 52–53, 101
ion, 222–23, 233–34, 247–48, 257, 265
ition, 265
ity, 92, 101, 140
ly, 82–83, 140
noun forming, 92, 140, 203, 222–23,
    247–48, 257, 265
or, 22, 33
part. (participle), 37–38, 43, 52–53, 56,
    101
past, 35–36, 101, 151
plural, 21–23, 101
possessive, 21–23, 101
pres. (present), 35–36, 101
review, 311–12
sup. (superlative), 48–49, 101, 326
tests, 28, 58, 114, 146, 178, 208, 240,
    270
verb forming, 43, 140
Myth, 96–99, 100

N

"Narrow Fellow in the Grass, A" (Dickinson), 31
Negative transformations, 64–65, 67
  review, 235, 315–16
  tests, 86
"Negro Speaks of Rivers, The" (Hughes),
  293
Nondefinite articles, *see* Articles, nondefinite
Nonsense rhymes, 50
Nonsense words, 121, 137
Noun phrases, *326*
  adjectives in, 174–75
  as adverbials, 75
  as complements, 16–17
  as object of verb, 16–17
  as subject, 6
  be and, 24–25
  determiners in, 7, 15
  expanding, 54–55, 122–23
  functions of, 6, 16–17

Simile, 26, 91

Singular, *325*

"Skeleton in Armor, The" (Longfellow), 45

Some, 7, 15, 297–99

Sonnet, 62

Spelling
  morphemes and, 22, 33, 43, 151, 163, 172, 173, 182–83, 193–94, 203, 222–23, 233–34, 247–48, 257
  plurals, 21, 42
  schwa, 14, 33, 43

Stanza, *326*

Statement, *326*

Stories:
  "Barking up the Wrong Tree" (Crockett), 124–26
  "Odysseus and Polyphemus" (Homer), 251–53
  "Trojan Horse, The" (Homer), 211–12
  writing a, 100, 214, 221

Stress, 3, 13, 14, *326*
  first, 3, 13
  in poetry, 50, 62, 108–09, 220–21
  middle, 3, 13, 14, 33
  morphemes that change, 101, 140, 183, 222
  tests, 28
  weak, 3, 13, 14, 33
  word classes and, 162

Structure, 6, 23–25

Subjects, *326*
  noun phrases as, 6, 17, 302
  nouns as, 6
  pronouns as, 6
  relative pronouns as, 122–23
  review, 302–03, 309–10

Subordinate clauses, 186–87, 204–05, 206–07, 258–59, 263, 264
  review, 294–95
  tests, 208–09, 301
  transformation, 196–97

Subordinators, 186–87, 196–97, 263, 264

Suffixes, *see also* morphemes, *326*

Suggestions, 224–25

Superlative transformation, 48–49, 318–19
  review, 289–90
  tests, 59

Syllables, 3, 13, 14, 21–23, 33

T

/ t / (sound), 234

Tennyson, Alfred Lord, 229–31

Tense, 34, *326*
  modals, 46–47
  morpheme, 35–36
  past, 34, 35–36, *324*
  present, 34, 35–36, *325*
  review, 309–10, 311–12
  tests, 58

Territorial Imperative, The (Ardrey), 68–71

Tests, *see* individual entries

the, 7, 15, 297–99

Titles, capitalization in, 5

Tom Sawyer, (Twain), 171

Transform, 55, *326*

Transformations, *326*
  comparison, 26–27, 48–49, 317–19
  deletion, 165–66, 174–75
  it, 204–05, 258–59, 266–67
  negative, 64–65
  noun modifier, 174–75, 196–97
  possessive, 54–55
  relative caluse, 130–31, 132–33
  review, 314–16
  subordinate clause, 196–97, 204–05
  superlative, 48–49
  tests, 29, 59
  using in writing, 245–46, 255–56, 296
  wh questions, 73–75, 82–85, 94–95, 104–05, 249–50
  yes/no question, 66, 67

"Trojan Horse, The" (Homer), 211–12

Twain, Mark, 171

U

/ u / (sound), 234

V

Verb phrase
  function of, 6
  review, 305–06
  structures in, 23–25, 112–13
  tests, 29

Verbs, 118–19, 129, 152–53, *327*
  have as, 56, 57
  object of, 16

333